The Survival
of North Korea

The Survival of North Korea

Essays on Strategy, Economics and International Relations

Edited by
Suk Hi Kim, Terence Roehrig
and Bernhard Seliger

McFarland & Company, Inc., Publishers
Jefferson, North Carolina, and London

Suk Hi Kim is the editor of the journal *North Korean Review* (McFarland; vol. 1–, 2005–) and author of *North Korea at a Crossroads* (McFarland, 2003)

Suk Hi Kim and Semoon Chang have edited *Economic Sanctions Against a Nuclear North Korea: An Analysis of United States and United Nations Actions Since 1950* (McFarland, 2007)

Terence Roehrig has also written *The Prosecution of Former Military Leaders in Newly Democratic Nations: The Cases of Argentina, Greece and South Korea* (McFarland, 2002)

LIBRARY OF CONGRESS CATALOGUING-IN-PUBLICATION DATA

The survival of North Korea : essays on strategy, economics and international relations / edited by Suk Hi Kim, Terence Roehrig and Bernhard Seliger.
    p.   cm.
Includes bibliographical references and index.

ISBN 978-0-7864-6463-0
softcover : 50# alkaline paper ∞

1. Korea (North)—Politics and government. 2. Korea (North)—Foreign relations. 3. Korea (North)—Foreign economic relations. 4. Korea (North)—Economic policy. 5. Korea (North)—Military policy. I. Kim, Suk H. II. Roehrig, Terence, 1955–   III. Seliger, Bernhard, 1970–
JQ1729.5.A58S87   2011
320.95193—dc22   2011014603

BRITISH LIBRARY CATALOGUING DATA ARE AVAILABLE

© 2011 Suk Hi Kim, Terence Roehrig and Bernhard Seliger. All rights reserved

No part of this book may be reproduced or transmitted in any form or by any means, electronic or mechanical, including photocopying or recording, or by any information storage and retrieval system, without permission in writing from the publisher.

On the cover: Propaganda artwork from the Democratic People's Republic of Korea, 1979 (photograph by Igor Golovniov)

Manufactured in the United States of America

McFarland & Company, Inc., Publishers
  Box 611, Jefferson, North Carolina 28640
  www.mcfarlandpub.com

Table of Contents

Introduction	1
1. North Korea: Yesterday, Today, and Tomorrow *Suk Hi Kim*	11
2. Will North Korea Be Able to Overcome the Third Wave of Its Collapse? *Suk Hi Kim*	28
3. Why Did So Many Influential Americans Think North Korea Would Collapse? *Bruce Cumings*	44
4. The Strategic Role of North Korea in Northeast Asia *Suk Hi Kim*	64
5. Inter-Korean Economic Cooperation *Semoon Chang* and *Hwa-Kyung Kim*	86
6. Economic Reform and Alternatives for North Korea *Thomas F. Cargill* and *Elliott Parker*	99
7. China–North Korea Relations *Dick K. Nanto* and *Mark E. Manyin*	116
8. North Korea's "Collapse" Pathways and the Role of the Energy Sector *Peter Hayes* and *David von Hippel*	137
9. Rethinking Special Economic Zones as a Survival Strategy for North Korea *Sung-Hoon Lim*	160

10. Violence from Within: North Korea's Place in East Asian
    Community Debates
    Mikyoung Kim   180

11. The Northern Limit Line and North Korean Provocations
    Terence Roehrig   198

12. Lessons Learned from the North Korean Nuclear Crises
    Siegfried S. Hecker   214

13. Channels of Engagement with North Korea: Academic
    Exchanges
    Bernhard J. Seliger and *Suk Hi Kim*   230

14. U.S. Policy Options on a Nuclear North Korea
    Suk Hi Kim and *Bernhard J. Seliger*   245

About the Contributors   257

Index   261

Introduction

Why do we need this sort of book? Before any country starts a battle or a war against another country, it needs to remember the three-sentence military strategy recommended by an ancient Chinese general Sun Tzu. "If you know the enemy and know yourself, you need not fear the result of a hundred battles. If you know yourself but not the enemy, for every victory gained you will also suffer a defeat. If you know neither the enemy nor yourself, you will succumb in every battle."[1] Sun Tzu was an ancient Chinese military general, strategist and philosopher who authored *The Art of War*, an influential book on military strategy considered to be a prime example of broad thinking on philosophical and religious tradition. Sun Tzu has had a significant impact on Chinese and Asian history and culture, both as an author of *The Art of War* and through legend. In fact, his theories have influenced not only Eastern Asia for more than two millennia but also have had a notable influence on the Western world since the nineteenth century. His guidance remains relevant for today, and a book that furthers understanding of North Korea will be very valuable to scholars, policymakers, analysts, and those who follow the region.

According to some observers, until the 1990s, North Korea's foremost goal had been the reunification of the Korean Peninsula on North Korean terms. But since that time, regime survival has replaced reunification as North Korea's most pressing objective. Can North Korea survive as a sovereign country? Most analysts think it depends on future economic conditions. If North Korea collapses, it will be because of its economic problems. Since the Soviet Union collapsed in 1990, North Korea has accepted humanitarian aid from the United Nations and individual donor countries, extracted economic aid through military threats, established a number of special economic zones to attract investment from South Korea and other countries, obtained a substantial amount of money through illegal or questionable methods, and attempted limited economic reform. In other words, North Korea has made numerous small attempts to boost its ailing economy, but to date, these measures have been peripheral and completely inadequate for pulling the economy out of its nose-dive. In addition, North Korea continues to test weapons of mass destruction, in part, to extract more economic aid from the United States, South Korea, and others.

The end of the Cold War in 1990 and the onset of food shortages strengthened the widespread belief that just like Eastern Europe, particularly East Germany, North Korea was doomed to collapse. The persistence of this belief, especially on the part of the United States and its allies, is part of the reason they failed to develop a coherent long-term policy toward North Korea. Instead, many approaches have been devised about the likelihood of North Korea's collapse. As a result, policies have often lacked a long-term vision and avoided the realities of dealing with a North Korea that may be around for quite some time.

In the middle of a precarious and tough neighborhood, a divided Korea stands as a strategic pivot. History and geography have consigned Korea to the position of a highly contested strategic crossroads, the site for over a century of recurrent collisions between great-power interests. However, four countries—Russia, China, Japan, and the United States—must eventually work together, because they will need each other's help on Korean issues for their national security, energy security, and economic security. In this book, we argue that North Korea's longevity and its role in Northeast Asia justify a strong case for a new way of thinking about the survival strategy of North Korea.

The Longevity of North Korea

A few years ago, North Korea faced its third wave of possible state collapse, a phenomenon largely rooted in Kim Jong-il's poor health, an impending power transition to his son, Kim Jong-un, North Korea's ongoing food shortages, and its failed currency and economic reforms. In fact, this latest speculation of North Korean collapse came from an array of intelligence analysts, Asian and American scholars, think tank specialists, and workers in relief organizations.[2] The first wave that predicted North Korea's collapse occurred in the 1980s, when the North Korean economy spiraled downward as the country's chief allies—the Soviet Union and China—discontinued new loans and demanded repayment of outstanding loans. The second wave came in the mid-1990s, when the great North Korean famine claimed the lives of between 200,000 and 3,000,000 people. Most communist countries except for North Korea either collapsed or carried out significant economic reform. Why should we assume that North Korea, one of the survivors that did not implement economic reform, will continue to be an exception to the pattern of history and survive?

Many scholars and analysts have tried to draw comparisons between Korea and Germany in an effort to assess the likelihood of Korean reunification. Some commonalities exist. Both Korea and Germany were created from the division of a homogeneous society, were part of the same Cold War alliance system, experienced similar tensions between a communist dictatorship and a capitalist democratic state, and had a national identity that was uprooted by a devastating war. However, when predicting a collapse, many observers ignore the cultural and historical differences that set the two nations apart. The Soviet occupation imposed an alien totalitarian model on East Germany, but North Korea's totalitarianism was home-grown, guided by principles based on Confucianism and an internally developed ideology such as *juche*, the concept of self-reliance. These guiding principles and other cultural factors have enabled North Korea to enjoy longevity contrary to widespread assumptions that the country would collapse in the conceivable future.[3] Moreover, Pyongyang continues to receive important economic and political support from China. Beijing does not wish to see a failed state on its border. Thus, it appears unlikely that North Korea will collapse any time soon.[4]

On June 12, 2009, the United Nations Security Council unanimously voted to expand and tighten sanctions against North Korea after its second nuclear test. In fact, the United Nations, the United States, South Korea, and others have taken a series of new hard-line actions—tougher sanctions, a stronger proliferation security initiative (PSI), and so on—to punish North Korea for its defiant May 25, 2009, atomic test and a barrage of earlier ballistic missile tests. Has this new round of tougher actions against a nuclear North Korea worked? These tougher actions have not succeeded so far. In fact, these sanctions have motivated North Korea to engage in more aggressive provocations. If history repeats itself, they will again undoubtedly fail. U.S. economic sanctions against North Korea began on June 28, 1950, three days after the outbreak of the Korean War. Since then, the United Nations, the United States, and its allies have increasingly imposed economic sanctions on North Korea in an attempt to contain, punish, and destabilize the regime. However, these sanctions and other hard-line measures have been largely ineffective in stopping North Korea from developing weapons of mass destruction (WMD). Despite China's efforts to revive the Six Party Talks, it appears unlikely that North Korea will give up its nuclear weapons ambitions any time soon.

Most North Korean experts split future predictions for North Korea into three broad scenarios of change: war, a North Korean collapse, or the continuation of the status quo with North Korea embarking on limited economic reforms.[5] The United States is highly unlikely to attack North Korea, because it remains heavily involved in both the Iraq and Afghanistan. North Korea will not dare to attack South Korea, because the U.S. and South Korean response would probably mean the end of the Democratic People's Republic of Korea. If the United States and South Korea hope that North Korea will either collapse or give up its nuclear weapons because of a U.S.–Republic of Korea policy of strangulation, the odds of success are remote. North Korea has survived for 20 years in a state of ongoing decline. The most likely scenario in any conceivable future appears to be a continuation of the status quo, possibly with some North Korean economic reform, largely because the neighboring countries wish to maintain North Korea as a viable state and avoid the dangers of a collapse.

Why have Western experts repeatedly predicted that North Korea would collapse only to see the country continue to muddle along?[6] Professor Alon Levkowitz listed 11 reasons Western experts are unable to make accurate forecasts about countries such as Iraq and North Korea: (1) analogies, (2) a "cold war mentality," (3) determinism, (4) idiosyncratic events, (5) a lack of facts, (6) political bias, (7) psychological warfare, (8) too many variables, (9) terminology or translation problems, (10) Western-style logic, and (11) wishful thinking.[7]

In the end, the difficult policy question remains. How should the United States, South Korea, China, and others that do not want a nuclear North Korea approach Pyongyang to maintain peace on the Korean Peninsula in light of its determination to retain its nuclear weapons capability without allowing North Korea to proliferate WMD? As noted, the collapse of North Korea or the military defeat of North Korea that would lead to reunification is unlikely. In addition, China has many reasons to retain a divided Korea. As a result, Western experts and policymakers need to have a clear understanding of North Korean survival strategy to better understand why Korea is different from Germany and to construct successful, long-term policy toward the DPRK.

The Strategic Role of North Korea in Northeast Asian Affairs

North Korea has blocked South Korea's overland access to China, Russia, and other Asian countries since the Korean War, thereby making South Korea an island for all practical purposes. North Korea stands as a strategic pivot in Northeast Asian security, energy security, and economic security mainly because of its location. If the land bridge that passes through North Korea can be restored, five Northeast Asian countries—China, Japan, Russia, and the two Koreas—can be connected through a land-based transportation network of railroads, highways, and undersea tunnels. The land transportation network can also be extended to cover Asia, the Middle East, and Europe via the Trans-Siberian Railway (TSR), the Trans-China Railway (TCR), the Trans-Korea Railway (TKR), and an undersea tunnel between South Korea and Japan. In addition, the reconnection of the TKR may revive a stalled UN railway project known as the Trans-Asian Railway (TAR) and a possible tunnel project between South Korea and Japan. The land bridge project for Northeast Asia and Europe will not be completed until some type of land transportation system can be extended to Japan. The major sticking point for the revival of the TAR and the tunnel between Korea and Japan has been the division of Korea.

Korea is the region where the interests and influences of the four global powers—China, Russia, Japan, and the United States—are most closely connected. The United States is not part of Northeast Asia geographically, but it has been deeply involved in all the important issues concerning this region since 1945. As a result, it is almost impossible for one to consider Northeast Asia without the United States. The peninsula has thus functioned as a land bridge between the Asian continental powers (China and Russia) and the oceanic powers (Japan and the United States) for cultural exchange and military aggression. However, this land bridge has been broken since the end of World War II because the peninsula has been divided into two separate states.

The spheres of influence of the regional powers—China, Japan, and Russia—along with the United States, overlap in Korea. The world's heaviest concentration of military and economic capabilities lies in Northeast Asia, with the three largest nuclear weapons states (China, Russia, and the United States), one fledgling nuclear weapons state (North Korea), two threshold nuclear weapons states (South Korea and Japan), and five of the world's largest economies (China, South Korea, Japan, the United States, and Russia).[8] Thus, Northeast Asia is a very important and dangerous region in the post–Cold War world.[9]

Many view Northeast Asia as being poised more for conflict than for international peace and cooperation, in part because of continuing North-South tension. We question this widely held view, because the strategic position of North Korea in Northeast Asia will compel the United States and other Northeast Asian countries to work together on the Korean issue for their own national security, energy security, and overall economic welfare. First, in the opinion of many observers, a divided Korea and a nuclear North Korea pose a more serious threat than the Middle East. As a result, the Northeast Asian countries and the United States need to work together to resolve the North Korean nuclear standoff through peaceful means in order to ensure their national security. Second, the Northeast Asian countries are likely to work together for their national energy security because this region is home to major energy consumers such as China and Japan, and for a major energy producer—Russia. The United States has an incentive to support regional cooperation to prevent these countries from increasing their dependence on Middle Eastern oil. Third, the economic integration of Northeast Asia and the United States is likely to grow further encouraging greater efforts to maintain regional peace and stability. Many observers argue that Northeast Asia has the potential to become the most important trading bloc in the future because of Japanese capital and technology, Chinese labor and money, Russian natural resources, and the Korean work ethic. In addition, the Northeast Asian countries and the United States have already established close economic ties over much of the postwar period and, in recent years, have become increasingly economically interdependent. Thus, there is significant economic motivation for peaceful management of the challenges posed by North Korea.

The Case for Confidence Building Between North Korea and the United States

It is important for social scientists and policymakers to discuss the survival strategy of North Korea in greater depth than academic, newspaper, and trade journal articles. North Korea will not collapse anytime soon and will continue to play a strategic role in relations between Northeast Asia and the United States, requiring in-depth knowledge of the ongoing challenge. According to Frank Rudiger, "Strategy games have been popular among world leaders for centuries. They all have one thing in common: to win, one needs a forward-looking strategy, must anticipate the developments in the next few rounds, and prepare in time to be able to react properly."[10] Like Sun Tzu, if you know the enemy and know yourself, you need not fear the result of a hundred battles. If you know yourself but not the enemy, for every victory gained you will also suffer a defeat. If you know neither the enemy nor yourself, you will succumb in every battle. Thus, it is time for the Western world to reexamine the survival strategy of North Korea and then develop a policy that better understands North Korea's strategy.

An approach that pursues dialogue and engagement may not be acceptable nor wise under the current environment in which recent North Korean provocations have become more militant and deadly. In March 2010, North Korea was found to have torpedoed a South Korean naval ship, the *Cheonan*, killing 46 crew members. In November 2010, Pyongyang revealed the existence of a sophisticated complex of centrifuges to enrich uranium, a program designed to produce more powerful nuclear weapons. Soon after, the North shelled South Korea's Yeonpyeong Island, killing two South Korean Marines and two civilians. This latest assault was the North's first to target a civilian area since the 1950–53 Korean War. Responses to such provocations by the United States and its allies included joint naval drills, threats of military retaliation to future North Korean provocations, condemnations, resolutions by legislatures, and increased military spending. In February 2007, the Six Party Talks concluded an agreement whereby North Korea would denuclearize in return for economic, political, and security concessions. It appears unlikely this agreement will ever be implemented, yet the security challenges on the Korean Peninsula remain. Moreover, the United States and South Korea remain adversaries with the North with little trust between themselves. Thus, to surmount these obstacles will require confidence building between North Korea and the United States.

It is unlikely North Korea will alter its foreign and defense policy until the United States and its allies adopt a long-term strategy of political and economic engagement with North Korea. Few consider a military solution as the answer given the likely costs to all involved. Sanctions have a role in addressing North Korea as a proliferation risk, but they have failed to stop North Korea from developing weapons of mass destruction and undertaking other provocative actions. The United States and its allies should consider engagement with North Korea as part of a long-term strategy to complement the short-term efforts to address North Korea's nuclear weapons capabilities. Several chapters of this book suggest or discuss a variety of channels for engagement with North Korea so aid cannot be diverted into its military forces: They include: (1) turn Korea's Demilitarized Zone into a UNESCO World Heritage Site; (2) perform an energy efficiency upgrade of buildings in Pyongyang; (3) undertake economic engagement through official contacts, unofficial country-to-country contacts, academic exchanges, NGO cooperation, and others; (4) replace armistice with a conditional peace treaty; (5) establish a cultural office in Pyongyang as a first step to normalize relations with North Korea; (6) increase engagement to include positive incentives for reform over the long term (loosen sanctions, encourage reforms, facilitate foreign investment, allow North Korea to join international financial institutions); (7) establish some sort of a standing committee under the auspices of the United Nations for negotiations over North Korea's nuclear standoff, along with other issues for these six countries; and (8) establish a development bank, the North Korean Bank for Reconstruction and Development. Such engagement policies would generate a vested interest in continued reform without strengthening the coercive power of North Korea, as is the case with foreign aid.

Synopsis of the Book

Since the end of the Cold War, scholars and analysts have been predicting the collapse of the communist regime in North Korea. Yet, despite a deteriorating economy characterized by declining industrial output, outdated technology, and difficulty feeding its people, the country has been able to persist in spite of these daunting obstacles and continues to plod along. How has North Korea been able to survive, and how long can it last without significant change to its economic and political structures? How can we peacefully resolve the North Korean nuclear standoff through constructive dialogue? This book examines North Korea's survival strategy and practical solutions to a fifty-year nuclear standoff through a series of essays written by thirteen of the world's foremost scholars and leading experts on strategy, economics, and international relations. *The Survival of North Korea*, edited by Kim, Roehrig, and Seliger, is essential reading for anyone interested in peace in Northeast Asia. The book will be invaluable in helping policy-makers, diplomats, politicians, researchers, and other North Korea watchers to understand the three closely related issues about North Korea: (1) why North Korea will continue to survive; (2) how the United States and North Korea can build a mutual confidence; and (3) why a dialogue is the only viable way to resolve the North Korea problem peacefully.

Notes

1. Sun Tzu's Art of War, http://en.wikipedia.org/wiki/Sun_Tzu, April 26, 2010.
2. Richard Halloran, "When Will North Korea Collapse?" http://www.realclearpolitics.com/articles/2008/08/when_will_north_korea_collapse.html, April 8, 2010.
3. Suk Hi Kim, *North Korea at a Crossroads* (Jefferson, NC: McFarland, 2003), Chapter 3.
4. Selig S. Harrison, *Korean Endgame* (Princeton, NJ: Princeton University Press, 2002).
5. Marcus Noland, ed., *Economic Integration of Korean Peninsula* (Washington, DC: Institute for International Economics, 1998).

6. Alon Levkowitz, "Why Do We Not Understand the DPRK?" *North Korean Review* (Fall 2007): 94–100.

7. Ibid.

8. Samuel S. Kim and Tai H. Lee, eds., *North Korea and Northeast Asia* (Lanham, MD: Rowman and Littlefield, 2003), p. 4.

9. Sandip Kumar Mishra, "Changing Landscape of Northeast Asian Security," *World Affairs* (Summer 2006): 60–71.

10. Frank Rudiger, "The Stability of North Korea and a Long-Term Strategy for Transformation," Nautilus Policy Online 10-019A: March 18, 2010, http://www.nautilus.org/fora/security/10019Frank.html.

CHAPTER 1

North Korea: Yesterday, Today, and Tomorrow

Suk Hi Kim[1]

ABSTRACT

The United States questions how to confront states, such as North Korea, that are sponsoring terrorism and developing weapons of mass destruction. Policy makers face two choices: engagement and confrontation. In the past, the Clinton administration had engaged with North Korea to prevent its development of nuclear, chemical, and biological weapons. The Bush administration quickly put North Korean relations on hold until a policy review was conducted. By early July 2001, the administration's policy, under the influence of Colin Powell, validated a continuation of the U.S.–North Korean dialogue. However, North Korea expressed its strong concern through other channels that the Bush administration operated under a different and more difficult set of principles than the Clinton administration. North Korea's view of the Bush administration's tougher line on relations was validated in 2002. In the past, the U.S. State Department had labeled North Korea, Iraq, and Iran as "rogue states" whose military policy and support of other groups threatened Washington's security. In his State of the Union address on January 29, 2002, however, Bush labeled Iran, Iraq, and North Korea as an "axis of evil," thus extending his war on terrorism. A series of one-sided hardline actions taken by both sides since then have caused their relationship to deteriorate to the point of no-return on the road to their eventual military confrontation.

On October 9, 2006, North Korea set off its first nuclear test, becoming the eighth country in history to join the club of nuclear weapons states. The UN Security Council voted unanimously on October 14 to slap North Korea with trade, travel, and other sanctions as punishment for its claimed nuclear weapons test. On May 25, 2009, North Korea conducted a second test of a nuclear weapon at the same location as the original test (not confirmed). The test weapon was of the same magnitude as the atomic bombs dropped on Japan during the Second World War.

On June 12, 2009, the United Nations Security Council unanimously voted to expand and tighten sanctions on North Korea after the nation's second nuclear test. In fact, the United Nations, the United States, and its allies have taken a series of new hardline actions—tougher sanctions, stronger proliferation security initiative (PSI), and so on—to punish North Korea for its defiant May 25, 2009 atomic test and a barrage of missile tests. Will this new round of tougher actions against a nuclear North Korea work? If history repeats itself, they will undoubtedly fail. U.S. economic sanctions against North Korea began on June 28, 1950, three days after the outbreak of the Korean War. Since then, the United Nations, the United States, and its allies have increasingly imposed economic sanctions on North Korea in an attempt to destabilize and manipulate the North Korean regime.

However, these sanctions and other hardline measures have been largely ineffective in stopping North Korea from developing weapons of mass destruction (WMD). North Korea has used these sanctions as an excuse for developing even more sophisticated weapons of mass destruction, while its economy has been getting worse. In fact, recent North Korean provocations have become more militant and deadlier. In March 2010, North Korea was found to have torpedoed a South Korean naval ship, the *Cheonan*, killing nearly 50 crew members. In November 2010, Pyongyang revealed the existence of a sophisticated complex of centrifuges to enrich uranium, a program designed to produce more powerful bombs, and then followed that with the shelling of South Korea's front-line island that killed four South Koreans. The latest assault on Yeonpyeong Island, home to both fishing communities and military bases, was the North's first to target a civilian area since the 1950–53 Korean War. Responses to such frantic provocations by the United States and its allies included joint naval drills, threats of military retaliation to future North Korean provocations, angry denunciations, resolutions by legislatures, and increased military spending.

Some experts think that the United States and North Korea will eventually make a deal that may stick for two major reasons: (1) after the North Korean nuclear tests in recent years, the United States had no other alternative but to reach an agreement; and (2) such an accord would neutralize a number of increasingly stringent economic sanctions and restrictions imposed by the United States, its allies, and the United Nations against North Korea in recent years. This chapter examines past, current, and future issues with North Korea. This chapter examines past, current, and future issues with North Korea.

Introduction

Given the gravity and urgency of North Korean issues, it is important for the United States to address the highly uncertain prospects in the North. Although Korea is a middle-size country—North and South Koreas are roughly the same size as Britain and have a combined population of 70 million—Koreans feel small because they live amid giants. Their geopolitical neighbors are China, Japan, Russia, and America—whose spheres of influence overlap in

Korea. As a result, the peninsula has been the site of recurrent collisions between great-power interests over the past 70 years. Nevertheless, recent events in the Korean peninsula—the death of Kim Il Sung, who had ruled North Korea for 45 years; the rise of his eldest son Kim Jong Il as the new leader of the North; a North Korean famine in 1990s; the U.S. treatment of North Korea as a terrorist sponsor; the development of weapons of mass destruction by North Korea; the rise of South Korea as a newly industrialized country; its financial crisis of 1997; North Korean nuclear tests of 2006 and 2009; and a series of frantic provocations by North Korea in 2010—have generated new attentions on Korea as one of global trouble spots.

Ever since the Korean War, two rival governments—the communist in the North and the capitalist in the South—have been locked in mortal combat. Half a century later, there is still no peace on the horizon. By American estimates, North Korea has 1.1 million troops; South Korea has 700,000, which are argumented by 28,500 Americans in a combined force structure. All men have military experience, and millions (the number of reserve troops is 4.7 million in North Korea and 4.5 million in South Korea) are eligible for call-up in case of war.[2] Since Kim Il Sung died of a heart attack on July 8, 1994, the future of North Korea became the core of Northeast Asian security issues. Arguments focus on North Korea's current situation, policy directions, and the results of its policies.

The history of contention between North and South dates back to World War II, when the Japanese emperor accepted the Allies' ultimatum of unconditional surrender on August 15, 1945. At the end of World War II, the United States and the Soviet Union agreed that U.S. forces would occupy South Korea and Soviet troops would occupy North Korea to disarm Japanese troops. This occupation was intended to be a temporary arrangement until elections supervised by the United Nations (UN) could be held to form one government for Korea. The U.S.–Soviet Joint Commission held a series of meetings in 1946 and 1947, but failed to reach any agreement. Then, in September 1947, the UN General Assembly adopted a resolution to hold general elections in Korea to insure immediate independence and unification. However, the Soviet Union and their communist followers in the North refused to comply with the UN resolution and obstructed the entry of the UN Commission on Korea (UNCK) into North Korea.

In order to accomplish its mission in Korea, the UNCK carried out national elections on the peninsula south of the 38th parallel on May 10, 1948. On August 15, 1948, the government of the Republic of Korea was officially proclaimed and Syngman Rhee took the oath of office as the first president of the Republic of Korea. Without UN involvement, the North Korean communists held their own elections under the tutelage of Russia in September 1948, and Kim Il Sung established the so-called Democratic People's Republic of Korea. Thus, the 38th parallel became the "Berlin Wall" in Korea.

Six decades after Korea was divided at the 38th parallel, South Korea has defeated North Korea economically. The only question remaining is whether victory will eventually eradicate North Korea, or the North will reconstruct itself as a modern state compatible with the economic and strategic realities of Northeast Asia. South Korea, the United States, China, Japan, and Russia will have to decide what Korean unification means, and thus maneuver to preserve the current partition or attempt to push the North into unification with the South through economic sanctions and other hostile actions. This important question can be addressed by examining past, current, and future issues with North Korea.

The Korean War: Causes and Consequences

On January 12, 1950, Dean Acheson, the U.S. Secretary of State, disclosed in a speech at the National Press Club in Washington D.C. that South Korea was outside the U.S. defense perimeter. His speech was viewed as a green light by the North Korean communists to cross the 38th parallel. On the morning of June 25, 1950, North Korea attacked South Korea, captured the South Korean capital of Seoul within four days, and subsequently overran two-thirds of South Korea within a short period of time. Five days after the North Korean invasion, President Harry S Truman sent American air and naval forces to assist South Korea. A few days later, he authorized the bombing of specific targets in North Korea, approved the use of ground forces in the fighting, and started a naval blockade of the entire Korean coast.

Both South Korean and U.S. forces took a last stand in the Pusan region, located in the southeastern corner of the peninsula. Realizing the grave danger to South Korea's existence, Truman requested the assistance of UN members. Consequently, troops from 14 other countries joined the South Korean and U.S. forces in the fight against North Korea. On September 15, 1950, UN forces made a successful amphibious assault far behind North Korean lines at Inchon forcing North Korean troops to retreat. The UN forces recaptured Seoul on September 28 and captured the North Korean capital of Pyongyang on October 19, 1950.

To prevent the defeat of North Korea, however, 150,000 Chinese troops poured into Korea in November and pushed the UN forces back to the 38th parallel. Inconclusive but fierce fighting continued for two years while truce negotiations were being held. An armistice agreement (July 27, 1953) between the warring parties ended three years of fighting and established a demilitarized zone near the original border at the 38th parallel. North and South Korea, however, remain in a technical state of war because later negotiations for a peace treaty between the two nations failed. To this date, a Military Armistice Commission (MAC) and a Neutral Nations Supervisory Commission (NNSC) continue to supervise the truce. The MAC is composed of five officers from North and South Korea, who supervise the armistice and settle any violations through negotiations. The MAC consists of officers from Sweden, Switzerland, Poland, and Czechoslovakia, who carry out specific functions of supervision, observation, inspection, and investigation.

North Korea's ambition to conquer South Korea by force fortunately failed, but the war caused enormous property damage and over 1.6 million combat casualties. Nearly 147,000 South Korean forces and 35,000 UN soldiers died during the bitter three-year war. North Korean and Chinese forces suffered approximately 1.42 million casualties over the same period.[3] These figures, however, cannot convey the horrors, which the war inflicted on the Korean people. Even to this day, the South is concerned by possible military actions by the North.

After the end of the Korean War, the United States adopted a general policy of military containment, diplomatic isolation, and economic sanctions against North Korea. In order to prevent another war, Washington signed a mutual security treaty with Seoul in 1953. To implement its anti-communist containment policy in Asia, furthermore, the United States signed a series of bilateral and multilateral security treaties with South Korea, Japan, the Philippines, Thailand, Australia, and New Zealand. The U.S.–led coalition with Japan and Korea, however, faced a counter-alliance of North Korea, the Soviet Union, and China. In the 30-year Treaty of Friendship, Alliance, and Mutual Assistance, signed in February 1950, the Soviet Union and China agreed to use "necessary means" to prevent the revival of Japanese imperialism. This Sino-Soviet treaty served as a model for North Korea's mutual defense treaties with the Soviet Union and China that were signed in 1961. These treaties by two rival camps fully integrated the Korean peninsula into the Cold War bipolar framework.[4]

However, a series of events since the late 1980s transformed the relations among the two Koreas and four pacific powers from confrontation to cooperation. The four Pacific powers—China, Japan, Russia, and the United States—significantly expanded the scope of their cooperation in military, diplomatic, and economic fields. South Korea increased its level of cooperation with these four powers during the same period. Even North Korea gradually improved its relations with South Korea, Japan, and the United States—until President Bush labeled North Korea as an "axis of evil" in his State of the Union address on January 29, 2002. In other words, the axis of evil remark by Bush effectively stalled many reforms in North Korea and reversed relations between North Korea and other countries from cooperation to confrontation.

When six nations (China, Japan, North Korea, South Korea, Russia, and the United States) reached a six-point agreement at the fourth round of talks in Beijing on North Korea's nuclear program in September 2005, some observers felt that the nuclear standoff might be resolved peacefully. A series of one-sided hardline actions taken by both sides since then, however, have caused their relationship to deteriorate making military confrontation more likely.

Juche Principle and Military-First Policy

Under the custodianship of Kim Il Sung and Kim Jong Il, *juche* (the principle of self-reliance) has guided North Korea's ideology. *Juche* is credited to Kim Il Sung, who is characterized in the 1998 socialist constitution and elsewhere as "a genius ideological theoretician." The first syllable, *ju*, means "the main or fundamental" principle; the second syllable, *che*, means body, self, or the foundation of something. Kim introduced *juche* in a speech to Korean Workers Party propaganda and agitation workers on December 28, 1955, when he was still trying to eliminate his rival politicians. *Juche*, repeated endlessly in classrooms and in the media, emphasizes national self-reliance, independence, and worship of the supreme leader. Although North Koreans often fail to follow the teachings of *juche* in their everyday lives, the ideology remains a powerful influence on their domestic and intentional policies.

Kim Jong Il transformed *juche* from a nationalistic ruling ideology to a cult ideology. Kim Jong Il was officially introduced as Kim Il Sung's successor in 1980. Not being a soldier, a statesman, or an economist, Kim Jong Il's role was to interpret and propagandize *juche* ideology and oversee cultural affairs. Because he was accountable to no one except his father, Kim Jong Il made *juche* an article of faith rather than a guide to practice all matters.[5]

North Korea's economy prominently adheres to the ideological principle of *juche* under the following three principles. First, the 1998 revision of North Korea's constitution stipulates that all means of production are owned solely by the state and cooperative organizations. All industrial facilities and commercial enterprises are state owned. Most farms operate as collectives under the strict guidance of the party. Under the second economic principle of central planning, the state formulates unified and detailed plans to guarantee a high rate of production growth and balanced development of the national economy. The third economic principle of *juche* is self-sufficiency, that is to say, socialist production relations are based upon the foundation of an independent national economy. In accordance with the *juche* principle, North Korea's foreign trade amounts only to around 10 percent of gross national product (GNP), far below that of most other economies.

Kim's speech also revealed a core concept of national self-reliance and pride. Thus, North Korea adapted Marxist-Leninist principles to Korean conditions, rather than accept them wholesale. However, the Western press ridiculed his appeal to nationalism because during the Korean War, China had saved North Korea as a state and Soviet aid strove to rebuild its economy. Of course, other measures of its dependence, such as reliance on foreign powers for economic aid and military support, eroded the belief that the North was a self-reliant country. Consequently, the original idea of self-reliance underwent revisions in the intervening years to make it compatible with evolving interpretations of *juche*. It is not unusual in North Korea to revise original texts for later publication to make them consistent with more recent ideological thought. For North Koreans, *juche* is inseparable from socialism, and is considered the only means by which the masses can gain independence. Still, whatever changes evolved in the *juche* concept over the years, North Korea's commitment to socialism as an organizational principle has never changed.

As *juche* developed, the principle addressed several major issues. First, it served to maintain North Korea's independence in the international community. Second, it modeled the North Korean people into ever-loyal disciples of the leader, but at the same time it gave them an individual purpose as "masters of society." Third, it glorified the solidarity of the people as a modern Confucian family around the party and its leader. Fourth, it defended North Korea's brand of socialism in the face of declining living standards and the collapse of the international communist bloc. Finally, under increasingly miserable conditions in the wake of Kim Il Sung's death, it gave the people a reason to live, or even to die, for the regime.

It seems that most people support the idea of *juche* as a principle of national sovereignty, pride, and self-sufficiency. Pride in one's own country and the desire to preserve its independence characterize all nations. National self-sufficiency appeals to everyone, but people with knowledge of economics realize that national economies must operate interdependently. However, North Korea has used *juche* to control the masses. *Juche* has been attached as a label to any idea promoted by the Kims. *Juche* farming, for example, prescribes when and how crops are to be planted; *juche* steel dictates the steelmaking process. In all cases, *juche* strives to make local production units self-sufficient as the nation progresses to self-sufficiency; *juche* ideology functions as an anchor to keep the North Korean state from moving with the times.

In the 1990s, the North Korean economy ground to a halt as its people faced disease and starvation, and communist countries elsewhere toppled like dominos. How, in hard times like this, did the North Korean masses accept or at least tolerate socialism, and the greatness of the leader who brought them to ruin? First, North Korea forced people to engage in endless study and self-criticism so that they would be loyal to the leader and the party indefinitely. Second, they have never experienced political or social freedom. During the Choson dynasty, many of them worked for landlords. Shortly after the turn of the century, the entire economy was geared to supply Japan. After World War II, the communists imposed a centralized form of nonparticipatory government. To the North Korean people, life in this autocratic society was business as usual. Third, the masses in North Korea differ in an important respect from those in the former Soviet Union and Eastern Europe—they are cut off from outside information. Because North Koreans have little information about life or thought outside, they have nothing else to believe if they reject what they are told. Finally, even if they were not committed to some ideological points and disbelieved others, they had no energy to pursue their own thoughts and no opportunity to discuss them. So, to avoid complicating life, they abandoned political thought and resigned themselves to repeating the political lessons they were taught.

Sŏn'gun, often spelled *Songun*, is North Korea's "military-first" policy, which prioritizes the Korean People's Army in the affairs of state and in the allocation of national resources.[6] This policy makes the case for an integrated approach to North Korea's guiding principle based on core concepts of both self-reliance and Confucianism, which values a patriarchal chain of command. This policy did not appear as an official government policy until after Kim Il Sung's death in 1994. In 1995, military-first policy was introduced both as a revolutionary idea of attaching great importance to the army, and as politics of emphasizing the perfect unity and the single-hearted unity of the party, army, and the people, with the role of the army as the vanguards. Military-first policy was designed to strengthen Kim Jong Il's absolute authority, mixing its tradition of self-reliance and Confucianism in the role of the army as vanguards for politics, economics, and international relations.

Why *songun*? Although many explanations have been offered on the reasons for North Korea's adoption of *songun as* its primary ideology, most views fall into two categories: external and internal affairs. First, one view of the debate points to North Korea's desire to increase its military strength due to its precarious international position. In this sense, *songun* is perceived as an aggressive, threatening move to increase the strength of the North Korean military at the expense of other parts of society. This argument points to the series of crises that befell North Korea in the early 1990s (i.e., the end of Cold War) and in the late 1990s (i.e., great famine). The other view focuses on internal North Korean politics as the cause for the move to military-first policy. When Kim Il Sung died in 1994, the most important position held by his son Kim Jong Il was second in command of the military. This left him with no choice but to use the Korean People's Army to consolidate his power. This line of argument points out that Kim Jong Il deliberately chose to sideline other aspects of the government in order to assert the primacy of the army.

Songun seems to fit very well with the possession of nuclear weapons, and can be seen as a way of making such weapons central to the government's ideology of self-governance with Kim Jong Il at the top of the supreme political structure. This leads to the concern that the longer the military-first ideology guides North Korea, the less likely the United States and its allies will be able to convince North Korea to give up its nuclear weapons program. In addition, North Korea could perceive attempts at de-nuclearization as a threat to the primacy of the military within North Korea, thereby casting doubt that North Korea is actually willing to give up its nuclear weapons program at all.

North Korea's Nuclear Weapons Program

In 1989, it became undeniably obvious that North Korea was assembling the elements of a nuclear weapons program. However, North Korea's program of nuclear technology emerged as early as the late 1950s; it gained momentum in the 1960s and again in the mid–1980s. North Korea initially obtained a small research reactor from Russia and later began construction on a larger reactor at the Yongbyon site. U.S. intelligence discovered this reactor under construction in 1984 and pressured Moscow to obtain North Korean agreement to the Nuclear Non-Proliferation Treaty (NPT) in late 1985. A series of delays kept the International Atomic Energy Agency (IAEA) inspectors away from Yongbyon for several years. In 1989, the U.S. Central Intelligence Agency obtained conclusive evidence of a North Korean reprocessing facility near the main reactor at Yongbyon.

The year 1991—the end of the cold war—inaugurated a new turn of events that are still unfolding; its culmination is still uncertain. In that year, both Russia and China moved toward a two–Korea policy, with obstacles to the South's joining the UN removed, thus forcing the long resistant North to accept dual membership. Consequently, the two Koreas became members of the UN in 1991. Now, North Korea had even greater reason to seek normalization of relations with the United States and Japan. At the same time, the U.S. tried to develop relations with North Korea, because it recognized that any outbreak of hostilities on the peninsula would constitute a serious blow to the region and its own economic security.

The United States, however, stipulated that progress on U.S.–North Korean relations had to be tied to advances in inter–Korean talks, and that North Korea had to permit the IAEA to inspect its nuclear facilities. By mid-1991, the North was prepared to move in these directions. The United States then withdrew its tactical nuclear weapons from South Korea in 1991. In January 1992, North Korea signed a nuclear safeguard agreement with the IAEA, which inspected its nuclear facilities six times between May 1992 and January 1993.[7] In spite of this improvement in North-South relations, U.S. and South Korean forces conducted Team Sprit 1993 war exercises to harass North Korea. North Korea announced its intention to withdraw from the NPT in March 1994, shut down its 5-megawatt reactor to unload fuel roads in May 1994, and rejected IAEA inspections of its military sites, thereby provoking an international crisis.

As President Bill Clinton considered military actions against North Korea in early June 1994, former President Jimmy Carter reentered the Korea saga to play another historic role. At 69 years of age, Carter had already played a post-presidential intermediary role in the Middle East, Ethiopia, Sudan, Somalia, and the former Yugoslavia. His trip to Pyongyang on June 15, 1994, set the stage for resolving this crisis peacefully, as North Korea agreed to freeze its nuclear program and permit the two remaining IAEA inspectors to remain in North Korea until the completion of the planned third round of U.S.–North Korea nuclear negotiations. In fact, his mission to North Korea saved President Clinton from the most catastrophic military crisis of his presidency. Jimmy Carter received a Nobel Peace Prize in 2002 in recognition of his contribution for world peace and charitable activities.

After a period of intense negotiations, the United States and North Korea reached the Agreed Framework in October 1994, which was one consequence of engagement.[8] Under this agreement, North Korea pledged to abandon its nuclear program ambitions and to remain in the NPT regime. In exchange, the U.S. agreed to offer North Korea two light-water reactors (LWR), interim deliveries of oil, and expanded contacts with the United States and other powers. As a result, the Korean Energy Development Organization (KEDO) was born to construct the LWRs and to provide North Korea with 500,000 tons of oil per year during their. This Agreed Framework created a mechanism for North Korea to interact in a constructive fashion with South Korea, the United States, and other participants in the arrangement.

In spite of many disputes over details of this agreement, it had served its purpose of capping North Korea's nuclear weapons program. North Korea had complied with the framework law, shut down its main Yongbyon reactor and the reprocessing facility, allowed repeated IAEA site visits, and done everything else the agreement called for. At the same time, the KEDO program had gone forward, with groundbreaking ceremonies taking place on August 19, 1997. Completion of the project was scheduled for 2004, with an estimated cost of about $5 billion.

On August 31, 1998, North Korea sent a three-stage rocket roaring into the heavens from a launch site on the shores of the Sea of Japan, which both North and South Korea call "The East Sea." As far as U.S. monitors could determine, the effort to launch a satellite failed. However, the range of the rocket, especially the third stage, was an unpleasant discovery for those concerned about North Korea's potential for launching ballistic missiles with highly lethal and destructive warheads. In mid–September 1999, North Korea agreed to a moratorium on further missile tests while talks continued. In return, President Clinton lifted some sanctions that banned most U.S. exports and imports to and from North Korea. However, it continued to develop a two-stage missile that would be capable of reaching parts of the western United States. Moreover, some analysts believed that North Korea was not only capable of developing many nuclear weapons, but that the country already had one or two nuclear weapons that could be mounted on those missiles. Thus, the United States used this kind of information to justify its plans for multi-billion-dollar missile defense systems capable of shooting down a limited ICBM attack on the United States. In other words, U.S. officials insisted that the missile defense program existed to defeat strikes by North Korea and other "rogue" nations.

In April 1996, the United States and South Korea proposed the four-party talks—the United States, North and South Koreas, and China—to solve the pending issues between the two Koreas. This format was a compromise between the two extreme options suggested by North and South Korea. North Korea has tried to bypass Seoul through direct negotiations with Washington. South Korea, on the other hand, has insisted on talks between the primary parties on the Korean peninsula.

The four-party talks had several advantages. First, they signaled the beginning of a face-to-face dialogue among the parties in the Korean War with the purpose of replacing the truce with a lasting structure for peace. Second, the talks provided an arena in which the United States and South Korea may use China as a lever against North Korea. Third, North Korea saw the talks as a vehicle to become closer to the United States. Fourth, China used this forum as a means to maintain good relations with the United States and other western powers for its own economic and security interests.

Though this four-party meeting seemed to have a high probability of success, these talks went nowhere. Until the second preliminary session, North Korea had reiterated its position that the agenda should include a permanent peace agreement between Pyongyang and Washington, along with withdrawal of U.S. troops stationed in South Korea—precisely the items that the U.S. and South Korea were not prepared to concede. Only after food aid was promised in 1998 did North Korea agree to attend the first formal meeting held in Geneva on December 9, 1999.

From October 3 to October 5, 2002, the U.S. and North Korea had their first high-level contact in Pyongyang after a nearly two-year hiatus, but they failed to reach any agreement on a range of security issues. In fact, this brief interaction effectively worsened U.S.–North Korean relations. North Korea charged that James Kelly, U.S. Assistant Secretary of State for East Asian and Pacific Affairs, visited North Korea not to negotiate but to make the following demands: the suspension of Pyongyang's nuclear weapons program, verifiable controls on missile production and exports, the reduction of conventional forces along the 38th parallel, and the improvement of human rights. To the Bush administration's surprise, North Koreans admitted to Kelly that his evidence about their secret nuclear weapons program was correct. The North's admission of these actions violates the 1994 Agreed Framework, in which it pledged to abandon its nuclear weapons program in return for a construction of two light-water reactors and 500,000 tons of oil each year until the reactors were completed.

North Korea offered talks with the United States to rectify the concerns over its nuclear weapons program. However, the Bush administration rejected these proposals, which were actually similar to North Korea's repeated offers over the last 50 years to give up its nuclear weapons program in exchange for a non-aggression pact with the United States. In addition, Japan, South Korea, and the European Union agreed that oil deliveries to North Korea should continue, as it represented the best available bait to lure the nation away from developing weapons of mass destruction. However, on November 14, 2002, the Executive Board of KEDO decided to end their monthly fuel deliveries to North Korea under heavy pressure from the Bush administration. In late

December 2002, North Korea evicted international nuclear inspectors in a move to restart its main nuclear weapons complex, which experts believed could produce several powerful nuclear weapons within months.

In 1968, Great Britain, the U.S., and the Soviet Union signed a Treaty on the Non-Proliferation of Nuclear Weapons, usually called the Non-Proliferation Treaty (NPT), to halt the spread of atomic weapons; the UN approved the treaty on March 5, 1970. Under the treaty, five permanent members of the UN Security Council—China, France, Great Britain, the Soviet Union, and the U.S.—agreed not to transfer nuclear weapons to other nations and not to assist other nations in the development their own nuclear devices. The IAEA, the UN watchdog that monitors the 1970 treaty, consists of 187 countries as signatories. Today only four other countries—Cuba, India, Israel, and Pakistan—are not signatories. South Korea joined the IAEA on April 23, 1975, while North Korea joined on December 12, 1985. On January 10, 2003, North Korea pulled out of the IAEA on the grounds that the U.S. continues to maintain its hostile policy toward the country.

Although six nations reached a six-point agreement at the fourth round of talks in Beijing on North Korea's nuclear program in September 2005, subsequent negotiations failed to make progress on implementing this agreement in which the North pledged to give up its nuclear programs in exchange for aid and security guarantees. On September 16, 2006, North Korea's No. 2 leader, Kim Yong Sam blamed the lack of world peace on the United States at the Nonaligned Movement Summit of the 118 countries held in Havana, Cuba. North Korea "has been left with no other choice but possess nuclear weapons as a self-defense deterrent," he said. Kim said U.S. financial restrictions aimed at Pyongyang had created a deadlock in six-party talks on its nuclear program. On October 9, 2006, North Korea tested a nuclear weapon, once again capturing the world's attention. On June 12, 2009, the United Nations Security Council unanimously voted to expand and tighten sanctions on North Korea after the nation's second nuclear test. In fact, the United Nations, the United States, and its allies have taken a series of new hardline actions—tougher sanctions, stronger proliferation security initiative (PSI), and so on—to punish North Korea for its defiant May 25, 2009 atomic test, and a barrage of missile tests. The latest standoff between the United States and North Korea on nuclear weapons created a climate for another potential war on the Korean peninsula. North Korea, though much poorer than South Korea, has a bigger army and is rapidly expanding its weapons of mass destruction. Experts fear it could threaten the continental U.S. with a nuclear, chemical, or biological missile in the foreseeable future.

The Future of North Korea

As with East and West Germany when the Berlin Wall fell in 1989, it is difficult to predict when and how the two Koreas will be united. However, most experts think that there are three broad alternative outcomes: war, a North Korean collapse, or the continuation of a two-state peninsula.[9] However, one can break down the future of North Korea into five scenarios of change: unification through the military defeat of North Korea, unification through collapse of North Korea, continuation of the status quo, reform without regime change, and reform with regime change.

North and South Korea may be united by a war. Will North Korea attack the South? This has been one of the key questions for the United States and South Korea in attempting to develop trilateral relations with the country over six decades. The usual argument for this possibility is that North Korean leaders will have no options but war against the South when their regime collapses. A conventional attack by North Korea, however, is highly unlikely—as long as the U.S. security umbrella over South Korea remains intact and North Korea receives economic assistance from South Korea, China, Russia, and other countries. Should North Korea launch a conventional attack, the combined forces of the United States and South Korea would be free to retaliate, which is likely to end the existence of North Korea.

If North Korea faces political and economic problems beyond its control, it is possible that North Korea will invade South Korea out of desperation. In fact, North Korea has repeatedly stated that if they will have to go under, they will drag South Korea along. Seoul's location just 25 miles south of the demilitarized zone makes it virtually impossible to protect from initial artillery attacks. Even with modern antibattery guided weapons, the greater Seoul metropolitan area could not escape damage that would wreak havoc where about a third of the South Korean population makes a living.

The North Korean collapse is the most undesirable outcome for North Korean leadership, who will thus try to avoid it at all costs. Moreover, South Korea might not want to absorb North Korea for a variety of reasons, such as the enormous cost of unification and the possible social chaos from a massive migration of Northerners into the already crowded South. In fact, some analysts believe that South Korea would try to prevent the collapse of North Korea if the regime appears to be teetering. South Korea's reluctance to absorb North Korea, and Chinese help, may preserve the longevity of the North Korean regime for quite some time. Nevertheless, some analysts believe that North Korea will eventually collapse mainly due to three sets of economic problems. The first concerns the stresses faced by war economies—economic systems on total war mobilization. The second involves severe exogenous economic shocks to centrally planned economies. Historically, such shocks have generated not only systemwide crises, such as the collapse of the Soviet Union, but also international sanctions or wartime embargoes. The third set of problems pertains to the stresses related to food shortages under communist economies.

Continuation of the status quo must also be counted among North Korea's future scenarios. Certainly, this is the option that North Korean leaders want most. When Kim Il Sung died in 1994, some experts suggested a time frame of two or three years within which North Korea must either attack South Korea or fall apart. But now, many people believe that North Korea's remarkable survival skills will enable it to continue to survive without overhauling its political-economic structure. North Korea has room to maneuver in foreign policy because the five governments that must contend most directly with Pyongyang—Seoul, Washington, Beijing, Tokyo, and Moscow—do not want an abrupt shift in the status quo.

Reform without regime change has been going on for some time. First, North Korean leaders seem to have realized that they can no longer ignore domestic and external pressures for change. Second, they may think that they can control the pace of economic liberalization and lessen the danger of East German style disintegration. South Korea and the United States had felt that the best way to minimize the risk on the Korean peninsula was to offer all possible inducements to North Korea to choose peace and reform. Some fruits of this policy include the summits of 2000 and 2007 between North and South Korean leaders, and several rounds of six-party talks between 2004 and 2008. However, the Bush administration's hardline policy toward North Korea and North Korea's tests of nuclear weapons in 2006 and 2009 have practically halted many North Korean reforms.

Reform with regime change is unlikely to occur soon, though it may be possible at some point in the future. North Korea must have learned a critical lesson from Eastern Europe's experience in the early 1990s. The lesson is that once you open the floodgate, no one can stop the flow. Thus, North Korean leaders will try to keep the country closed for as long as possible. However, forces for change, such as North Korean economic problems and the growing globalization, are almost impossible to ignore. The North Korean military or a group it supports is most likely to seize power if there is any new regime in the North.

The future of Korea boils down to a struggle for power between the two camps: South Korea, Japan, and the U.S. on one hand; and North Korea, China, and Russia on the other. China and Russia will stand by the North

Korean regime to prevent any radical changes on the peninsula. Clearly, South Korea, Japan, and the U.S. prefer that North Korea liberalize its economy. North Korea knows that such reforms may contain the seeds of its defeat or demise. The painful fact is that North Korean patrons—China and Russia— may not have the ability either to withstand the pressures from the Western camp or to match the assistance it offers. Nevertheless, analysts believe that North Korea is likely to muddle through with support from China, Russia, and South Korea, which would like to avoid its collapse.

Conclusion

North Korea's nuclear weapons program has been a major headache for the United States throughout the post–Cold War era. Pyongyang's development of nuclear weapons created serious problems with the Clinton administration (1993–2001) and the George W. Bush administration (2001–2009), as both U.S. administrations maintained that the non-proliferation of nuclear weapons was essential for the preservation of the existing international order. Although the United States succeeded in persuading North Korea to give up its nuclear weapons program through the six-party talks by September 2005 (i.e., the September 19th Joint Statement), Pyongyang did not fulfill its commitment on denuclearization by the end of 2008. As a result, the Obama administration has inherited the unfinished task of implementing the agreement on North Korea's denuclearization.

The inauguration of the Obama administration in January 2009 aroused expectations in Pyongyang that the strained relationship between North Korea and the United States would improve under the new U.S. administration, because Obama had indicated during the 2008 presidential campaign his willingness to meet even with leaders of rogue nations, such as Kim Jong Il of North Korea, if that was what it took to resolve the North Korean nuclear issue. However, contrary to North Korea's expectations, the bilateral relationship between the two countries has not improved but has deteriorated further, mainly because North Korea conducted missile and nuclear tests in the spring of 2009 and the United Nations imposed economic sanctions against North Korea in the fall of 2009.[10]

Notes

1. Published in an earlier version as Chapter 1 of *Economic Sanctions Against a Nuclear North Korea: An Analysis of United States and United Nations Actions Since 1950* by Suk Hi Kim and Semoon Chang, eds. (Jefferson, NC: McFarland, 2007).

2. R. Ratnesar, "How Dangerous Is North Korea?" *Time*, January 13, 2003, pp. 21–29.
3. Korean Overseas Information Service, *Focus on Korea: This Is Korea* (Seoul: Seoul International Publishing House, 1986).
4. N. Eberstadt, "Disparities in Socioeconomic Development in Divided Korea," *Asian Survey* (November/December 2000): 867–893.
5. Oh Kongdan and R.C. Hassig, *North Korea Through the Looking Glass* (Washington, DC: Brookings Institution, 2000).
6. Many parts of this section explicitly draw on "Songun," http://en.wikipedia.org/wiki/Songun, April 8, 2010; and Koga, Kei, "The Anatomy of North Korea's Foreign Policy Formulation," *North Korean Review* (Fall 2009): 21–33.
7. J.M. Swomley, "North Korea's Military Threat Has Been Exaggerated," in William Dudley, ed., *North and South Korea* (New York: Greenhaven, 2002), pp. 26–33.
8. M.J. Mazarr, "Predator States and War: The North Korea Case," in Dong Whan Park, ed., *The United States and Two Koreas: A New Triangle* (Boulder, CO: Lynne Rienner, 1998), pp. 75–96.
9. M. Noland, ed., *Economic Integration of the Korean Peninsula* (Washington, DC: Institute for International Economics, January 1998).
10. H.N. Kim, "U.S.–North Korea Relations Under the Obama Administration," *North Korean Review* (Spring 2010): 20–36.

CHAPTER 2

Will North Korea Be Able to Overcome the Third Wave of Its Collapse?

Suk Hi Kim*

ABSTRACT

This chapter addresses the problem of the third wave of the North Korean collapse in the first decade of the 2000s and asks if North Korea will overcome it. The author explains that a combination of unique cultural and historical factors, including the part played by Neo-Confucianism, the principle of self-reliance (*Juche*), and the military-first policy (*Songun*), have contributed to the survival of the crisis-ridden and impoverished North Korean state in the post–Soviet era. Examining these factors in conjunction with established prediction scenarios, this chapter argues that the collapse of North Korea in the near future is unlikely. Because North Korea will be around for some time to come, confidence-building initiatives are needed to resolve long-standing security, energy, and economic issues between the country, the major powers, and other regional actors.

Introduction

In the first decade of the 2000s, North Korea faced the third wave of its collapse, a phenomenon triggered by food shortages, failed currency-economic reforms, and Kim Jong Il's declining health. The first wave occurred in the 1980s, when the North Korean economy spiraled downward as its chief allies—

---

*Originally published in Nautilus Policy Forum Online, Policy Forum 10-041: July 27, 2010, http://www.nautilus.org/publications/essays/napsnet/policy-forums-online/security2009-2010/will-north-korea-be-able-to-overcome-the-third-wave-of-its-collapse.

the Soviet Union and China—discontinued new loans and demanded payment for outstanding debts. The second wave came in the late 1990s, when the great North Korean famine claimed anywhere between 200,000 and 3,000,000 lives. Every Communist country either collapsed or carried out significant economic reforms following the fall of the Soviet Union, except for North Korea. Renewed speculation of a North Korean collapse has come from numerous intelligence analysts, scholars, think tank specialists, and relief organizations.[1] Why should one assume that North Korea, the only Communist country today without significant economic reforms, can defeat the pattern of history and survive?[2]

The termination of the Cold War in 1991 and the onset of food shortages in North Korea strengthened the widespread belief that, just like East Germany, the Pyongyang regime was doomed to collapse. The persistence of this belief, especially by the United States and its allies, is the main reason why they failed to develop a coherent long-term policy toward North Korea. Instead, these actors have relied on short-term fixes while waiting for a collapse. Admittedly, there may be several similarities in the recent histories of Korea and Germany, even commonalities in the last fifty years, but a collapse of North Korea is unlikely anytime soon.[3] Similarities between the two nations include the occupation and division of societies with a long history, the Cold War and participation in the Soviet alliance and trading bloc, tensions between a dictatorial Communist system and a liberal capitalist system, and a traumatized sense of postwar national identity. When predicting a collapse, however, many observers overlook the unique cultural and historical factors that distinguish the two nations. The Soviet military occupation imposed an alien totalitarian Stalinist model in East Germany, whereas Stalinist totalitarianism in North Korea was reinforced by centuries of feudal autocracy and guided by Neo-Confucianism and the concept of national self-reliance (*Juche*). On the basis of Neo-Confucian and *Juche* principles, along with sociohistorical factors, North Korea might experience longevity, contrary to widespread assumptions that the country will collapse in the conceivable future, thus justifying a strong case for a new way of thinking about the possible solution of the United States–North Korean nuclear standoff.

Neo-Confucianism

Before the division of the Korean peninsula in August 1945, Korea was home to a population with tendencies of ethnic and linguistic homogeneity, coupled with a history of exclusionism as a result of numerous invasions and territorial claims by powerful countries, for example, the Chinese and Mongol empires and, in more recent history, the Japanese Empire. That is a legacy with reverberations in North Korea today. Besides premodern and twentieth-century imperialism, a history of Neo-Confucianism and a top-down bureaucratic and administrative structure continue to assert influence in North Korean governance. Confucianism, the source of Korean Neo-Confucianism, is an ideology and value system rooted in ancient China and derived from the social-political philosophy of K'ung Fu Tzu (551–479 B.C.), better known as Confucius. Born during a period of social crisis in the Chinese Empire, Confucius was deeply concerned by the unstable state of affairs in his country and sought the reformation of Chinese social life.

As a secular political-philosophical doctrine, Confucianism promotes a value system based on harmony in human relations structured around the so-called "three bonds and five relations." The three bonds are (1) ruler-minister, (2) parent-child, and (3) husband-wife. The five relations are (1) ruler-subject, (2) father-son, (3) husband-wife, (4) elder-younger brothers, and (5) friend-friend. These relations are based on ideals of righteousness, affection, respect, faithfulness, and the separation of social functions. Societies deeply affected by Confucian ethics and statecraft include, most notably, the Northeast Asian countries of China, Japan, and Korea. Politically, Confucianism promotes a type of virtuocracy (government by virtue), emphasizing moral education, self-cultivation, family regulation, and harmony in social relationships.[4]

Confucius had some 3,000 disciples who recorded his thought in volumes of commentary and dialogs. Although the philosopher and his followers traveled throughout China as political advisors, Confucius never held a government position to test his theories. He lived primarily as an itinerant scholar and teacher. Despite the fact that Confucius avoided metaphysical and supernatural questions for human affairs, social order, and good government, his thought nevertheless came to function as a substitute religion. Subsequent followers venerated the sage and his greatest disciples, such as the Neo-Confucian Chu Hsi (1130–1200), in an effort to spread Confucian doctrine.

Chu Hsi Neo-Confucianism, introduced to Korea in the fourteenth century, became the predominant philosophical system of the Choson dynasty (1392–1910) and greatly influenced the political and social order of the peninsula. The ethical and social-political philosophy was accepted so eagerly and strictly by the Koreans that the Chinese came to regard Korea as "the country of Eastern decorum."[5] Neo-Confucianism thoroughly influenced education, ceremony, and civil administration. More specifically, the doctrine became the guiding precept of the state, presiding over social reform and the development of judicial systems. The deeply ingrained legacy of Neo-Confucianism is still an important feature of Korean life, and South Korean academics, for example, attempt to make Confucian values relevant to modern, post-industrial society, stressing reverence for learning and culture, social stability, and respect for the past. Korea is thus a nation built on strictly defined relationships centered on the idea that one person is naturally superior to another. Several factors determine status, and the social rules are so extensive that there is nearly always something to distinguish two people. Even the firstborn among twins has superior status. While determining social status can be complex, Koreans know how to identify their place in the vertical social hierarchy.

The Neo-Confucian tradition in Korea also includes worship of ancestors, continuity of family bloodlines, and proper burial of patriarchs and matriarchs. Burial of an ancestor is of considerable importance in Korean Neo-Confucianism. That is because the place of rest of the deceased is believed to affect posterity. Therefore, "ancestral remains are sometimes moved to a more propitious location several years after internment. This is especially true if a lack of preparation or a lack of financial resources mandated less than suitable arrangements at the time of death."[6] Respect for the dead also comes in the form of continued ancestral rites and memorial ceremonies. Many South Koreans, for instance, hold memorial rites for their deceased parents before important events in the belief that the duly departed can help them obtain their wishes. South Korean presidential candidates have even visited their parents' graves beseeching good fortune. Also, in an April 10, 2010, case, former Prime Minister Han Myung-sook visited the grave of President Rho Moo-hyun when a Seoul court dismissed bribery charges against her. She said she visited Rho's grave to express appreciation for his help with the court finding her not guilty. Han served as a primer minister under Rho, who committed suicide on May 23, 2009, following bribery charges that tarnished his reputation.

Since the beginning of Japanese colonialism over Korea in 1910, the U.S.-Soviet liberation and division of the peninsula in 1945, the Korean War of 1950 to 1953, and the post–Korean War period, Neo-Confucianism has had a continued historical presence in Korea. Despite sixty years of nationally adapted Marxism-Leninism, North Korea still consciously appropriates the Neo-Confucian traditions of political centralization and obedience to authority. Neo-Confucianism, like its predecessor Confucianism, teaches that every person has a place in the social order and that the preservation of harmony in society is paramount. Under the influence of Neo-Confucian thought, inferiors in North Korea are expected to be obedient to superiors and superiors benevolent to inferiors. In practice, the obedience component is emphasized over the benevolence component in order to maintain the status quo. In addition, the emphasis on preserving harmony results in a lack of mobility between levels in the social hierarchy. Especially since the 1970s, the regime of Kim Il Sung and Kim Jong Il has consciously sought to wrap itself in the mantle of pre-modern Neo-Confucian values. The state constantly depicts the late leader and his son-successor as benevolent fathers of the nation. North Korean propaganda also refers to the country as one large family. Appeals for social and political support use metaphors designed to draw on the feelings of duty toward one's parents, seeking to transfer these feelings to a national father figure.[7] As a result of the peculiar historical situation on the Korean peninsula, the tightly controlled North Korean system has lasted longer than any other twentieth-century dictatorship, with the North Korean leadership carrying over traditions of centralized authority inherited from the Neo-Confucian Korean dynasties of the past.

Principle of Self-Reliance (Juche)

Under the auspices of Kim Il Sung and Kim Jong Il, *Juche*, not to mention its recent development as *Songun* (military-first) ideology, has served as the programmatic guide for North Korean politics. Officially, *Juche* was conceived by Kim Il Sung, who is described in the 2009 constitution as "a genius in ideology and theory." The word *Juche* (*zhŭtĭ* in Chinese) literally means agent, main part, subject. The first Chinese character *ju*/*zhŭ* means master, lord, primary, to host, to own. The second Chinese character (*che*/*tĭ*) means body, form, style, system. Kim Il Sung's first major official use of *Juche* appeared in his December 28, 1955, party speech in opposition to the Soviet campaign of "de–Stalinization" (bureaucratic self-reform), "On Eliminating Dogmatism and Formalism and Establishing the Subject in Ideological Work." Kim declared that the "subject" (*juche*) of the party ideological program was the Korean revolution, and he maintained a core belief in national self-determination and national pride. Thus, Soviet Marxist-Leninism was adapted to Korean conditions rather than accepted wholesale. Since China saved North Korea during the Korean War and Soviet and Eastern Bloc aid rebuilt the war-shattered national economy, North Korea was never regarded in the Western press to possess complete national self-determination. Dependence on fraternal aid and military support also confirms that the autarkic state was never, for that matter, a completely self-sufficient country.

The *Juche* slogan eventually emerged as an independent line and doctrine of national self-reliance in response to the Sino-Soviet split in the 1960s. As is well known, Kim advanced three key principles of *Juche* in his April 14,

1965, speech "On Socialist Construction and the South Korean Revolution in the Democratic People's Republic of Korea." These principles are (1) independence in politics (*chaju*), (2) self-sustenance in the economy (*charip*), and (3) self-defense in national defense (*chawi*). Kim Jong Il, who was officially designated as Kim's successor in 1980, transformed *Juche* into a cult ideology from the mid–1970s. Not being an economist, military man, or political leader, his role was to interpret and propagandize his father's doctrine and manage cultural affairs. Kim Jong Il was accountable to no one except Kim Il Sung and made *Juche* a fundamental belief in all matters.[8] Since its inception in 1955, *Juche* has undergone several pragmatic revisions, as seen in republished works by the Kims. Revision of authoritative texts is a common practice in North Korea, making the works consistent with and thereby justifying the changing political tactics. Ideologically, *Juche* is inseparable from socialism in the eyes of most North Koreans and is considered the only way the masses of people can maintain national independence. Yet, whatever modifications have been made in *Juche* over the past fifty-five years, the North Korean commitment to the program of nationally self-contained socialism has never changed.

Juche has several functions: (1) it serves to maintain the political independence of North Korea in the international community; (2) it simultaneously indoctrinates citizens to be loyal followers of the leader and to believe that they are the "masters of society"; (3) it promotes popular solidarity by uniting the people as a modern Neo-Confucian family headed by the "father leader" and "mother party"; (4) it justifies the North Korean conception of socialism amid economic decline in the post–Soviet era; and (5) finally, under adverse material conditions since the death of Kim Il Sung in 1994, it gives the people a reason to live, even to die for the regime. Apparently, most North Koreans seem to support *Juche* in principle. National pride and the desire to safeguard independence characterize all modern nations, and national self-sufficiency appeals to people in general, even though the world economic system makes it objectively necessary for national economies to operate interdependently.

Despite the apparent public support for *Juche* in principle, the North Korean leadership exploits it to preserve its own social interests. *Juche* is literally attached to anything sanctioned by Kim Il Sung and Kim Jong Il. For example, there is *Juche* art for the state-approved style, *Juche* farming for the prescribed planting of crops, and *Juche* steel for the steelmaking process. These notions create the idea that North Korea is self-sufficient. Unfortunately, *Juche* is an anchor that prevents the state from moving forward. Although it is propagated in the media and in classrooms, regular North Koreans often do not observe *Juche* teachings in day-to-day life. Nevertheless, the ideology exerts considerable influence on North Korean domestic and foreign policy. With Neo-Confucian elements, nationalist populism, and a quasi-religious appeal, *Juche* explains in part why the North Korean regime is able to command popular support in the eroding totalitarian system.

The North Korean economy continues to apply the three ideological principles of *Juche*. Even though the regime has made concessions to capitalism since the fall of the Soviet Union in 1991 and is being structurally reintegrated into the international profit system, the 2009 revised North Korean constitution still maintains that "the means of production are owned by the state and social cooperative organizations." State ownership of industries and enterprises continues to be a cornerstone of the system. Therefore, although farmers, for example, have begun producing crops privately, most farms operate as collectives under government supervision. Furthermore, while central control of the economy is eroding, the state still formulates coordinated plans for production growth and balanced national economic development. As per the *Juche* principle of self-sustenance in the economy, self-contained socialist production relations are based on an independent national economy. The result of *Juche* economics is that trade volume in 2008 was 3,820 million dollars ($1/244$ that of South Korea), and the nominal gross national income (GNI) was 27,347 billion won ($1/38$ that of South Korea).[9]

Military-First Policy (Songun)[10]

Songun (military-first) policy is a North Korean adaptation of *Juche* to the present domestic and world political situation and places the Korean People's Army at the head of state and economic affairs. As with *Juche* ideology, *Songun* advocates self-reliance, national familism, and patriarchalism. The military-first policy was introduced in the North Korean media in 1998; however, official North Korean histories have backdated it to a visit Kim Jong Il made to a military unit in 1995, even claiming the policy originated with Kim Il Sung in the 1930s anti-colonial guerrilla struggle against Imperial Japan. Coming after the death of Kim senior, *Songun* legitimizes rule under Kim Jong Il and the National Defense Commission, which became the highest organ of the state in 1998, contemporaneous with the inauguration of the military-first policy.

Why *Songun*? Although many explanations have been offered as to why North Korea has adopted *Songun* as its primary ideology, the views tend to fall into two general categories: external affairs and internal affairs. The first view points to the need to increase military strength in response to a precarious international situation. In this sense, *Songun* is perceived as an aggressive policy that privileges the North Korean military at the expense of other sectors of society. This argument points to the chain of crises that afflicted North Korea with the fall of the Soviet Union in the early 1990s and the great famine in the late 1990s. The second view focuses on internal politics as the reason behind the military-first policy. When Kim Il Sung died in 1994, the two most important positions held by his son, Kim Jong Il, were supreme commander of the Korean People's Army and chairman of the National Defense Commission (NDC). Consequently, Kim sidelined other areas of government and used the armed forces to consolidate personal power.

When North Korea adopted its revised constitution in 1998, the chairmanship of the NDC was elevated to the highest position of state authority. This new position gave Kim Jong Il a basis to legitimize his power. Under *Songun*, three functions of the military are as follows: (1) the military must live and die with the leader to the end; (2) the military will achieve its assigned goals at all costs; and (3) the most admirable quality of a soldier is to stay with the leader to defend the nation. Because *Songun* is now pervasive in North Korea and deeply integrated into the lives of the masses, it is highly unlikely that the North Korean regime will collapse as a result of an internal rebellion.[11] *Songun* also accommodates possession and production of nuclear weapons to ensure governance of the North Korean state. There is the concern that the longer the military-first ideology guides North Korea, the U.S. and its allies will be less able to coax the regime into relinquishing its nuclear arsenal and program. In addition, North Korea could perceive insistence to denuclearize as a threat to the ruling position of the military elite, thus casting doubt that North Korea will ever give up its nuclear weapons program. The military-first policy formulates domestic politics, foreign policy, and decision making in North Korea.

Analysts assert that *Songun* has been instrumental in transforming the country into a nuclear-armed state, despite international sanctions and worsening economic conditions. The core concepts of *Songun* are consistent with the presumed conviction in North Korea that only a "nuclear deterrent," to the use the North Korean phrase, will prevent a U.S. invasion. Some experts argue that North Korea will never surrender its nuclear weapons under any concessions with the U.S. and its allies. According to some observers, the foremost goal of North Korea until the 1990s was reunification of the Korean peninsula on its own terms. Since then, however, regime survival with the military-first policy has replaced reunification as the single most important prerogative of the state. Can North Korea survive as a sovereign country? Most analysts think that depends on its future economic conditions and problems.

With dissolution of the Soviet Union, North Korea began appealing for and accepting humanitarian assistance from the U.N. and other donor countries, extracted economic aid through brinkmanship diplomacy and missile tests, established a number of capitalist Special Economic Zones to attract foreign investment, allegedly earned a substantial amount of cash through narcotics sales, and carried out limited economic reforms. In other words, North Korea has made numerous small attempts to jumpstart its ailing economy, but these measures have been superficial and completely inadequate for pulling the economy out of its nosedive.

On October 9, 2006, North Korea conducted its first nuclear test, becoming the ninth member of the international "nuclear club." A second test with the same magnitude of the U.S. atomic bombs dropped on Japan in 1945 was conducted on May 25, 2009, at an unconfirmed location. A number of missile tests followed. Afterwards, the U.N. Security Council voted unanimously on June 12 to expand and tighten sanctions against North Korea. Altogether, the United Nations, the United States, and its allies have taken a series of hard-line actions (e.g., tougher sanctions and a stronger proliferation security initiative) to punish North Korea. Rather than being anything new, this is a continuation of policies that began with U.S. sanctions against North Korea on June 28, 1950, three days after the outbreak of the Korean War, in an attempt to destabilize the North Korean regime. Has the latest hard-line stance worked, or will it work? If history repeats itself, the new round of sanctions are bound to fail. Sanctions and other hard-line measures have been largely ineffective in forcing North Korea to change its domestic and foreign policy.

Before any country starts a battle or a war against another country, it needs to remember the three-sentence military strategy recommended by an ancient Chinese general Sun Tzu. "If you know the enemy and know yourself, you need not fear the result of a hundred battles. If you know yourself but not the enemy, for every victory gained you will also suffer a defeat. If you know neither the enemy nor yourself, you will succumb in every battle."[12] North Korea watchers who are anticipating the collapse of the state in the near future are encouraged to read *The Art of War*, an influential Chinese military manual written by Sun Tzu (ca. 544–496 B.C.) in the sixth century during the Warring States period (475–221 B.C.). Sun Tzu was a strategist and pragmatist committed to efficient and decisive military operations. His thirteen-chapter work examines different aspects of war, such as strategy, planning, and psychological warfare, and is a standard military text with a profound influence in Northeast Asian history. Sun Tzu, moreover, has had an important presence in the West since his introduction in the nineteenth century, and he is even studied in American military colleges. Given its historical and military significance, *The Art of War* is, no doubt, a work that is read in North Korea and likely instrumental in the logic behind the North Korean military-first policy.

Will Kim Jong Eun's Succession Go Smoothly?[13]

On September 27, 2010, North Korean leader Kim Jong Il anointed his third son, Kim Jong Un, as his successor. At first glance, the road ahead for the young age 27 and inexperienced Kim Jong Un, does not look smooth; however, Jennifer Lind at Dartmouth College argues that several factors, both internal and external, will work in his favor. He will rely on the system designed by his grandfather, the founder of North Korea, Kim Il Sung—a system that was designed for resilience.

1. Xenophobia is an ideological tool that helps prevent revolution. The regime's propaganda inspires fear of dire threats from the United States and it allies—justifies the powerful political role of the military.

2. The risk of popular rebellion is reduced by Kim Il Sung's social engineering. In the communist system that Kim Il Sung created, North Korea has neither a middle class nor a clergy—groups that are frequently instrumental in fomenting revolution.

3. Indeed, perhaps the most important factor deterring revolution in North Korea is the government's threat or use of force. Informants from multiple security agencies watch for any stirrings of dissent. North Korea's would-be freedom fighters know that they risk arrest, incarceration, torture, and death not only of themselves but also of their parents and children.

4. The odds of a military coup in North Korea have been significantly reduced by Kim Il Sung's measures to "coup-proof" his government. To maximize the intelligence he received about any brewing disloyalty, he designed multiple internal security agencies that competed with and watched one another, and all reported to him. In the event that these measures failed and a coup occurred, Kim Il Sung created a parallel military force to protect himself from the Korean People's Army.

5. Another factor reducing the likelihood of military coups is North Korea's class system, which is divided into three tiers—the core, wavering and hostile. The "core" class consists of favored elites who have impeccable pro-regime credentials. A "wavering" class has more questionable bloodlines. Consigned to the "hostile" class are people whose relatives fought for the South in the war or supported the Japanese occupation of the peninsula.

6. North Korea's greatest deterrent lies in its weakness. The collapse of the Kim regime in the event of war carries with it a grim specter of potential chaos which has led neighboring countries to prefer the status quo.

Despite all of the obstacles Kim Jong Un must overcome as he ascends the throne, powerful forces will encourage stability. Because of the regime's many tools of authoritarian control, revolutions or military coups will likely be deterred, detected, or quashed. Because of the dread of collapse, North Korea's neighbors will likely continue, at least to a certain point, to allow the regime to run its pathetic kingdom. The alternative is too dangerous.

Prediction Scenarios

Most North Korean experts divide predictions for North Korea into three broad scenarios: war, collapse, or the continuation of a two-state peninsula with some reform.[14] The United States is unlikely to attack North Korea, in view of the logistic and political problems it is confronting with the military occupations of Afghanistan and Iraq. North Korea will also not likely attack South Korea, because that would inevitably turn into a bigger war involving the United States and China, spelling the end of North Korea as it is known today. If the United States foresees North Korea as either collapsing or giving up its nuclear weapons through a policy of economic strangulation, the odds of success seem remote. Realistically, the most likely scenario in any conceivable future appears to be the continuation of a two-state peninsula with limited reforms, largely because China and South Korea presently wish to maintain North Korea as a viable buffer state.

One should ask why repeated collapse predictions by Western experts have not materialized in the North Korean case. If one studies reports prior to the North Korean missile and nuclear tests, one sees that some experts predicted that the country would not conduct these tests. North Korea is not conforming to analysis. Of course, North Korea is not the only case study in which social science predictions have failed. One can observe predictions preceding elections in countries worldwide and see results that are sometimes completely different from original forecasts. Forecasts concerning the Iraqi attack on Kuwait or the Chinese intervention in the Korean War are examples of how social science researchers can err. Miscalculations by analysts and incorrect predictions in the North Korean case occur for several specific reasons. Alon Levkowitz, a professor of international relations at the Tel Aviv University, has listed eleven reasons why Western experts are unable to make accurate forecasts about countries such as Iraq and North Korea: (1) analogies, (2) cold war mentality, (3) determinism, (4) idiosyncratic events, (5) lack of facts, (6) political bias, (7) psychological warfare, (8) too many variables, (9) terminology or translation problems, (10) Western-style logic, and (11) wishful thinking.[15]

How can the United States, China, and other countries that do not want a nuclear North Korea maintain the status quo on the Korean peninsula? The above discussion has ruled out predictions of unification through collapse or unification through military defeat. In addition, China will never allow the United States to unite the Korean peninsula on American terms. Western experts and policymakers will benefit from studying cultural, historical, political, and situational factors in order to see why what happened in East Germany is unlikely to be repeated in North Korea in the conceivable future. Unlike the East German case, attention should be given to the fact that North Korea has become increasingly dependent on China as its greatest economic benefactor—negotiating economic aid, inward investment, foreign trade, and political support—especially now that the Six-Party Talks are at a standstill and with U.S. and UN economic sanctions. There is no doubt that Chinese aid and support are designed to prevent a sudden North Korean collapse.

Chinese objectives toward North Korea are geared towards protecting Chinese national interests. That makes military-strategic environment, border security and stability, and economic development and political stability in bordering North Korean provinces a vital necessity. Understandably, international efforts to bring about a North Korean crisis or foreign regime change will face Chinese resistance. Although Chinese calculations for intervention are unknown, China will become involved and restore stability and political order in North Korea if circumstances run out of control.[16] Therefore, complete downfall in the third wave of the North Korean collapse might be wishful thinking on the part of those who want to see the country abandon its nuclear weapons program. Ironically, the U.S. strangulation policy may actually increase the probability that Pyongyang will produce more nuclear weapons and sell such weapons to the highest international bidder so as to replenish the impoverished North Korean economy. Oddly enough, the United States, its allies, North Korea, and many North Korean experts believe that the United States should hand out economic aid and a security assurance (replacement of the armistice agreement with a peace treaty) if North Korea dismantles its nuclear program to settle the nuclear deadlock.

The problem is that the United States and North Korea have been key enemies since the Korean War and naturally do not trust each other. Washington demands that North Korea destroy all its nuclear weapons in a complete, verifiable, and irreversible manner before substantial rewards are delivered. Pyongyang, however, insists that only if the United States first provides economic assistance and a security guarantee, will it gradually dismantle its nuclear weapons.[17] In view of the cold facts, the United States and its allies should acknowledge that North Korea will not collapse, nor will it surrender its nuclear weapons until the country gets what it wants. North Korea, too, should acknowledge that the United States and its allies will not give economic aid and security assurances until the country abandons its nuclear program. Psychiatrists explain that the most difficult part of their job is to convince their patients that they have problems beyond their control and need professional help. Likewise, some type of mechanism is needed to convince the United States and North Korea to admit that each party will never accept the other's demands, thus enabling each side to understand their respective positions more objectively. The problem is that any type of mechanism for such a task requires years of confidence-building.

Building Mutual Confidence

In the middle of a precarious and tough regional neighborhood, divided Korea stands as a pivot. History and geography have consigned the peninsula to the position of a highly contested strategic crossroads, the site of over a century of collisions between great power interests. Yet the four major powers—China, Japan, Russia, and the United States—will eventually have to work together, because they will need each other's help on Korean issues for their national security, energy security, and economic security needs. Where North Korea is concerned, it is imperative for one to step back and see the forest instead of the trees. The North Korean nuclear standoff must be taken on the premise that the United States and respective Northeast Asian countries will have to learn to work together. First, they have no other choice but to resolve the nuclear standoff through peaceful negotiations, since a nuclear North Korea poses a greater threat than that posed by the Middle East. Second, the Northeast Asian countries are likely to cooperate for their national energy security, as the region is home to major energy consumers, such as China, as well as major energy producers, such as Russia. The United States is likely to support such regional cooperation because it does not want these countries to depend excessively on Middle Eastern oil. Third, scholars argue that Northeast Asia is a region that has every possibility of becoming the best trading bloc in the future, given Japanese capital and technology, Chinese labor, Russian natural resources, and the Korean work ethic. In addition, the Northeast Asian countries and the United States have already had close economic ties for many years and are increasingly interdependent economically. Eventually, these factors are likely to compel the China, Japan, Russia, South Korea, and the United States to collaborate on security, energy, and economic issues, even if they have some differences.

An important implication of U.S. relations with North Korea is the impact of those relations on other nations in the region. If North Korea were to face political and economic problems beyond its control as a consequence of U.S. containment, there is a possibility, even if remote, that the threatened and desperate state could invade the South. North Korea, to be sure, has frequently declared that it will not capitulate without bringing South Korea into a conflict. With Seoul located a mere 25 miles below the Demilitarized Zone, it would be impossible to shield the city from North Korean artillery bombardment. Even without a direct invasion of the South, a hypothetical collapse of North Korea through U.S. containment policies would lead to insurmountable problems for South Korea. In short, North Korea stands as one of the few countries in the world that could involve the four major powers in major military operations. In view of the gravity of the situation, it is important for North Korea watchers to take a long-term view on North Korean affairs and promote mutual confidence-building initiatives.

If the land bridge that passes through North Korea were to be restored, not only Northeast Asian countries but also other parts of Asia, the Middle East, and Europe could be connected through a land transportation network with highways, railroads, and undersea tunnels. Such a network would open the possibility of direct travel between Tokyo and London by train, car, and truck. But before a transportation network comes into being, confidence-building with North Korea and billions in investments in its degraded rail and highway systems are needed. Of course, this future may not be possible until North Korea compromises on its nuclear weapons program and resolves reported human rights abuses. Such moves will help build public support in South Korea and other countries for substantial investment and enable international development aid.

Conclusion

This chapter has argued that the longevity of North Korea, owed to cultural, historical, political, and situational factors, and its role in Northeast Asia justify a strong case for a new way of thinking about the possible solution of the U.S.–North Korea nuclear standoff. Presently, no stable and authoritative institution exists for the deliberation and development of multilateral security, energy, and economic cooperation in Northeast Asia. One potential candidate for the role of driving Northeast Asian energy and economic cooperation is the Six-Party Talks, informally established to solve the nuclear dispute. Given the vital role of energy supply and economic growth in stabilizing the Korean peninsula, it is conceivable that the Six-Party Talks grouping could develop into a more formal economic institution even before solutions to present challenges emerge. For example, the six participating countries could establish some sort of standing committee under the auspices of the U.N. for negotiations over the nuclear standoff, along with other issues. Six-Party Talks and bilateral talks have produced quite a few agreements, but not all of them have materialized, mainly because these agreements have been reached in a hurry without confidence-building. The European Union provides another precedent, as its origin lies in political and security concerns.[18]

Although Asia does not have a strong trading bloc like the North American Free Trade Agreement or the European Union, it does have two loose affiliations: ASEAN Plus Three and the Asia Pacific Economic Cooperation (APEC). Created in 1967, ASEAN consists of Southeast Asian countries such as Indonesia, the Philippines, Singapore, and Vietnam. The ASEAN Plus Three was institutionalized in 1999 when ASEAN leaders and their Chinese, Japanese, and South Korean counterparts issued a Joint Statement on East Asia Cooperation at their Third ASEAN Plus Three Summit in Manila. Formed in 1989, APEC includes China, Japan, South Korea, and the United States. ASEAN Plus Three and APEC do not, however, focus on contemporary issues in Northeast Asia. Economic patterns are complementary and can be transformed into a force that drives regional cooperation. North Korea can also become a potential market, because it is one of only a few countries still untapped by multinational and transnational corporations.

The establishment of a development bank, a "North Korean Bank for Reconstruction and Development," may be another workable idea to resolve the half-century-old U.S.–North Korean conflict. This bank can be funded by China, South Korea, the United States, and other countries. But for political credibility and stability, it may be better for it to be run by three countries, namely, China, the United States, and a neutral third country, such as Switzerland. The bank can encourage development and construction in North Korea through loans, guarantees, and equity investments in private and public companies. The establishment of such a bank may convince North Korea that other member countries are indeed ready to provide a security guarantee and economic aid in exchange for the abandonment of its nuclear program.

Notes

1. Richard Halloran, "When Will North Korea Collapse?" *Real Clear Politics*, August 17, 2008, http://www.realclearpolitics.com/articles/2008/08/when_will_north_korea_collapse.html (accessed June 24, 2010).

2. On April 1, 2009, North Korea adopted a new constitution that dropped all references to "communism" for Kim Jong Il's *Songun* ideology, which was placed alongside the *Juche* ideology. See Alzo David-West, "North Korean Newsbriefs," *North Korean Review* 6, no. 1 (Spring 2010): 120–127; p. 125.

3. Selig S. Harrison, *Korean Endgame* (Princeton, NJ: Princeton University Press, 2002), pp. 21–24; and Alon Levkowitz, "Why Do We Not Understand the DPRK?" *North Korean Review* 3, no. 2 (Fall 2007): 94–100.

4. See Young Whan Kihl, "Taking Culture Seriously: Confucian Tradition and Modernization," in *Transforming Korean Politics: Democracy, Reform, and Culture* (Armonk, NY: M.E. Sharpe, 2005), pp. 39–61.

5. Yushin Yoo, *Korea the Beautiful: Treasures of the Hermit Kingdom* (Los Angeles, CA: Golden Pond, 1987), p. 137.

6. Stephen W. Linton, "Life after Death in North Korea," in *Korea Briefing: Toward Reunification*, ed. David R. McCann (Armonk, NY: East Gate, 1997), pp. 83–108; p. 92.

7. Harrison, p. 21.

8. Kong Dan Oh and Ralph C. Hassig, *North Korea through Looking Glass* (Washington, DC: Brookings Institution, 2000), p. 201.

9. "Gross Domestic Product of North Korea in 2008," *Bank of Korea Economic Statistics System*, http://ecos.bok.or.kr/jsp/use/reportdata/ReportDataSelectCtl.jsp?actionType=registerDetailFileDown&informSeq=1794&fileSeq=1 (accessed June 24, 2010).

10. Parts of this section are based on discussion of *Songun* in Kei Koga, "The Anatomy of North Korea's Foreign Policy Formulation," *North Korean Review* 5, no. 2 (Fall 2009): 21–33.

11. Han S. Park, "Military-First Politics (Songun): Understanding Kim Jong-Il's North Korea," *2008 Academic Paper Series on Korea* 1 (2009): 118–130.

12. Sun Tzu's Art of War, http://en.wikipedia.org/wiki/Sun_Tzu, April 26, 2010.

13. This section is a summary of Jennifer Lind, "The Once and Future Kim," *Foreign Affairs*, October 25, 2010, http://www.foreignaffairs.com/articles/66870/by-jennifer-lind/the-once-and-future-kim.

14. Marcus Noland, "Why North Korea Will Muddle Through," *Foreign Affairs* 76, no. 4 (July/August 1997): 101–117.

15. Levkowitz, pp. 94–100.

16. Bruce Klingner, "Leadership Change in North Korea: What It Means for the U.S.," *The Heritage Foundation*, April 7, 2010, http://www.heritage.org/Research/Reports/2010/04/Leadership-Change-in-North-Korea-What-it-Means-for-the-US (accessed June 24, 2010).

17. Kongdan Oh and Ralph C. Hassig, "North Korea's Nuclear Politics," *Current History* 103, no. 674 (September 2004): 273–279.

18. Philip Andrews-Speed, Xuanli Liao, and Paul Stevens, "Multilateral Energy Cooperation in Northeast Asia: Promise or Mirage?" *Oxford Energy Forum* 60, (February 2005): 13–17.

CHAPTER 3

Why Did So Many Influential Americans Think North Korea Would Collapse?
Bruce Cumings

ABSTRACT

This chapter attempts to explain why the collapse scenario was, is, and will be wrong. It is now twenty years since a bipartisan consensus emerged inside the Beltway that North Korea would soon "implode or explode," a mantra that began with Bush I and lasted through Clinton and Bush II, right down to the present. This was the hidden premise of the American pledge to build two light-water reactors to replace the North Korean plutonium complex in the 1994 Framework Agreement: since they would not come onstream for eight or ten years, by then they would belong to South Korea. When does the statute of limitations run out on being systematically wrong? North Korea's coming collapse is still the dominant opinion today. This chapter briefly examines this Washington consensus, and then attempts to explain why the collapse scenario was, is, and will be wrong.

Introduction

If "know your enemy" is the *sine qua non* of effective warfare and diplomacy, the United States has been badly served by those who claim expertise on North Korea in Washington. It is now twenty years since a bipartisan consensus emerged inside the Beltway that the Democratic People's Republic of Korea (DPRK) would soon "implode or explode," a mantra that began with Bush I and lasted through Clinton and Bush II, right down to the present. This was the hidden premise of the American pledge to build two light-water reactors to replace the Yŏngbyŏn plutonium complex in the 1994 Framework Agreement: since they wouldn't come onstream for eight or ten years, by then they would belong to the Republic of Korea (ROK).

Iraq War architect Paul Wolfowitz journeyed to Seoul in the aftermath of the apparent American victory over Saddam to opine (in June 2003) that "North Korea is teetering on the brink of collapse." In intervening years we heard Gen. Gary Luck, commander of U.S. forces in Korea, say (in 1997) that "North Korea will disintegrate, possibly in very short order;" the only question was whether it would implode or explode.[1] In this he was plagiarizing another of our commanders in Korea, Gen. Robert Riscassi, who never tired of saying Pyongyang would soon "implode or explode." (Riscassi retired in 1992.)

When does the statute of limitations run out on being systematically wrong? But I know from experience that any attempt by outsiders to break through this Beltway groupthink merely results in polite silence and discrete headshaking. North Korea's coming collapse is still the dominant opinion today.[2]

In what follows I want to briefly examine this Washington consensus, and then attempt to explain why the collapse scenario was, is, and will be wrong. But my argument can be stated simply:

- North Korea is *sui generis* and not comparable to any other communist regime.
- It is much less communist than nationalist, and less nationalist than Korean.
- It draws deeply from the well of modern and pre-modern Korean political culture.
- Its nationalism traces back 75 years, to a never resolved conflict with Japan.
- Its legitimacy is entirely wrapped up with this anti–Japanese struggle.
- It is a garrison state the likes of which the world has never seen.
- Its military leaders take pride in having faced up to the U.S. military for six decades.
- If it probably can't defeat anyone, it is still militarily impregnable.[3]
- No foreign troops have been stationed in the DPRK since 1958.
- It has always had close backing from China.
- It also got backing from Moscow, but never had close relations with it.
- It is run by a gerontocracy of solipsists who care nothing for what the outside world thinks.
- This elite proved itself capable of starving hundreds of thousands to death while retaining power.

- This elite has proved for more than 60 years that it knows how to hold onto power.

Collapse or Overthrow?

The leading Washington pundit on North Korea is Nicholas Eberstadt, who has been with the American Enterprise Institute for about twenty years, and initially distinguished himself by using demographic data to pinpoint the wretched health care system and dramatic declines in life expectancy of the Soviet Union, several years before it fizzled. Since at least June 1990 he has been predicting the impending collapse of North Korea,[4] but his views are best sampled in his 1999 book, *The End of North Korea*. (When a *New York Times* reporter asked John Bolton what the Bush administration's policy was on the DPRK, he strode to his bookshelf and handed him Eberstadt's book: that's our policy, he said.)

The flaws in Eberstadt's "end-of-North-Korea" theme can help us understand the DPRK's post–cold war endurance. He enjoys arguing throughout the book that North Korea has been *wrong-wrong-wrong* in all of its strategies from the word go, but he does not tell the reader that he brings purely liberal and capitalist assumptions to bear on a society that constituted for most of its existence the highly self-conscious *anti-capitalist*, somewhat as if Milton Friedman were to describe how stupid the Ayatollahs have been for not charging interest on loans. Thus we hear about how the "amazingly naïve" North Koreans just couldn't understand what a World Bank official meant when he used terms like "macroenomics" and "microeconomics." But Eberstadt has also been *wrong-wrong-wrong* since the Berlin Wall fell in his prognostications of North Korean collapse: Why? Because he sees the DPRK entirely through the lens of Soviet and East European communism and therefore cannot grasp the regime's very different history, the pragmatic shrewdness of its post–Soviet foreign policy, the desperate survival strategies it is willing to undertake, let alone the anti-colonial and revolutionary nationalist origins of this regime and those in Vietnam and China, yielding no significant break since 1989 in Asian communism.

Beginning with his first attempt to predict the North's coming collapse, Eberstadt has seen North Korea as a Soviet implant comparable to the defunct European communist regimes, and especially East Germany. The Honecker regime hosted fully 360,000 Soviet troops when the regime fell and if Mikhail Gorbachev had chosen to mobilize them, the German Democratic Republic would still exist. Meanwhile the last foreign troops left the DPRK when China pulled out in 1958, leaving an independently-controlled military more than one million strong (indeed the fourth largest army in the world). Eberstadt repeats the cold war mantra that Moscow saw everything in the world through the Marxist-Leninist doctrine of "the correlation of forces" ("*sootnoshenie sil*"), and argues that this is also the basis of North Korea's global strategy. If so, P'yŏngyang should have folded its hand and cashed in its chips in 1989; no other state has faced such a hostile "correlation of forces" and unbroken string of seemingly insurmountable crises in the years since then, with little help from anyone (until the late 1990s) amid universal hopes that it simply erase itself and disappear.

Eberstadt understands North Korea to be an industrialized economy in an urban society, unlike the frequently-quoted ignoramuses who compare it to Albania or Cambodia or Somalia. Although routinely denounced as "Stalinist," North Korea, he says, always had "too few farmers to permit a policy of 'squeezing the countryside' any realistic chance of success." Eberstadt is particularly good at depicting a systematic decline in either importing or investing in capital goods after 1975, an odd thing given the regime's previous heavy-industry-first strategy and its desire to keep up with a rapidly-industrializing South. In the past decade the DPRK's deepest economic problems have arisen because of its obsolescent industrial structure and the collapse of its energy regime, which left the massive chemical sector unable to supply the huge doses of fertilizer that used to be laid on the fields, resulting in declining food production that became catastrophic when the worst flooding in decades hit in 1995 and 1996.

Eberstadt does not pretend to know how many North Koreans died as a result of food shortages, citing claims of two to three million but suggesting that it might be closer to the DPRK's official figure of 200,000. He does not point out, though, that in its worse phase the famine only began to approach India's year-in, year-out toll (in proportionate terms) of infant mortality and deaths from malnutrition or starvation, which I mention only because of the media's habit of depicting Kim Jong Il frolicking amid a heap of starved cadavers.

Until former dissident Kim Dae Jung came to power in early 1998, the official line in Seoul was also that everyone should prepare for a North Korean collapse, followed by its absorption into the Republic of Korea. In particular, oceans of ink were spilled in the 1990s on the "German model" of Korean reunification. Study teams went off to Germany to examine its unification after the Honecker regime fell, and came back with worrisome stories about how much the process had cost, and therefore how expensive it would be to bring northern Korea up to the level of the rest of the country. Any number of foreign reporters also thought this would be Korea's future—if an expensive one—and one still reads about it all the time.

Unfortunately the German model of unification was the wrong one. Korea's main difference from Germany is that it suffered a terrible civil war, with millions killed, in recent memory. It is very hard to believe that People's Army commanders who fought the South in such a bloody fratricidal war would allow the ROK to overwhelm the DPRK, by whatever means. As we have seen, East Germany collapsed because Gorbachev chose to do what none of his predecessors would ever have done, namely, to keep Soviet troops in their barracks rather than mobilize them to save the Honecker regime. Although Gorbachev sought similarly to pull levers against North Korea, he had none but the relatively small amounts of aid which Moscow had provided, and which he eventually cut off. South Korea also flattered itself by comparing its status to West Germany: many Easterners could see in West Germany some approximation to their socialist ideals, in its democratic politics, its social safety net, its widespread unionization (about 40 percent compared to 12 percent in the United States and less than that in the ROK), its early and favorable retirement benefits, and its good public order and strong civil society. By contrast North Korean citizens could look forward to little or none of this in union with the South, but instead to the longest hours of labor in the industrial world on terms that South Korean firms would set—until Kim Dae Jung set in motion a very different strategy of reconciliation.

Eberstadt eventually got tired of predicting the DPRK's collapse and decided to do something about it: he argued that America and its allies should waltz in and, in his Reaganesque flourish, "tear down this tyranny."[5] At the time he had excellent backing for such views in Vice President Dick Cheney's entourage, and especially Paul Wolfowitz and John Bolton. With the demise of the Bush vision, if one can call it that, enthusiasm for such a course has waned. But it was the preferred policy of hard-liners for several years, amid the internal civil war that shaped Bush's policies toward North Korea.[6]

In 2005 Jasper Becker produced a wretched-excess of a book called (with impeccable originality) *Rogue Regime*, where he joins Eberstadt in arguing for a forced collapse of the regime.[7] This book would not be worth mentioning except that it comes praised and highly recommended by a reviewer in the *New York Review of Books*, and was echoed in many ways by all-purpose pundit Robert Kaplan's 2006 article in *The Atlantic*, where Kaplan provided levity by taking seriously the words of octogenarian "wise man" Paek Sŏn-yŏp on the future of North Korea.[8] (Paek sought to track down Kim Il Sung for the Japanese in the 1930s, and was Washington's choice to replace Syngman Rhee in the American *coup d'etat* plan in 1953 called "Operation Eveready.") If these are indeed our top intellectual journals, then we really have a case of the blind leading the blind.

Becker, a reporter with much experience in Asia, peered over the fence (the Chinese border) at North Korea and excoriated the suffering that "short, pudgy, cognac-swilling Kim Jong Il" had imposed on his people, "an unparalleled and monstrous crime."[9] This statement appears on the same page with the following body counts: five million people lost to Lenin's erroneous launching of the Bolshevik Revolution, eight million to Stalin's terror, thirty million in the famine Becker believes Mao imposed on China after 1958 (see his earlier book, *Hungry Ghosts*), and millions more at the hands of Pol Pot. He left Genghis Khan off this list, but never mind: Kim Jong Il is worse than all of them—insane, evil, dangerous, a drunkard, and a lecher (among other epithets).[10] Indeed, Kim is so bad that Becker advocates another one of those vintage American "shock and awe" campaigns to get rid of the regime—not right now, of course, but if he goes ahead and tests an atomic bomb. It's a moral issue, he says again and again: this regime has to be got rid of.

The book begins with a quotation from George W. Bush tutoring cadets at The Citadel about "rogue states" in December 2001, and then launches into a "fictional scenario" taking up sixteen pages about a preemptive strike against every nuclear, military, industrial, and governmental facility in North Korea—in other words another preventive war. Just like Iraq, dozens of F-117 Stealth fighter-bombers open the campaign by trying to solve Kim Jong Il's perpetual bad hair day through decapitation, followed by phalanxes of F-16 fighters launched from several nearby American aircraft carriers (which Kim somehow failed to notice as they steamed 6,000 miles), B-1 and B-52 bombers, Tomahawk cruise missiles, thousands of JDAM blast munitions and "high-intensity, heat-generating BLU-118Bs" are unleashed, "designed to penetrate reinforced bunkers." Finally 60,000 Marines rush in from Okinawa to march on Pyongyang.

Don't worry about the North Koreans striking back: Americans and South Koreans will be protected because "following the Second Gulf War in 2003," then Secretary of Defense Donald Rumsfeld and his deputy Wolfowitz had presciently upgraded American and Korean high-tech weaponry: "new generation" PAC3 Patriot missiles, "Defense Secretary Donald Rumsfeld's missile Defense system" (described as "up and running, although not tested in wartime conditions"), and air-to-ground "HARPY" guided missiles.

If the reader finds this war game preposterous, it is strangely prefigured in the Pentagon's real-world "OPLAN 5027." Shortly after the invasion of Iraq began, Donald Rumsfeld demanded revisions in the basic war plan for Korea (called "Operations Plan 5030"). The strategy, according to insiders who have read the plan, was "to topple Kim's regime by destabilizing its military forces," so they would overthrow him and thus accomplish a "regime change." The plan was pushed "by many of the same administration hardliners who advocated regime change in Iraq." Unnamed senior Bush administration officials considered elements of this new plan "so aggressive that they could provoke a war." Short of attacking or trying to force a military coup, Rumsfeld and company wanted the U.S. military to "stage a weeks-long surprise military exercise, designed to force North Koreans to head for bunkers and deplete valuable stores of food, water, and other resources."[11]

This is how the 1950 invasion began: North Korea announced a long summer military exercise along the 38th parallel, mobilizing some 40,000 troops. In the middle of these war games, several divisions suddenly veered south and took Seoul in three days; only a tiny handful of the highest officials knew that the summer exercises were prelude to an invasion. Half a century later came Mr. Rumsfeld with his plans, a man who according to two eyewitnesses was surprised to learn when he joined the Pentagon that we still had nearly 40,000 troops in Korea.

Larry Niksch, a long-time specialist on Asian Affairs at the Congressional Research Service and a person never given to leaps toward unfounded conclusions, cited Rumsfeld's war plans and wrote that "regime change in North Korea is indeed the Bush administration's policy objective." If recent, sporadically-applied sanctions against the DPRK and interdiction of its shipping do not produce a regime change or "diplomatic capitulation," then Rumsfeld planned to escalate from a preemptive strike against Yŏngbyŏn (which Clinton came close to mounting in 1994) to "a broader plan of massive strikes against multiple targets."

Jasper Becker was all for it: "Victory would be swift and total," he assures us, but he still cannot guarantee that this wholesale onslaught will kill or capture the mad, evil, corpulent, cognac-drenched, altitudinally challenged Kim Jong Il.[12] But, on Becker's behalf, we recall that many moons passed before Saddam was flushed out of his gopher hole. Becker's book is simply nonsense, but that does not render his scenario for battle out of the question because he belongs to a faith-based fraternity of pundits who still believe in things like "the 'shock and awe' campaign that quickly defeated Iraq," Rumsfeld's missile defense fantasies, the verisimilitude of "the axis of evil," the steady, experienced leadership of Bush, Rumsfeld and Cheney as opposed to pusillanimous Bill Clinton or Barack Obama. At the end of the book we again encounter scenarios for violent "regime change:" Dark Neo-Con Force Richard Perle thinks Americans should be able to inspect anything they want to in the North, and remove their nuclear physicists to a neutral spot for interrogation. Failing that, the U. S. "should take decisive military action."[13]

Omniscience in Langley

When I was growing up, major highlights included trips to Washington to visit my Aunt, who spent her entire career in the OSS and the CIA. With a Ph.D. from Bryn Mawr, a husband whom she dispatched after only a few years of marriage, a fascinating career that she couldn't talk about (making it all the more interesting), and a conquering-dowager way of getting around the capital city, I thought she was not only a sterling example of a liberated professional woman, but an *eminence gris* like the many others at CIA headquarters (all of her friends were CIA people, and I met many of them, too). It took me decades to get out of my head the idea that somewhere in the bowels of Langley is a person who knows all there is to know about North Korea. Then I read Helen Louise Hunter's book.

Another Beltway mantra is that no one knows anything about North Korea—except possibly in our intelligence agencies. Former Congressman Stephen Solarz, long interested in Korean affairs, found a "brilliant and breathtaking" study by a CIA analyst and concluded that it was for North Korea "what the Rosetta stone was to ancient Egypt." So rare and privileged was the author's knowledge that it took him a decade to get the CIA to declassify the book. Helen-Louise Hunter was for two decades "a Far East Specialist" in the CIA, which is where her book first appeared (if that is the right word) as a long internal memorandum. This is "a country about which we knew virtually nothing," in Solarz's words; that is, we have trouble penetrating and surveilling them: how scary!

Hunter's work has some excellent information on arcane and difficult to research subjects like North Korean wage and price structures, the self-sufficient and decentralized neighborhood living practices that mostly eliminated the long lines for goods that characterized Soviet-style communism, and the decade of one's young life that almost every North Korean male is required to devote to military service in this garrison state. Ms. Hunter points out many achievements of the North Korean system, in ways that would get anyone outside the CIA labeled a sympathizer—compassionate care for war orphans in particular and children in general, "radical change" in the position of women ("there are now more college-educated woman than college-educated men"), genuinely free housing, preventive medicine on a national scale accomplished to a comparatively high standard, infant mortality and life expectancy rates comparable to the most advanced countries until the recent famine, "no organized prostitution" and "the police are difficult, if not impossible, to bribe" (also no longer true, since the famine).The author frequently acknowledges that the vast majority of Koreans did in fact revere Kim Il Sung, even the defectors from the system whose information forms the core evidence for her book. According to Prince Norodom Sihanouk, for decades a close friend of Kim's who frequently stayed for months at a time in the North, "Kim had a relationship with his people that every other leader in the world would envy;" he described it as "much closer" than his own with the Cambodian people (where he is both venerated and highly popular.)[14]

In her account of the DPRK when its economy was still reasonably good, about twenty years ago, she found that daily necessities were very low priced, luxuries vastly overpriced. Rents were so nominal that most housing was effectively free, as was health care, and "the government subsidizes the low prices of rice, sugar, and other food necessities, as well as student uniforms and work clothes." All homes in the country had electricity by 1968, far ahead of where the South was at the time. To take a measure close to home, she estimates that a husband and wife who were both university professors would be able to save about 50 percent cent of their monthly salaries. Rice and corn, the major staples, were rationed by the state, as were cooking oils, meat, soy sauce, bean curd and *kimch'i*. Other things—fruits, vegetables, nuts, noodles, beer—could be purchased at low prices, with meats and luxury foods overvalued. The general egalitarianism of the society was remarkable, in her view, even if the elite lived much better than the masses.[15]

It is interesting to see Ms. Hunter come to conclusions about North Korea similar to those of outside experts, but I had to read to page 68 before learning anything new: Kim Il Sung University has a baseball team—which must mean other universities do, too (although KISU no doubt wins all the time). What this book really tells us is how far the DPRK has fallen in the last two decades, precisely the period when South Korea conquered one advanced industry after another. For a top leadership that prided itself on its rapid industrial growth a generation ago, watching the ROK take off in their rearview mirror while they stagnate must be a terrible pill to swallow.

Things go downhill when Ms. Hunter examines North Korean politics. Her big theme: North Korea is a "cult society" akin to the folks trundling along behind Jim Jones or Charles Manson.[16] But this analogy merely betrays her lack of knowledge about the society she spent so many years studying, presumably with the best intelligence materials that the U.S. Government can muster at her fingertips. She ought to know just how extensive kingly worship, paeans of praise to the King's fount-of-knowledge, wisdom and metaphysical idealism, abject obeisance to authority, the people being "of one mind and one body" with the King, and veneration of leaders and elders to seemingly absurd lengths was (and is) in Korean patriarchal society. A knowledgeable scholar put it this way: "The religion-like cult surrounding Kim Il-sung ...

appears to be in large part an unplanned outgrowth of Confucian values placed in a new context;" more broadly, it is "a new and well-integrated family-state that, in certain respects, resembles Confucian society."[17]

In 1997, after Ms. Hunter had retired, the CIA convened a panel of government and outside experts and concluded that North Korea was likely to collapse within five years. Robert A. Wampler of the National Security Archive obtained this report under the Freedom of Information Act.[18] In his essay Dr. Wampler cited senior Foreign Service officer David Straub's observation that one expert after another came through the Tokyo Embassy in the early 1990s, "pontificating on their prognoses for the inevitable collapse of the North Korean regime, giving odds that allowed Pyongyang anywhere from a few months to perhaps two years before falling." Eight years after the Berlin Wall opened, the assembled CIA experts anticipated a longer scenario for the same outcome, as part of a CIA inquiry that had already included a government-wide simulation of "alternative Korean endgames." Kim Jong Il, the conferees thought, was likely to have just "a brief window of time" to cope with all his difficulties before suffering a probable "hard landing." Unless major reform happened, some "catalyst" would come along "that will lead to [the North's] collapse."

The majority of the group doubted that Kim's regime could persist "beyond five years," yielding a "political implosion." But many of them expressed surprise that in spite of the degraded economy and the beginnings of a famine that would soon grow much worse, somehow the "delusionary" Kim Jong Il "remained firmly in control."

Among those outsiders whom the CIA invited to this exercise were Nicholas Eberstadt, academics Kenneth Lieberthal and Robert Ross, and Daryl Plunk and James Przystup from the Heritage Foundation. No recognized experts on North Korea from outside the government were there (Lieberthal and Ross are China experts), but more surprisingly, neither was anyone from Brookings or Johns Hopkins–SAIS—the liberal anchors of the remarkably narrow spectrum of Beltway opinion. Here was the CIA under the Clinton administration reaching out to the right for guidance on North Korea's coming collapse, probably in search of a Beltway political consensus rather than anything substantive. (If they really had wanted a prescient judgment, they could have called in Eason Jordon, the president of CNN International who had made many visits to Pyongyang: "When you hear about starvation in North Korea, a lot of very level-headed people think, 'There is no way a country like that can survive.' Well, I can guarantee you this: I'm here to tell you with absolute certainty those guys will tough it out for centuries just the way they are. Neither the United States nor any other country is going to be able to force a collapse of that government."[19])

The DPRK Did Collapse

The irony is that North Korea's economy and most of its "iron rice bowl" social safety net did collapse in the 1990s. After the death of Kim Il Sung in 1994 the North faced one terrible crisis after another: it was visited with a near collapse of its energy system in the early 1990s (which then caused many factories to close, which in turn meant little fertilizer was available the fields), two years of unprecedented floods (in 1995 and 1996), a summer of drought (1997), and a resulting famine that some say claimed the lives of two million people. Here is a textbook example of the calamities that are supposed to mark the end of the Confucian dynastic cycle, and North Korean citizens must wonder how much more suffering they will endure before the economy returns to anything like the relatively stable situation that foreigners like myself observed in the 1980s. Kim Jong Il waited out the three-year traditional mourning period for the first son of the king before assuming his father's leadership of the ruling party, which also enabled him to avoid direct blame for the various catastrophes. On the 50th anniversary of the regime's founding in September 1998 he became the maximum leader, but chose not to become the titular head of state (that is, President of the Democratic People's Republic of Korea)—probably because he appears to be uncomfortable in meeting foreign leaders.

The collapse of the socialist bloc deprived P'yŏngyang of major export markets, leading to several years of declining GNP in the early 1990s. South Korean figures put these declines in the two to five percent range, and U. S. Government analysts thought that the worst was over for the North Korean economy by the end of 1993. But this was a major crisis for the leadership well before the floods and droughts, to the degree that at the 21st Plenum of the Worker's Party in December 1993 P'yŏngyang for the first time publicly acknowledged "big losses in our economic construction" and "a most complex and acute internal and external situation." Most of the blame was attributed not to North Korea's ponderous socialist system, but to "the collapse of socialist countries and the socialist market of the world," which "shattered" many of P'yŏngyang's trade partners and agreements.[20] The 1995 floods wiped out 40 percent of the DPRK's arable land, a natural disaster that would have demolished any economy. But it was worsened by hare-brained agricultural policies and widespread deforestation, leading to massive water runoffs. Flood and drought came successively in the next two years, bringing the economy to its lowest point in 1998.

Unlike similar catastrophes and humanitarian emergencies around the world, however, this one has provided little evidence of a collapse of state power, except for breakdowns at the local level in the delivery of goods and services (necessities are heavily rationed, and the state could no longer provide them). There have been few significant changes in the North Korean leadership since Kim died. There have been defections, many of them hyped in the South Korean press and the world media, but only one—that of Hwang Chang-yŏp in February 1997—was truly significant, and although the regime was embarrassed and demoralized by Hwang's departure, he had never been a central power-holder and the core leadership still appears to be unshaken. In August 2001 Kim Jong Il chose to spend three weeks on an armored train while traveling to Moscow and back, presumably a junket meant to indicate that his hold on power back home is firm and secure. Nothing has occurred since then to lead to a different judgment.

In the midst of this collapse, much has changed since the famine years. For the first time in a generation, the North's economy grew more than the South's in 2008—3.5 percent to 2 percent, the latter a reflection of the financial collapse. Markets, which began functioning out of absolute necessity at the bottom of society, now operate everywhere (there are more than 2,000 in P'yŏngyang). Small groups of Korean experts have come out of the country for high-tech training or basic information about the functioning of world commerce and trade, with China and Sweden being preferred destinations. Kim Jong Il is said to be a denizen of the Internet (even if hardly anyone else is).

All along, though, Kim has been the prime advocate of reeducation campaigns designed to make sure that a communist collapse along East European lines does not happen: in a central essay called "Abuses of Socialism,"[21] Kim took a tour through the history of communism and the causes for its collapse in "some countries," arguing that this happened mainly because of a failure to indoctrinate the young. He goes on, "consciousness plays a decisive role in the activity of a human being.... The basic factor which gives an impetus to social development must always be ascribed to ideological consciousness."

North Korea's Hermit Kingdom policies of self-reliance were a response to a prolonged 20th century crisis in the country. Put in place to insulate the country against the disasters of colonization, depression, and war, they seem irrelevant now. But one can imagine Kim Il Sung looking at his politburo friends in 1989 when the Berlin Wall fell, or in 1991 when the USSR collapsed, and asking them where North Korea would be had it integrated with the Soviet bloc and participated in the international division of labor that Moscow fostered in Eastern Europe.

North Korean ideologues like to use the term "mosquito net" as a metaphor for letting advanced technology come in, while keeping capitalist ideas out: "It can let in breezes, and it also can defend against mosquitoes." This is the same metaphor Deng Xiaoping used when he began to open up China in 1978; the North of course was much more shrill in denouncing the infiltration of liberal and capitalist ideas:

> It is the main strategy of the imperialists to dominate the world with corrupt ideas which they had failed to bring under their control with atomic bombs and dollars. This poisoning is aimed at doing harm to the excellent national character of each country and nation and making hundreds of millions of people across the world mentally deformed.... Corrupt ideas ... are more dangerous than atomic bombs ... ideological education is our life line ... to pay exclusive attention to economic construction and abandon ideological work is just a suicidal act of opening the door for imperialist ideology and culture to infiltrate.... It is imperative to set up a mosquito net in all realms of social life.

After flailing "vulgar" bourgeois society—"narcotics addicts, alcoholics and degenerates seeking to satisfy abnormal desires"—the article said "the collapse of the erstwhile Soviet Union and East European countries is entirely attributable to their flinging the door open to imperialist ideological and cultural poisoning."[22] The overall burden of this missive, though, was to let in joint ventures and keep out bad ideas.

The unending crises forced North Korea to think seriously about the future of its autarchic system, resulting in a host of new laws on foreign investment, relations with capitalist firms, and new zones of free trade. Many new banking, labor and investment laws were promulgated over the past fifteen years.[23] If East Asian development in recent decades has demonstrated anything, it is that rapid capitalist growth is not incompatible with strong central state power. Thus it is quite predictable that North Korean reformers told reporters that they "would like to take Singapore as a model," which combines "great freedom in business activities" with "good order, discipline and observation of laws."[24] It is also easier to use Singapore as an example than China or Vietnam; they of course would be more relevant, but Korean pride gets in the way of acknowledging that. Most important is the deep interest of many South Korean firms in cheap but intelligent and disciplined North Korean labor, which can help South Korea recoup comparative advantages in the world market while moving both Koreas slowly toward reconciliation. The best example of this is the large Kaesŏng export zone, just across the DMZ, which by 2010 employed around 45,000 North Koreans in factories built by the South, but is expected eventually to employ hundreds of thousands.

Kim Jong Il assumed the mandate of heaven in 1998 (a classical term that the North Koreans used repeatedly after Kim Il Sung died) with the regime's future shaky and with his people still starving. Confucian civilization put power in the hands of the morally superior man who would govern well; people were happy when a good king rules and nature was bountiful. Equality, too, is found in the emphasis on every person being capable of education and moral improvement. Since he assumed full power the people of North Korea have been misled by Kim Jong Il and victimized by a cruel Mother Nature, with an equality that consists of sharing their portion of stark misery. Quite apart from the wretched rural areas where the annual harvest is half of what it was in the 1980s, entire industrial cities have ceased to function, power can't even be supplied reliably to the elite and model capital city, P'yŏngyang, and a state of nature has existed for over a decade along the border with China—desperate people going back and forth, traffic in women, and an economy—such as it is—increasingly dominated by China.

The DPRK's Claim to Legitimacy

Successive administrations and Beltway pundits get North Korea so wrong because they know next to nothing about its origins, view it through the lenses of Soviet satellite behavior, and cannot come up with any North Korean interests that they deem worthy of respect. For many, it is an outrage that the regime continues to exist at all. But that doesn't make much difference; the DPRK is not going to erase itself because the American Enterprise Institute thinks it should do so. Besides, Americans are seen as a disease of the skin, Japanese militarists and their South Korean allies a disease of the heart.

On April 25, 2007, the *New York Times* carried a photo of North Korean soldiers goose-stepping through P'yŏngyang, on the seventy-fifth anniversary of the founding of their army. The *Times* noted that the regime itself was only founded in 1948, but carried no more information. On another page was an article about Japanese Prime Minister Abe Shinzo arriving in Washington to visit George W. Bush. Neither there, nor in any article that I have seen in the press after Abe came to power, were these two events connected. Abe is the grandson of class A war criminal and postwar Prime Minister Kishi Nobosuke, who was head of munitions in the puppet state of Manchukuo in the 1930s. Kim Il Sung began fighting the Japanese in Manchuria the spring of 1932 and did not stop for a decade, and his heirs trace everything back to that distant beginning. After every other characteristic attached to this regime—communist, nationalist, rogue state, evil enemy—it is first of all, and above all, an anti–Japanese entity run by the most hoary-minded nationalists in the world.

A state narrative runs from the early days of the anti–Japanese resistance down to the present, and appears everywhere from their favorite revolutionary operas to the face of their currency. It is drummed into the brains of everyone in the country by an elderly elite that believes anyone younger than them cannot possibly know what it meant to fight Japan in the 1930s or the United States in the 1950s (allied with Japan and utilizing bases all over Japan) and, more or less, ever since. When you combine deeply ingrained Confucian patriarchy with people who have been sentient adults since the Korean War began in 1950, you have some sense of why North Korea has changed so little at top levels in recent years, and why it is highly unlikely to collapse before this elite—and its relentlessly nationalist ideology—leaves the scene.

The average age of the top leaders in North Korea is usually in the mid-70s (in 2007 it was 76). Of the top forty leaders in 2000, only one was under 60: Kim Jong Il. In 2010 the Politburo had twenty-five members; thirteen were 80 or older. This gerontocracy draws a straight line from 1932 onward, brooking no deviation from this most important of all North Korean legitimations. You would think the regime's solipsistic focus on all this would be well known, since their dollar bill-equivalent has an icon of a woman wielding a pistol, heroine of their most famous opera set in April 1932, but it is not. Diane Sawyer may not be the best example, but when she took an ABC crew to North Korea in late 2006, she interviewed General Yi Ch'an-bok, who commands the DMZ on the northern side. How long have you been commander, she asked sweetly. "Forty years," he replied, to her amazement .He has been getting up every morning to riffle through the enemy's order of battle since the year before the Pueblo was seized, since the year before the Tet offensive effectively ended the American effort in Vietnam.

For decades the South Korean intelligence agencies put out the line that Kim Il Sung was an imposter, a Soviet stooge who stole the name of a famous Korean patriot. The real reason for this smoke screen was the pathetic truth that almost the entire high command of the South Korean military in 1950 had served the Japanese (as did Park Chung Hee, the militarist who ruled from 1961 to 1979), including even high-ranking officers who had tried to chase down Kim in Manchuria at the Japanese behest. They succeeded in convincing most of their own people—and all too many foreigners—of this canard. Meanwhile the North Koreans took Kim's admirable record and surrounded it with hagiography and myth that has to be sampled to be believed. But somewhere along the yawning chasm between the desperate lies of former South Korean governments and the ceaseless exaggeration of the North Koreans, there is a truth.

Careful scholarship in recent years, made possible by the availability of new Korean, Chinese, Japanese and Soviet documentation and by the hard labors and open minds of a younger generation of historians, has now made clear that Koreans formed the vast majority of resisters to the Japanese takeover of Manchuria, native place for the rulers of the Qing Dynasty (1644–1911). By the early 1930s half a million Koreans lived in the prefecture of Kando (Jiandao in Chinese) alone, long a Korean immigrant community just across the border in China, and since 1949 an autonomous Korean region in the People's Republic of China (PRC). After the establishment of Manchukuo around 80 percent of anti–Japanese guerrillas and upwards of 90 percent of the members of the "Chinese Communist Party" were Korean. Most Koreans had moved to Kando in hopes of escaping Japanese oppression, although some previous emigrants had also gotten wealthy developing the fertile soils of Manchuria, yielding tales that farming families could double or triple their income there. By and large, though, these Koreans were very poor and thoroughly recalcitrant in their hatred of the colonizers, and remained so in 1945 when U.S. intelligence estimated that 95 percent of the nearly 2 million Koreans in Manchuria were anti–Japanese, and only 5 percent were sympathizers and collaborators.

The puppet state of Manchukuo was born in March 1932 on the first day of the month, just to stick the March 1, 1919, Korean independence movement—which shook Japanese imperialism to its roots—back in their craw. Japanese officials saw the Korean colony as a model for Manchuria, and encouraged Korean allies to think that if they helped colonize Manchuria, Korea itself might get closer to independence. Japanese forces launched their first major anti-guerrilla campaign in April 1932 in Kando, killing anyone said to be a "communist," or aiding communists; many victims were innocent peasants. Korean sources at the time said 25,000 died, perhaps an exaggeration, but it surely was an unholy slaughter. This experience became the *locus classicus* for the most famous North Korean opera, "Sea of Blood" (*P'ibada*),[25] and it happened amid a drastic fall in peasant livelihoods, brought on by the depression and the collapse of the world economy. By the end of 1934 after successive waves of attack the number of Korean mass organizations linked to the insurgents had dropped from nearly 12,000 in 1933 to barely 1000, and only the number of guerrillas had increased—but not by much (guerrilla bases held about 1000 insurgents; 80 percent were still Koreans). A Japanese police chief remarked that "if you killed a hundred Koreans, there was bound to be at least one communist among them."[26]

Kim Il Sung took a leading role in trying to forge Chinese-Korean cooperation in the Manchurian guerrilla struggle, helped along by his fluency in Chinese and his long association with Chinese guerrillas leaders. He was not alone, though, working with other Korean guerrilla leaders with their own detachments like Ch'oe Yong-gŏn (Minister of Defense when the Korean War began), Kim Ch'aek, and Ch'oi Hyŏn. By February 1936 a formidable army had emerged, with Kim Il Sung commanding the 3rd Division, and several Chinese regimental commanders under him. Koreans still were the largest ethnic force, constituting 80 percent of two regiments, 50 percent of another, and so on. By this time Kim was "the leader of Korean communists in eastern Manchuria with a great reputation and a high position."[27]

Kim's reputation was also plumped up by the Japanese, whose newspapers featured the conflict between him and the Korean Quislings whom the Japanese employed to track him down and kill him, like Col. Kim Sŏk-wŏn (who commanded ROK forces along the 38th parallel in 1949). Kim Sŏk-wŏn was known then as Col. Kaneyama Shakugen; he reported to Gen. Nozoe Shotoku, commander of the "Special Kim Detachment" of the Imperial Army. Col. Kim's greatest success came in February 1940, when he killed Yang Jingyu, a famous Chinese guerrilla and close comrade of Kim Il Sung. In April Nozoe's forces captured Kim Hye-sun, thought to be Kim's first wife; the Japanese tried in vain to use her to lure Kim out of hiding, and then murdered her.[28]

"Kim Il Sung fought all during 1938 and 1939," the leading scholar of Korean communism Dae-Sook Suh wrote, "mostly in southern and southeastern Manchuria. There were numerous [published] accounts of his activities, such as the Liudaogou raid of April 26, 1938, and his raid into Korea once again in May 1939." In September 1939, the month when Hitler invaded Poland and started World War II, a "massive punitive expedition" combining Japanese forces from the Kwantung and Manchukuo Armies as well as paramilitary police, destroyed many cadres and units in the insurgent armies and forced the remnants ever northward, until Korean and Chinese guerrillas finally crossed the Soviet border a year later.[29]

In other words, massive counterinsurgency punctuated the last two years of this conflict, which lasted until the eve of the German onslaught against the Soviet Union. Kim Il Sung, Kim Ch'aek, Ch'oe Hyŏn, Ch'oe Yong-gŏn, and about 200 other key Korean leaders, were the fortunate survivors of pitiless campaigns that soaked the hills of Manchukuo with Korean blood. By the time of Pearl Harbor, the Korean insurgency was reduced to minor forays into Manchuria, and the Korean Left—a strong force everywhere in the Korean diaspora, including the United States—was nearly demolished by a combination of severe Japanese repression at home and in Manchukuo. But in 1945 these 200 people came back to P'yŏngyang, colonized the regime, and in typical Korean fashion began intermarrying, producing children, and putting them through elite schools. Their descendants are the power-holders in North Korea today, and everything they have depends on and privileges events that began seventy-five years ago.

Ultimately the legitimacy of this regime depends upon what its own people think of it. In the absence of elections and open discussion, one can never know. It may be that the DPRK remains in power only because of its enormous repressive apparatus. The mass protests over the Iranian election in 2009 could never happen in North Korea, because they have no valid elections and any hint of protest is met with draconian force. But the very willingness to use force and be successful at it—something witnessed time and again under the military dictatorships in the South—is a sign both of weakness (you can't trust your own people) and of regime morale. They show no signs of giving up, or even acknowledging the world's judgment on communism twenty years ago. Here is another thing the CIA should have thought of when they never tired of predicting the DPRK's collapse.

Conclusion

In his classic book, *Knowledge and Politics*, Roberto Unger distinguished between an inner and an outer circle in contemporary politics. The inner circle represents power and domination, exercised everywhere by the few. The outer circle includes all the rest, and their search for community, decency, and participation through the architecture of politics. Nowhere has the problem of the inner circle been resolved, he argued, and therefore in the outer circle "the search for community is condemned to be idolatrous, or utopian, or both." In Unger's sense, the inner circle—the Kim family nucleus—is the critical problem in North Korea; in the absence of a non-family and impersonal principle for constituting the core, the outer circle is condemned to idolatry, while the inner core searches for a successor among Kim's sons. It may be that the apparent stability of this state masks instability at its center, in the failure to constitute a politics that can extend beyond the circle of family and personal relations. Or perhaps the North Korean leaders know their people better than we do, and with their singular meld of pre-modern, nationalist, and communist politics, will weather the problems that bedeviled and finally destroyed other communist systems.

Since 1991 the world has been more inhospitable to P'yŏngyang's policies than at any point since 1948. Yet this cloistered regime faced the death of its founding king and remained stable, while passing on the baton to Kim Jong Il—in spite of three decades of predictions that Kim's death would lead to revolt and the collapse of the system. With party elders like Pak Sŏng-ch'ŏl and Yi Chong-ok leading the way for the younger Kim, the core of high politics again showed itself to be cohesive and strong. Meanwhile the outer circle hangs in the balance, as the North Korean people put up with another "Sun-

King" and a very different world closes in upon this modern Hermit Kingdom. What will happen to the DPRK? It's anybody's guess. But in the past foreign observers have gone wrong, in my view, by underestimating North Korea in nearly every way possible. Meanwhile, predictions based on the idea that this regime draws deeply from the well of Korean tradition and anti-colonial nationalism, and will therefore have staying power in the post–cold war world, have so far been correct.

Notes

1. Naewoe Press, *North Korea: Uneasy, Shaky Kim Jong-il Regime* (Seoul: ROK Government, 1997), p. 143.

2. I attended a State Department conference on North Korea in the spring of 2009, and this was still the dominant opinion.

3. The American war plan has assumed for decades that half a million American troops would have to be in Korea before the North could be defeated, and even today a victory would take six months. *Occupying and stabilizing* the North would require at least as many troops, and there would be no guarantee of success. Ergo: the cost of defeating the North is still, even today, prohibitive.

4. See his "The Coming Collapse of North Korea," *The Wall Street Journal*, June 25, 1990. In some parts of this essay I draw on *Korea's Place in the Sun* (W.W. Norton, rev. ed., 2005), *North Korea: Another Country* (New Press, 2004), and from recent articles of mine in the *London Review of Books* and *The Nation*. For those who may have read any or all of it, my apologies—North Korea is still around, which either proves that I'm right, or that I don't know what else to say.

5. Eberstadt, "Tear Down This Tyranny," *The Weekly Standard* (November 29, 2004).

6. The best account of the internal struggles is Mike Chinoy, *Meltdown: the Inside Story of the North Korean Nuclear Crisis* (New York: St. Martin's, 2008).

7. Jasper Becker, *Rogue Regime: Kim Jong Il and the Looming Threat of North Korea* (New York: Oxford University Press, 2005). See Richard Bernstein's review of this "excellent book," in his "How Not to Deal with North Korea," *New York Review of Books*, March 1, 2007.

8. Robert Kaplan, "When North Korea Falls," *The Atlantic* (October 2006), pp. 64–73.

9. Becker, pp. 4, 31.

10. Becker, pp. ix, xiv.

11. Bruce B. Auster and Kevin Whitelaw, "Pentagon Plan 5030, A New Blueprint for Facing Down North Korea," *U.S. News and World Report*, July 21, 2003.

12. Becker, pp. 9–10.

13. Becker, p. 260.

14. Helen-Louise Hunter, *Kim Il-song's North Korea* (Westport, CT: Praeger, 1999), pp. 26–7.

15. Hunter, pp. 146–51. She has a full price list of daily necessities on p. 147.

16. Hunter. p. 34.

17. Mun Woong Lee, *Rural North Korea Under Communism* (Rice University Special Studies, 1976), pp. 130–31.

18. Robert A. Wampler introduced the collection with his essay "North Korea's Collapse? The End Is Near—Maybe" (October 26, 2006). I am part of Dr. Wampler's

declassification project, and appreciate his making these documents available to me. The CIA's January 21, 1998, report (about the 1997 conference) is entitled "Exploring the Implications of Alternative North Korean Endgames: Results From a Discussion Panel on Continuing Coexistence Between North and South Korea," which is mostly declassified except for some redacted names.

19. From Jordan's lecture at Harvard in 1999, quoted in Selig S. Harrison, *Korean Endgame: A Strategy for Reunification and U.S. Disengagement* (Princeton, NJ: Princeton University Press, 2002), p. 3.

20. Korean Central News Agency (KCNA), December 9, 1993.

21. Kim Jong Il, "Abuses of Socialism," *Kûlloja* [The Worker], March 1, 1993, KCNA, P'yŏngyang, March 3, 1993.

22. "Combating Imperialist Ideology and Cultural Poisoning Called For," KCNA (June 1, 1999), reporting a joint article in the *Nodong Sinmun* (Worker's Daily) and *Kûlloja* (The Worker), the two leading ideological organs.

23. The first new laws are summarized in Eui-gak Hwang, "North Korean Laws for the Induction of Foreign Capital and Practical Approaches to Foreign Investment in North Korea," *Vantage Point*, v.xvii, nos. 4 and 5 (Seoul, March, April 1994). See also the relatively liberal labor regulations for foreign-funded enterprises, published by KCNA on January 11, 1994. I wrote about more recent reforms in *North Korea: Another Country*.

24. *Far Eastern Economic Review*, September 30, 1993.

25. Hong-koo Han, "Kim Il Sung and the Guerrilla Struggle in Eastern Manchuria," Ph.D. diss. (University of Washington, 1999), pp. 8, 13.

26. Han, p. 162.

27. Han, pp. 324–26.

28. Kim Se-jin, *The Politics of Military Revolution in Korea* (Chapel Hill: University of North Carolina Press, 1973), pp. 48–57. Syngman Rhee came to rely on a small core of Manchurian officers after coming to power in 1948, mainly those having experience in counterinsurgency.

29. Charles K. Armstrong, *The North Korean Revolution, 1945–1950* (Ithaca, NY: Cornell University Press, 2003), p. 31.

CHAPTER 4

The Strategic Role of North Korea in Northeast Asia
Suk Hi Kim

ABSTRACT

Northeast Asia consists of China, Japan, the two Koreas, the Russian Far East, and Mongolia. The Korean peninsula stretches southward from the northeastern section of the Asian continent and faces the islands of Japan. Korea is the country where the interests and influences of the four global powers—China, Russia, Japan, and the United States—are closely interlocked. The United States is not part of Northeast Asia geographically, but it has been deeply involved in all of the important issues of this region since 1945. As a result, it is almost impossible for one to think of Northeast Asia without the United States. The peninsula has thus functioned as a land bridge between the Asian continental powers (China and Russia) and the oceanic powers (Japan and the United States), for both cultural exchange and military aggression. However, this land bridge has been broken since the end of World War II, because the peninsula has been divided into two separate states, North Korea and South Korea. Northeast Asia is arguably considered to be the most dangerous region in the post–Cold War world, where the interests of three nuclear powers (the United States, Russia, and China) and three threshold nuclear countries (North Korea, South Korea, and Japan) are engaged.[1]

Many view Northeast Asia as poised more for international conflict than for international peace, because this region manifests the more general global North-South divide based on the divergence between market countries (United States, Japan, and South Korea) and socialist or transitional countries (China, Russia, and North Korea). This chapter questions this widely held view, because the strategic role of North Korea in Northeast Asia will compel the United States and other Northeast Asian countries to work together on the Korean issue for their national security, energy supply, and economic welfare. First, in the opinion of many observers, a divided Korea and a nuclear North Korea pose a more serious threat than the Middle East. As a result, the Northeast Asian countries and the United States have little option but to work together to resolve the North Korean nuclear standoff through peaceful negotiations in order to ensure their national security. Second, the Northeast Asian countries are likely to work together for their national energy security, because this region is home to major energy consumers such as China and Japan and a major energy producer—Russia. The United States has an incentive to support regional cooperation to prevent these countries from increasing their dependence on Middle Eastern oil. Third, there is a good possibility that the Northeast Asian countries and the United States will work together for their joint economic interests. Many observers argue Northeast Asia has the potential to become the most important trading bloc in the future because of Japanese capital and technology, Chinese labor and capital, Russian natural resources, and the Korean work ethic. In addition, the Northeast Asian countries and the United States have already established close economic ties over much of the postwar period and, in recent years, have become increasingly economically interdependent. One wonders why U.S. Secretary of State Hillary Clinton once said "We should try to step back and see North Korean issues as the forest instead of the trees."

Introduction

Northeast's heavyweight neighbors' spheres of influence (China, Japan, and Russia), along with that of the United States, overlap in Korea (see Table 1). Consequently, the world's heaviest concentration of military and economic capabilities is in Northeast Asia, with three of the four large nuclear weapons states (China, Russia, and the U.S.), three threshold nuclear weapons states (North Korea, South Korea, and Japan), and five large economies (China, South Korea, Japan, the U.S., and Russia).[2] In the middle of this precarious and tough neighborhood, divided Korea stands as a strategic pivot. History and geography have consigned Korea to the position of a highly contested strategic crossroads, the site for over a century of recurrent collisions between

Table 1: The Vital Economic Statistics of the Northeast Asian Countries

Country	Area (million km²)	Population (millions)	GDP (PPP) ($ billion)	Exports ($ billion)	Reserves ($ billion)
China	9,569 (4)	1,339 (1)	8,789 (3)	1,941 (2)	2,206 (1)
Japan	378 (61)	127 (10)	4,137 (4)	516 (5)	1,011 (2)
Mongolia	1,564 (19)	3 (136)	9 (150)	2 (130)	n.a.
Russia	17,098 (1)	140 (9)	2,116 (8)	296 (14)	439 (3)
North Korea	121 (98)	23 (50)	40 (97)	2.1 (127)	n.a.
South Korea	100 (108)	49 (25)	1,356 (14)	355 (9)	245 (6)
U.S.	9,826 (3)	307 (4)	14,267 (2)	995 (4)	77(n.a.)
EU	4,325 (n.a.)	491 (2)	14,510 (1)	1,952 (1)	(n.a.)

( ) Country comparison to the world.
Source: The *World CIA Factbook*, April 14, 2010.

great-power interests. Consequently, many view Northeast Asia as primed more for international conflict than for international peace, because this region replicates the global North-South divide, with its sharp divergence between capitalist countries (the U.S., Japan, and South Korea) and socialist or transitional countries (China, Russia, and North Korea).

However, this chapter argues that these countries will eventually work together, because they will need each other's help for their national security, energy security, and economic security. First, many analysts insist that all the Northeast Asian countries and the United States will use divided Korea as a bridge for their national security. The continental powers on the northwest side of Korea and the oceanic powers on the southeast side of Korea have no choice other than to work together to resolve the North Korean nuclear stand-off through peaceful negotiations, because a nuclear North Korea poses a greater threat than that posed by the Middle East. China, Russia, and North Korea already have nuclear weapons. South Korea and Japan have the technology and the money to develop nuclear weapons quite quickly if necessary, in order to defend themselves against possible attacks by a nuclear North Korea. A U.S. military strike on the nuclear facilities might eliminate North Korea's plutonium reprocessing capacity. However, such a strike would risk a North Korean counterattack that could devastate South Korea, subject Japan to missile attacks, and even trigger a broader regional war involving China.

On October 9, 2006, North Korea set off its first nuclear test, thus becoming the eighth country in history to proclaim that it has joined the club of nuclear weapons states. On May 25, 2009, North Korea conducted a second test of a nuclear weapon at the same location as the original test (not confirmed). The test weapon was of the same magnitude as the atomic bombs dropped on Japan in World War II. In April 2010, both the International Atomic Energy Agency (IAEA) and the United States publicly acknowledged that North Korea had a number of nuclear weapons.

On June 12, 2009, the United Nations Security Council unanimously voted to expand and tighten sanctions on North Korea after the nation's recent nuclear test. In fact, the United Nations, the United States, and its allies have taken a series of new hard-line actions—tougher sanctions, a stronger proliferation security initiative (PSI), and so on—to punish North Korea for its defiant May 25, 2009, atomic test and a barrage of missile tests. Will this new round of tougher actions against a nuclear North Korea work? If history repeats itself, they will again undoubtedly fail. U.S. economic sanctions against North Korea began on June 28, 1950, three days after the outbreak of the Korean War. Since then, the United Nations, the United States, and its allies have increasingly imposed economic sanctions on North Korea in an attempt to destabilize and manipulate the North Korean regime. However, these sanctions and other hard-line measures have been largely ineffective in stopping North Korea from developing weapons of mass destruction (WMD). In fact, North Korea has used these sanctions as an excuse for developing more sophisticated weapons of mass destruction, while its economy has been getting worse.

First, some experts think that, sooner or later, the United States and North Korea will make a deal that may stick for two major reasons: (1) after the North Korean nuclear tests in recent years, the United States has no other alternative but to reach an agreement; and (2) such an accord would neutralize a number of increasingly stringent economic sanctions and restrictions against North Korea, imposed by the United States, its allies, and the United Nations in recent years.

Second, the Northeast Asian countries are likely to work together for their national energy security, because this region is home to major energy consumers such as China, as well as major energy producers such as Russia. This region has become a principal driver in the world energy markets, largely due to China's remarkable growth in demand. As the gap between consumption and production levels in Northeast Asia expands, the region's economic powers appear to be increasingly anxious about their energy security, and concerned that tight supplies and consequent high prices may constrain economic growth. The Russian Far East, with its vast proven energy reserves and relative geographic proximity to the Northeast Asian markets, is already an arena for competition between the Asian powers. On the other hand, energy has recently emerged as an area of regional cooperation. Such cooperation is expected to facilitate a wider spectrum of regional cooperation and sharpen the competitive edge of the whole region. A peaceful solution to the North Korean nuclear issue will be essential to build up the political trust and institutions needed for such cooperation.

Third, there is a good possibility that the Northeast Asian countries and the United States will work together for their economic interests. The world has been swiftly moving toward trading blocs in recent years. Economists divide trading nations into three groups based on the euro, the dollar, and the yen-yuan. The world's future economic landscape will see that companies will compete within the boundaries of trading blocs—whether in Europe, North America, or Asia. Asia does not have a strong trading bloc, such as the North American Free Trade Agreement or the European Union. However, the so-called "ASEAN Plus Three" (the Southeast Asian nations plus China, Japan, and South Korea) has recently emerged as a potential trading bloc. Scholars argue that Northeast Asia is a region with every possibility of becoming the best trading bloc in the future, because of Japanese capital and technology, Chinese labor, Russian natural resources, and the Korean work ethic. In addition, the Northeast Asian countries and the United States have already had close economic ties for many years and have been becoming increasingly economically interdependent.

North Korea has blocked South Korea's overland access to China, Russia, and other Asian countries since the Korean War, thereby making South Korea an island for all practical purposes. North Korea stands as a strategic pivot in Northeast Asian security, energy security, and economic security mainly because of its location. Thus, we will discuss the importance of North Korea's location first.

The Strategic Location of North Korea

The Korean peninsula stretches southward from the northeastern section of the Asian continent and faces the islands of Japan. The peninsula has thus functioned as a land bridge between the Asian continental powers (China and Russia) and the oceanic powers (Japan and the United States), for both cultural exchange and military aggression. However, this land bridge has been broken since the end of World War II, because the peninsula has been divided into two separate states, the Democratic People's Republic of Korea in the north and the Republic of Korea in the south. All of the Northeast Asian countries and the United States may wish to restore this land bridge in the interests of economic and energy cooperation.

If the land bridge that passes through North Korea is restored, five Northeast Asian countries—China, Japan, Russia, and the two Koreas—can be connected through a land transportation network, such as railroads, highways, and undersea tunnels. In addition, this land transportation network can also be extended to cover Asia, the Middle East, and Europe via the Trans-Siberian Railway (TSR), the Trans-China Railway (TCR), the Trans-Korea Railway (TKR), and an undersea tunnel between South Korea and Japan.

In simultaneous ceremonies on the western Kyongui Line and the eastern Donghae Line, at 1:00 P.M. on June 14, 2003, the two Koreas reconnected the lines of the Trans-Korean Railway (TKR) for the first time since the Korean War. Fifty officials from the North and South presided at a ceremony in which 25 kilometers (about 15.5 miles) of new rail was laid on either side of the sensitive Military Demarcation Line (MDL), which runs down the center of the 14 kilometer (about 8.5 mile) wide Demilitarized Zone (DMZ).[3] The northern parts of the TKR, known as the Gyeongui Line (Seoul-Shinuiju) and the Donghae Line (Cheojn-Najin) were severed immediately after the breakout of the Korean War, thereby blocking South Korea's overland access to China and other Asian countries, which makes South Koreans "feel as if we live on an island." For South Korea, the restoration of rail travel would help end its virtual island status, given that the only land route is through North Korea. The reconnection of railway lines along with that of roads severed during the 1950–53 Korean War was another hole punched through the DMZ since the two Koreas embarked on unprecedented reconciliation, with their first summit in June 2000.

The first railway link for 53 years between the previously hostile countries of North and South Korea was officially completed in June 2003, following a new era of cooperation. Then, trains crossed the heavily fortified border between North and South Korea on May 17, 2007, for the first time in 57 years, in what was hailed by both countries as a key step toward reconciliation on the divided Korean peninsula. Although these were one-time test runs on the two short stretches of railroad that were linked through the DMZ a few years earlier, they were highly symbolic for Koreans. South Korea stressed that the connection of these two lines is not only in the deep interests of the people of both Koreas, but that it is also for the good of the people of the entire Eurasian Land Bridge, and indeed the world. The immediate attention of Northeast Asian officials is to not only connect the North-South rails, but to help connect, strengthen, and upgrade the entire route for the rails all along both the TCR and the TSR. Thus, this one-time test run on May 17, 2007, has created a focus of world attention not only on Korea, but also on the entire Eurasian Land Bridge project and the movement of people and goods across Eurasia. Both the TSR and the TCR, which link Asia and Europe, can connect with the TKR. This would become the world's largest overland transportation route, bringing together the European and Northeast Asian markets.

The TKR would offer a faster and cheaper way for South Korea to deliver exports that are presently shipped by sea to China and Europe. It would also provide a shortcut for Russian oil and other natural resources that are transported to South Korea. South Korean officials state that such a rail system would save South Korea $34 to $50 per ton in shipping costs. In addition, this connection would reduce shipment times for goods and materials from South Korea to Europe by as much as by 15 days. Similar benefits would also be available to China, Europe, and Russia if they were to ship their exports to South Korea through this rail system.[4]

The reconnection of the TKR could revive the stalled TAR UN railway project known as the Trans-Asian Railway (TAR), and a long-shot tunnel project between South Korea and Japan. The Land Bridge project for Northeast Asia and Europe will not be completed until some type of land transportation system can be extended to Japan. Some scholars and politicians in both South Korea and Japan have been talking about the construction of an undersea tunnel between the two countries for years, just like the Eurotunnel between England and France. The major sticking point for the construction of such a tunnel has been the division of Korea, which has prevented the South Koreans and the Japanese from shipping or receiving goods via land routes. If North Korea opens up its territory for highways and rail lines, the feasibility study of this project may be accelerated, because South Korea and Japan are trade-oriented economies, and they currently have to ship and receive all goods in foreign trade via air or sea. Exports and imports among the Northeast Asian countries and the Eurasian markets by air, or otherwise by sea, are either expensive or time-consuming. Even without a land bridge between Korea and Japan, the restoration of the TKR offers logistical opportunities to Japan because of its geographic proximity to the Korean peninsula.

The idea of building a fixed link to connect England and France is a very old one, the first proposal having been presented to Napoleon in 1802. From the late nineteenth century until 1975, the project went through several starts and stops. Construction finally got under way in 1987; in 1990, engineers and diggers from the two sides met under the Channel waters, and the official opening was held in May 1994.

This impressive undersea structure, the Eurotunnel System, is the only service that provides a direct link between the highway networks of England and France. Train shuttles and freight shuttle services carry both passenger cars and trucks. In addition, it also allows the Eurostar passenger train service and various freight rail carriers to cross the Channel using its infrastructure. These carriers pay Eurotunnel for the right to use the tunnel and can use up to half of its paths. In 2006, Eurotunnel carried 1,296,269 trucks, 2,021,543 cars, and 67,201 coaches on its shuttle services. It also provided access through the Tunnel for 7,858,337 Eurostar passengers and 1,569,429 tons of rail freight.[5]

In fact, on October 20, 2000, Japanese Prime Minister Yoshiro Mori had publicly proposed an undersea tunnel between the western part of Kyushu and the southern tip of the Korean peninsula, thus opening up the possibility of direct travel between Tokyo and London by train. The tunnel would be some 173 kilometers (about 107.5 miles) long, almost four times the length of the Eurotunnel, and it would link up with the TKR. This line would eventually link up with both the TSR and the TCR.

"The construction is technically possible, but the problem is money," Mr. Mori said, during a meeting of leaders at the Asia-Europe Summit (Asem) in Seoul. This project has been a dream of railway officials in both South Korea and Japan for many years. Reports said that some Japanese experts estimated that the project would cost more than $77 billion. If we assume that the cost of construction would go up by 10 percent per year, its cost should be more than $200 billion by now (as of August 2010). Mr. Mori suggested calling the tunnel the Asem Railway in honor of the summit, as it would eventually link Japan to Europe. Japan already has the world's longest undersea tunnel, which connects the islands of Honshu and Hokkaido and is 53.9 kilometers (about 33.5 miles) long. The Eurotunnel between England and France is about 50 kilometers (about 31 miles). If realized, the project would help Japan become a part of the Asian continent, not an isolated island state. Some Korean and Japanese officials and researchers have a dream of seeing an "Iron Silk Road" in the form of the TAR, which would take South Korean and Japanese people and goods across Siberia and China to Europe.[6]

The TAR, a project of the United Nations Economic and Social Commission for Asia and the Pacific (UNESCAP), is aimed at creating an integrated freight railway network across Europe and Asia. The project was initiated in the 1960s, with the objective of providing a continuous 14,000 kilometer (about 8,699 mile) rail link between Singapore and Istanbul, Turkey, with possible further connections to Europe and Africa. At the time, shipping and air travel were not as well developed, and the project promised to significantly reduce shipping times and costs between Europe and Asia. Progress in developing TAR was hindered by political and economic obstacles throughout the 1960s, 1970s, and early 1980s. By the 1990s, the end of the Cold War and normalization of relations between some countries improved the prospects for creating a rail network across the Asian continent.

The TAR was seen as a way of accommodating the huge increases in international trade between Eurasian nations and facilitating the increased movements of goods between countries. It was also seen as a way of improving the economies and accessibility of landlocked countries such as Laos, Afghanistan, Mongolia, and the Central Asian republics.

Much of the railway network already exists, although some significant gaps remain. A big challenge is the differences in rail gauge across Eurasia. Four different major rail gauges (which measures the distance between rails) exist across the continent: most of Europe, as well as Turkey, Iran, China, and the two Koreas, use the 1,435 mm gauge, known as Standard gauge; Finland, Russia, and the former Soviet republics use a 1,520 mm gauge; most of the railways in India, Pakistan, Bangladesh, and Sri Lanka use a 1,676 mm gauge;

and most of Southeast Asia has a meter-gauge. For the most part, the TAR would not change national gauges; mechanized facilities would be built to move shipping containers from train to train at the breaks of gauge. By 2001, four corridors had been studied as part of the plan[7]:

- The Northern Corridor would link Europe and the Pacific, via Germany, Poland, Belarus, Russia, Kazakhstan, Mongolia, China, and the two Koreas, with breaks of gauge at the Poland/Belarus border (1,435 mm to 1,520 mm), the Kazakhstan/China border (1,520 mm to 1,435 mm), and the Mongolia-China border (1,520 mm to 1,435 mm). The 9,200 kilometer (about 5,716 mile) Trans-Siberian Railway covers much of this route and currently carries large amounts of freight from East Asia to Moscow, and on to the rest of Europe. Due to political problems with North Korea, freight from South Korea must currently be shipped by sea to the port of Vladivostok to access the route.
- The Southern Corridor would go from Europe to Southeast Asia, connecting Turkey, Iran, Pakistan, India, Bangladesh, Myanmar, and Thailand, with links to China's Yunnan Province and, via Malaysia, to Singapore. Gaps exist in eastern Iran, between India and Myanmar, between Myanmar and Thailand, between Thailand and Cambodia, between Cambodia and Vietnam, and between Thailand and Yunnan. Breaks of gauge occur, or will occur, at the Iran/Pakistan border (1,435 mm to 1,676 mm), the India/Myanmar border (1,676 mm to 1,000 mm), and in connections to China (1,000 mm to 1,435 mm).
- A Southeast Asian network would link the sub-regional network covering the ASEAN and Indo-China sub-regions. The ASEAN countries include Indonesia, Malaysia, Singapore, and Thailand (south of Bangkok), while the Greater Mekong Area includes Cambodia, southern China (Yunnan province), Myanmar, Lao, Thailand (north and east of Bangkok), and Vietnam.
- The North-South Corridor would link northern Europe to the Persian Gulf. The main route would start in Helsinki, Finland, and continue through Russia to the Caspian Sea, where it would split into three routes: a western route through Azerbaijan, Armenia, and western Iran; a central route across the Caspian Sea to Iran via ferry; and an eastern route through Kazakhstan, Uzbekistan, and Turkmenia to eastern Iran. The routes would converge in the Iranian capital of Tehran and continue to the Iranian port of Bandar Abbas.

In early November 2006, transportation and railway ministers from 41 countries participated in the week-long conference held in Busan, South Korea; these countries signed the Trans-Asian Railway Network Agreement on November 10, 2006. This agreement reaffirmed among other things that the Northern Corridor would connect to not only Russia, Mongolia, and Kazakhstan, but also South Korea. Of course, this corridor will not connect to South Korea until the TKR has been completed. It cannot be said that the TAR project has been a success so far. Very little railway has been built along the corridors during the past 50 years. The Northern Corridor was already working in the 1960s, but only for trade between the Soviet Union and China.

Before the dream of the TKR comes true, however, transportation officials and government officials say that years of confidence-building talks and billions of dollars in investments in North Korea's decrepit rail system will be needed. Observers acknowledge that such a dream will not be made real until North Korea gives up its nuclear weapons and improves its human rights. Those moves would help build public support in South Korea for large cross-border investments and would open the way for international development aid. The reconnection of roads and train lines severed during the 1950–53 Korean War was one of the inter–Korean rapprochement projects agreed upon following the historic 2000 summit between then South Korean President Kim Dae-jung and North Korean leader Kim Jong-il. For quite a few years after the summit, reconnected roads have been used to transport South Korean workers to a joint industrial complex in the North Korean border city of Kaesong, as well as to transport South Korean tourists to North Korea's scenic Mount Geumgang.

Rising Energy Competition and Energy Cooperation in Northeast Asia

The enormous potential of East Asia's energy market has been an American preoccupation almost from the time when Secretary of State John Hay proclaimed the Open Door policy in 1900. It even became the theme for an improbably successful novel, *Oil for the Lamps of China*, by Alice Tisdale Hobart, which was a bestseller in the United States during the early 1930s. Drawing on her own experiences as the wife of a Standard Oil executive in China, Hobart turned the clash of corporate and Confucian cultures into a drama so compelling that it inspired two Hollywood movies and won her a loyal audience for a dozen other novels, travel books, and a memoir, most of them set in the Far East.

Almost a century later, a real-life Asian drama is unfolding about oil and geopolitics that is likely to be unfamiliar even to devotees of financial journalism. This time, Russia—not the U.S.—is cast in the leading role. With the emergence of Russia as a major oil and gas exporter, China, Japan, and the two Koreas have turned to nearby Russian sources of petroleum in Siberia and on Sakhalin Island.[8]

Apart from their need to keep pace with rapidly growing energy needs, all of these countries are anxious to offset their dependence on faraway Arab producers. They not only want a hedge against possible supply disruptions resulting from war and revolutions; equally importantly, they want to reduce what they find to be an increasingly uncomfortable reliance on the United States for the protection of tanker traffic through potentially hazardous sea lanes. For environmental reasons, the addition of Russian natural gas to their energy mix is particularly attractive as a way to cut down on an appalling level of pollution resulting from the use of coal and oil.

Rising competition for energy and Asian government conceptions of energy security in China, Japan, and South Korea are of interest to policymakers for these three countries and the United States for three primary reasons.[9] First, the surge in China's oil demand has emerged as a major factor influencing world oil prices. Second, the tightening global oil market could increase the bargaining power of the oil-exporting countries, possibly driving a wedge between the United States and its Asian allies over important foreign policy issues. Third, competition in Asia over access to energy supplies could significantly alter the geopolitics of the region, with important implications for U.S. foreign policy.

China, previously almost entirely dependent on coal, has turned increasingly to oil to satisfy its soaring energy demand. Although China still depends on coal to meet more than half of its energy consumption, in 2003 it surpassed Japan to become the world's second-largest oil-consuming country after the United States (see Table 2). If China reaches per capita consumption levels comparable to those of South Korea, its demand will be twice that of the United States and will push up the worldwide demand for oil by at least 20 percent.[10]

As the world's third-largest consumer of oil, Japan, with almost no oil reserves, has long depended on external sources to keep its economy running. Since the 1970s, Japan has embarked on a focused campaign of diversification of suppliers and forms of energy, conservation, and research devoted to alternative sources. Despite attempts at diversification, Japan still imports most of its oil from the Middle East. Observers point out that Japanese policymakers are increasingly linking energy policy and security policy, citing threats to the

Table 2: Oil Production, Consumption, and Reserves for the Northeast Asian Countries

Country	Production*	Consumption*	Known reserves
China (million bbl)	3.795	7.999	12,550
Japan (million bbl)	0.133	4.785	44
South Korea (million bbl)	0.030	2.175	0
Russia (million bbl)	9.810	2.800	79,000
Total (million bbl)	13.760	17.849	91,594

*Per day consumption and production for the Northeast Asian countries.
Source: *The World CIA Factbook*, April 18, 2010.

Persian Gulf or to the area of the sea lanes that bring oil to Japan. South Korea, the world's tenth-largest consumer of oil, has a strikingly similar energy portfolio to that of Japan, but its production and consumption of energy are less efficient, less advanced, and less environmentally friendly. For example, the South Korean economy is much smaller than that of either the United Kingdom or France, but its oil consumption is larger than that of either country. Because most of the imported oil comes from the Middle East, South Korea has taken measures to diversify its sources by seeking equity states in energy exploration worldwide and has built up a strategic oil reserve.

Rising Competition over Access to Energy in the Russian Far East

The United States has recently sounded alarm bells as China, Japan, and South Korea have competed to make separate energy deals with U.S. adversaries such as Venezuela and Iran. Furthermore, as these three countries have scrambled to meet their energy needs while reducing their dependence on the Middle East; the largely undeveloped resources of neighboring Siberia have become the prize. Although the promise of the Russian Far East is significant, many analysts have cast doubt on the commercial viability of tapping the Far Eastern reserves. This has not discouraged China and Japan from engaging in a bidding war over Russian projects to bolster their energy security.[11]

The opening round of the contest has centered on negotiations on proposed pipeline routes from the eastern Siberian oilfield of Angarsk. An agreement between Russia and China, endorsed by presidents Putin and Hu in May 2003, cleared the way for the pipeline from the city of Angarsk to Daqing, China's flagship oilfield, with refining facilities, in the industrial northeast. The arrangement stalled, however, after the arrest of Russian oil tycoon Mikhail Khodorkovsky, chairman of Yukos, the company that brokered the deal and planned to construct the pipeline. In 2005, Moscow changed course and designated the route preferred by Japan to terminate in the Russian port of Nakholdka, near Vladivostok on the Sea of Japan, and a short tanker trip away from Japan. Analysts say that this pipeline would only pass through Russian territory, facilitating construction and maintenance. However, the pipeline would reportedly cover 2,580 miles of harsh terrain and cost up to $18 billion. China's alternative proposal to bring the oil to the Daqing refineries would stretch for 1,400 miles and cost only $2.5 billion.[12]

Energy-hungry Asian consumers have also targeted Russian gas. As the world's largest exporter of natural gas, and with abundant reserves, Russia is poised to be a natural gas superpower. Projects under development now in Sakhalin and for the massive Kovykta gas field in the eastern Siberian region of Irkutsk also hold promise for Asian consumers, while indicating the potential for further political competition over Russian energy sources. The initial proposal for a gas pipeline, running from Irkutsk through Beijing and under the Yellow Sea to South Korea, would have served the Chinese and South Korean markets. In June 2004, however, Japan emerged as a potential buyer, and Russian negotiators suggested an alternative pipeline that would parallel the proposed Angarsk-Nakhodka oil pipeline, and therefore serve the Japanese market.

In addition, with natural gas reserves estimated at 96 trillion cubic feet and oil reserves at 14 billion barrels, the Russian island of Sakhalin, north of Japan, is primed to become a major gas supplier to the region as well as an important oil producer. The question of whether to transport gas by pipeline or in the form of liquefied natural gas (LNG) is linked to broader issues of national energy security. Japan prefers the pipeline option because it ensures an exclusive supply and helps to diversify its energy sources away from the Middle East. LNG producers, on the other hand, wish to have other potential markets, such as China, South Korea, and the United States Oil pipeline politics could develop similarly to the competition over gas transportation routes.

Will Russian oil and gas pipelines lead to China, Japan, or South Korea? As the Iraq war drags on, the international market sees a constant rise in oil and gas prices. Russia, a major exporter of both oil and gas, naturally draws considerable attention from the rest of the world in every action taken. However, its government has not made a firm commitment to any project, and claims that it will try to satisfy both Japan and China for relatively close-by energy supplies. Moscow, with its huge reserves of both gas and oil, has played Tokyo and Beijing off against one another to maximize concessions for itself since the early 2000s. Although China and Japan have expressed frustration with Russia's frequent changes in its energy deals, the proximity of Siberian energy supplies remains attractive. In May 2008, China and Russia revived a third plan, originally proposed by Russian president Vladimir Putin in 2005, which would combine the aforementioned two routes: from Siberia to the Russian Far East, and then on to China and the Asia-Pacific region. The first leg of the pipeline, estimated at $11 billion, would be built first from Taishet to Skovorodino, near the Chinese border, and then on to Daqing. Later, the second leg of the pipeline, which will stretch for 1,304 miles, would be extended to Nakhodka and the Asia-Pacific market, in order to diversify Russian exports.[13] However, most analysts caution that the decision is far from finalized and that significant obstacles remain before any arrangement can be realized.

At a Kremlin summit on September 29, 2008, South Korean President Lee and Russian President Medvedev agreed to work together to send Russian natural gas through a pipeline to South Korea via North Korea, and to link the inter–Korean railway with the Trans-Siberian Railway (TSR), for its eventual connection to Europe.[14] The agreement calls for building a South Korea—North Korea—Russia natural gas pipeline for exclusive use by South Korea. In addition, the agreement also calls for linking the inter–Korean railway to the TSR, which will help South Korea to drastically reduce its international logistical costs. The two countries expect that the railway and pipeline projects will help stabilize the security situation in Northeast Asia and eventually become a cornerstone for an economic community in the region.

Long-Term Consequences

The ongoing negotiations may yield more political tension as consumers compete for more assured access to energy supplies. The long-term consequences of increasing energy competition in Northeast Asia range from dire predictions of military conflict to scenarios for unprecedented regional cooperation. Optimistic analysts point out the potential for unprecedented cooperation between the Asian countries, with the shared goal of enhancing energy security for the region. Various regional groupings, including ASEAN Plus Three (Southeast Asian nations plus Japan, South Korea, and China), APEC (the Asia Pacific Economic Cooperation forum), and the East Asia Summit, have introduced programs for enhancing energy cooperation as high oil prices have continued. At the 2007 East Asia Summit, leaders pushed for concerted efforts to explore nuclear, hydropower, and biofuel alternatives. If institutions devoted to sharing infrastructure and information are developed, East Asia may find the mechanisms helpful for other political, economic, and security-related issues. Although such a development may lessen dependence on the United States for stability, which could threaten the influence of the United States in the region, stronger regional dialogue might also allow for a drawdown of the costly U.S. military presence in the region.

The North Korea Factor

The uncertain future of the Korean peninsula makes it difficult for the Northeast Asian countries to consider long-term strategies for energy security. With or without Korean unification, Korea would certainly face rising demands for energy, and North Korea—with an economic recovery under way—already has a critical energy deficit.

Energy has played a central and controversial role in the ongoing Six-Party Talks (China, Japan, the two Koreas, Russia, and the United States) to deal with North Korea's nuclear weapons programs. The United States and North Korea reached the Agreed Framework in October 1994, in which North Korea pledged to abandon its nuclear ambitions in return for the construction of two light-water reactors and 500,000 tons of fuel oil each year until the reactors were completed. Under the February 2007 agreement, China, Russia, South Korea, and the United States promised to provide heavy fuel oil to North Korea in exchange for disablement of key nuclear facilities.

Proponents of engagement with North Korea may support the construction of oil/gas pipelines or other forms of energy infrastructure through North Korea to link the peninsula and other Asian markets with resources from the Russian Far East. Such arrangements would provide North Korea with foreign exchange in the form of transit payments, and could provide energy for the country without relying on the controversial nuclear energy program. In addition, they could reduce the cost of construction and maintenance for pipelines, ease rising energy competition in Northeast Asia, and lessen intra–Asian tension over energy supplies. Some of those who support the expansion of the Six-Party Talks have pointed to energy as a potential platform for region-wide cooperation.

There is a catch. Although these pipelines could greatly enhance regional stability and provide a cheap alternative to oil imported from the Middle East, the United States seems uneasily wary of pipeline networks in Northeast Asia. In the case of Korea, for ideological reasons, the United States actively opposes pipelines crossing from North Korea to South Korea. In other words, the United States opposes such a project without the complete and verifiable dismantling of the existing nuclear weapons programs. Should North Korea satisfy these requirements, the dream of a proposed pipeline passing through North Korea may be realized. In fact, some have long suggested that the proposal for oil and gas pipelines from the Russian Far East with China in transit to North Korea could create unprecedented cooperation among the Northeast Asian countries, because it will be a win-win project for every country involved.

Globalization and Economic Cooperation in Northeast Asia

Globalization is the idea of integrating the world marketplace, creating a so-called "borderless world" for goods, services, knowledge, and capital. To some extent, such a world is already a reality. Consider physical communications (mail, the telephone, the Internet, and airline and ocean shipping networks); entertainment (film, TV, music, news, and sports); economic and business exchange (banking and insurance networks, dependable foreign exchange and stock markets, and reciprocal trade arrangements); and even ideas and competing spiritual values through evangelical Christianity, Islam, and other religions.[15]

The increasing integration of goods, services, and financial markets presents both opportunities and challenges for governments, businesses, and individuals. Although business operations in countries across the globe have existed for centuries, the world has recently entered an era of unprecedented worldwide production and distribution. Worldwide production and distribution are critical for the survival of the multinational corporation—its ability to produce products and sell them at a profit. International finance is an integral part of total management and cuts across functional boundaries because it expresses inputs, outputs, plants, and results in monetary terms.

A trading bloc is a preferential economic arrangement among a group of countries that reduces interregional barriers to trade in goods, services, investment, and capital. Trading blocs have emerged as the most debated topic in world trade. While countries around the world are making efforts to suppress national interests in favor of trading blocs, these groupings are also seen as evidence of difficulties in preserving the current global trading system under the World Trade Organization (WTO). Historically, trading blocs have consisted of member countries with similar levels of per capita income, geographic proximity, comparable trading regimes, and political commitment to regional organization.[16] While the European Community displayed all of these characteristics in its early stages with six members, recent developments have shown that political will to cooperate does overcome consequences of dissimilarity in the first three characteristics. The admission of Greece and Poland into the European Union and the bilateral trade agreement between Chile and Korea indicate that a united political will can overcome the consequences of most dissimilarity.

When we consider major examples of economic integration, such as the North American Free Trade Agreement (NAFTA) or the European Union (EU), the concept of geographic proximity stands out. Neighboring countries tend to become involved in integrative activities for several reasons[17]:

1. The distances to be traversed between such countries are shorter.
2. Consumers' tastes are more likely to be similar.
3. Distribution channels can be more easily established in adjacent economies.
4. Neighboring countries may have a common history, awareness of common interests, and so forth, and may be more willing to coordinate their policies.

Indeed, China, Japan, Korea, and the Russian Far East have much in common: geography, history, culture, ethnic background, and even the use of Chinese characters as part of their language. Ideological differences are one major reason for the lack of a strong trading bloc in Northeast Asia. However, there are strong indications that political will may overcome such ideological differences once the North Korean nuclear issue has been resolved peacefully.

Although Asia does not have a strong trading bloc, such as NAFTA or the EU, it has two loose affiliations: ASEAN Plus Three and APEC. Created in 1967, ASEAN consists of Southeast Asian countries, such as Indonesia, the Philippines, Vietnam, and Singapore. The ASEAN Plus Three was institutionalized in 1999 when the ASEAN leaders and their counterparts in China, Japan, and South Korea issued a Joint Statement on East Asia Cooperation at their third ASEAN Plus Three Summit in Manila. Formed in 1989, APEC includes the United States, Japan, China, and South Korea. Current economic patterns in Northeast Asia are, in fact, complementary and can be transformed into a force that drives regional cooperation. Japan and South Korea are rich in capital and knowledge, China in labor, and Russia and Mongolia in natural resources. North Korea can also become a potential market, because it is one of only a few countries that are still untapped by multinational companies.

Although the economic and trade ties among China, South Korea, Japan, and the United States have grown substantially in recent years, the potential is greater still.[18] We can draw a number of inferences from Table 3, which will support the above argument.

First, the Northeast Asian economies depend far more on exports than the United States. The ratio of exports to gross national product for these Northeast Asian countries is 1.8 to 20.9 times larger than that of the United States.

Second, China, Japan, and South Korea are each others' major export markets. These statistics appear to at least partly support the argument that multinational companies largely operate within their home-based markets in each part of the "triad" of North America, the European Union, and Asia.[19] In other words, most of sales of global companies are made on a "triad" regional basis. Apparently, this argument is true for Japan, China, and South

Table 3.
The Ratio of Exports to Gross National Product (GDP) for Five Countries (billions of U.S. dollars)

Country	GDP (A)	Exports (B)	B/A (%)	Major partners*
China	4,814	1,941	40.32	U.S., Hong Kong, Japan, and South Korea
Japan	5,108	516	10.11	U.S., China, South Korea, and Hong Kong
Russia	1,232	296	28.85	Netherlands, Italy, Germany, and Turkey
S. Korea	810	355	43.83	China, U.S., Japan, and Hong Kong
U.S.	14,430	995	6.89	Canada, Mexico, China, and Japan

*The major partners are listed in order of the size of export market for each country. For example, the U.S. is listed first in the column of major partners for China because the U.S. is the largest export market for China.

Source: *The World CIA Factbook*, April 18, 2010.

Korea if one excludes the United States, which is the largest export market for many countries around the world.

Third, the Northeast Asian countries, except for Russia, depend heavily on U.S. markets for their exports. The United States is the second-largest export market for South Korea and the largest export market for both China and Japan. These three countries are far more dependent economically on the United States than the United States is on them, because they enjoy large trade surpluses with the United States. Consequently, China, Japan, and South Korea now belong to a bloc of countries that holds $5.6 trillion in foreign exchange reserves—more than half of the world's total (see Table 4). China, Japan, and other countries in the region have stabilized their currencies by buying U.S. dollars. In doing so, these countries have effectively become the primary source of funding for the growing U.S. fiscal deficit and current account deficit. Japan has played that role since the 1980s, but in the past few years China has been funding U.S. deficits for the first time.

Table 4: Reserves of Foreign Exchange and Gold for Selected Countries

Country	Reserves ($ billions)	Percentage of world total
China	2,447	27.16
Japan	1,074	11.92
Taiwan	355	3.94
South Korea	273	3.03
Singapore	190	2.11
Hong Kong	258	2.86
U.S.	83	0.92
Other countries	4,328	48.06
World total	9,008	100.00

Source: http://en.wikipedia.org/wiki/List_of_countries_by_foreign_exchange_reserves, accessed April 18, 2010.

Although there are many different types of international transactions, such as foreign direct investment, portfolio investment, and offshore banking and insurance, foreign trade still stands out. According to the World Trade Organization, world trade has grown about twice as fast as output in recent years. It appears that the excess of trade over output will be greater in the future, as national economies steadily become more integrated. Technological barriers have fallen as transportation and communication costs have dropped. Government-made barriers have also fallen as tariff and nontariff barriers have been drastically reduced in a series of multilateral negotiations and trading blocs. Economists say that the gap between exports and output is "the handiest practical measurement of the globalization of the world economy." Thus, strong trade relations among China, Japan, South Korea, and the United States are likely to eventually compel these countries to work together on the economy, security, and energy, even if they have differences on those issues.

China-U.S. Relations

The China-U.S. relationship is the most significant factor affecting the political and economic conditions of Northeast Asia. For China, the United States is not an enemy. But it is not a friend either. Many Chinese still view the United States as a major threat to their nation's security and domestic stability. Yet, the United States is still a global leader in economics, education, culture, technology, and science. China, therefore, must maintain a close relationship with the United States if its modernization efforts are to succeed.[20] Indeed, a cooperative partnership with the United States is of primary importance to China, where economic prosperity and social stability are now top concerns.

Fortunately, greater cooperation with China is also in the interests of the United States—especially since the attacks of September 11, 2001. The United States now needs China's help on issues such as counter-terrorism, nonproliferation, and the maintenance of stability in the Middle East, and a peaceful resolution of North Korean nuclear standoff. More and more, the United States has also started to see the need for China's cooperation in fields such as trade and finance, despite increased friction over currency exchange rates, intellectual property rights, and trade imbalances.

One focal point in China-U.S. relations is the North Korean nuclear issue. On this question, the United States has little choice but to rely on the Six-Party Talks to stop North Korea from developing and exporting nuclear weapons and technology. The United States and China have shared interests on the Korean peninsula. Both the United States and China want neither another Korean War nor a nuclear North Korea. Their long-term interests in relation to Korea are no longer incompatible. With the Cold War over, the only vital American interest on the Korean peninsula is that North Korea should not be allowed to threaten the United States and its allies with missiles and weapons of mass destruction. China's vital interest on the peninsula is to exercise maximum influence over the process of reunification. The last thing China wants to see is a strong and independent state on its northern frontier. Thus, China prefers the status quo and to keep North Korea as a strategic buffer.[21]

Conclusion

Given the gravity and urgency of North Korean issues, it is important for the world to address the highly uncertain prospects in North Korea. Although Korea is a middle-sized country—the two Koreas are of roughly the same size as the United Kingdom and have a combined population of 70 million—the two Koreas feel small because they live amidst giants. The geographic neighbors are China, Japan, Russia, and the United States, whose spheres of influence overlap in Korea. As a result, the future of Korea boils down to a struggle for power between two camps: South Korea, Japan, and the United States on one hand, versus North Korea, China, and Russia on the other. China, Japan, Korea, and the Russian Far East have much in common: geography, history, culture, ethnic background, and even aspects of their languages.

Northeast Asia is the region where the United States is most likely to come into close contact with China, leading to either major conflicts or real cooperation, simply because the primary focal point in China-U.S. relations is the North Korean nuclear issue. On this question, the Bush administration had little choice but to rely on the Six-Party Talks to stop North Korea from developing and exporting nuclear weapons and technology. China, in its own way, has tried to dissuade North Korea from developing nuclear weapons.

This essay has listed and discussed a number of reasons why North Korea will play a strategic role for Northeast Asian peace, stability, and economic welfare. First, many analysts insist that all of the Northeast Asian countries and the United States will use a divided Korea as a bridge for their national security. The continental powers on the northwest side of Korea and the oceanic powers on the southeast side of Korea have no choice other than to work together to resolve the North Korean nuclear standoff through peaceful negotiations, because a nuclear North Korea poses a greater threat than that posed by the Middle East. Second, the Northeast Asian countries are likely to work together for their national energy security, because this region is home to major energy consumers such as China, as well as major energy producers such as Russia. The United States is likely to support such a region's cooperation because the United States does not want these countries to become too highly dependent on Middle Eastern oil. Third, there is a good possibility that the Northeast Asian countries and the United States will work together for their economic interests. Scholars argue that Northeast Asia is a region with every possibility of becoming the best trading bloc in the future, because of Japanese capital and technology, Chinese labor, Russian natural resources, and the Korean work ethic. In addition, the Northeast Asian countries and the United States have already had close economic ties for many years and have been increasingly economically interdependent.

No stable and authoritative institution exists for the deliberation and development of multilateral energy and economic cooperation in Northeast Asia. One potential candidate for the role of driving Northeast Asia's energy and economic cooperation is the Six-Party Talks, informally put together to solve the North Korean nuclear dispute. Given the vital role of energy supply and economic growth in stabilizing the peninsula, it is conceivable that this grouping could develop into a more formal economic institution once solutions to the challenge emerge. The European Union provides a precedent, as its origin also lays in political and security concerns.[22]

Notes

1. Sandip Kumar Mishra, "Changing Landscape of Northeast Asian Security," *World Affairs* (Summer 2006): 60–71.

2. Samuel S. Kim and Tai H. Lee, eds., *North Korea and Northeast Asia* (Lanham, MD: Rowman and Littlefield, 2003), p. 4.

3. Kathy Wolfe, "Trans-Korean Rail: These Lines Will Go Through," *Executive Intelligence Report*, http://www.larouchepub.com/other/2003/3025koreas_connect.html, accessed August 10, 2007.

4. Choe Sang-Hun, "Korean Train Crossing Seen as Sign of Progress," *The New York Times*, http://www.nytimes.com, accessed May 18, 2007.

5. http://www.eurotunnel.com/ukcP3Main/ukcCorporate/ukcMediaCentre/ukcNewsReleases/ukcNews2007/ukcJanuary2007.

6. http://news.bbc.co.uk/1/hi/world/asia-pacific/982289.stm, accessed May 20, 2007.

7. http://www.unescap.org/ttdw/index.asp?MenuName=TheTrans-AsianRailway, accessed May 20, 2007.

8. Selig Harrison, "Gas and Geopolitics in Northeast Asia: Pipelines, Regional Stability, and the Korean Nuclear Crisis," *World Policy Journal* (Winter 2002/2003): 23–36.

9. Emma Chanlett-Avery, "Rising Energy Competition and Energy Security in Northeast Asia: Issues for U.S. Policy," CRS Report for Congress, Order Code RL 32466, May 13, 2008.

10. "Japan: Underpowered," Economist Intelligence Unit, December 1, 2003.

11. Emma Chanlett-Avery, "Rising Energy Competition and Energy Security in Northeast Asia: Issues for U.S. Policy," CRS Report for Congress, Order Code RL 32466, February 9, 2005.

12. Emma Chanlett-Avery, "Rising Energy Competition and Energy Security in Northeast Asia: Issues for U.S. Policy," Report for Congress, Congressional Research Services, Library of Congress, Washington, DC, updated May 13, 2008, p. CRS 13.

13. "Russia, China Close to Deal on ESPO Oil Pipeline Branch," *Mobile SMS Alert*, May 22, 2008.

14. Yonhap News, "Seoul, Moscow Agree on Gas Pipeline Projects Involving Pyongyang," *Vantage Point*, October 2008, pp. 28–29.

15. Suk Kim and Seung H. Kim, *Global Corporate Finance*, 6th ed. (New York: Wiley-Blackwell, 2006), pp. 4–5.

16. Suk Kim and Hassan Moussawi, "A Proposed Korea-U.S. Free Trade Agreement and the Kaesong Industrial Complex," *North Korean Review* (Spring 2007): 59–71.

17. John D. Daniels and Lee H. Radebaugh, *International Business* (New York: Addison-Wesley, 1998), pp. 283–285.

18. Ruan Zongze, "China's Role in a Northeast Asian Community," *Asian Perspective* 30, no. 3 (2006): 149–157; and Mel Gurtov, "Northeast Policy Under George W. Bush: Doctrine in Search of Policy," *North Korean Review* (Spring 2007): 72–85.

19. Alan M. Rugman, "Multinational Enterprises Are Regional, Not Global," *Multinational Business Review* (Spring 2003): 3–12.

20. Wang Fisi, "China's Search for Stability with America," *Foreign Affairs* (September/October 2005): 39–48.

21. Robyn Lim, "The U.S.-Japan Alliance in the Korean Crucible," *American Asian Review* (Fall 2003): 1–27.

22. P. Andrews-Speed, X. Liao, and P. Stevens, "Multilateral Energy Co-operation in Northeast Asia: Promise or Mirage?" *Oxford Energy Forum* (2005): 13–17.

CHAPTER 5

Inter-Korean Economic Cooperation
Semoon Chang and *Hwa-Kyung Kim*

Abstract

Meaningful economic cooperation between North Korea and South Korea began in the late 1980s, but took off when then President Kim Dae-jung initiated the sunshine policy in 1998. Against the numerous provocative acts by North Korea, South Korea refrained from imposing tough economic sanctions against North Korea until a South Korean tourist was shot to death by a North Korean soldier at Mt. Kumgang in July 2008 after which South Korea closed the Mt. Kumgang tourism project.

Further, South Korea imposed a variety of additional sanctions against North Korea when North Korea was found guilty of sinking a South Korean Navy ship on May 24, 2010. In the meantime, North Korea's dependence on China as a trading partner has increased dramatically since 2001. This chapter concludes with the recommendation that, for the sake of eventual unification, South Korea lifts any and all existing economic sanctions against North Korea and expands economic cooperation with North Korea.

Introduction

Fluctuating political relations between North and South Korea made it difficult, at least in the past, to sustain any meaningful and lasting economic cooperation between the two Koreas. This chapter reviews the history and the scope of economic cooperation between the two Koreas, leading to the conclusion that economic cooperation between North and South Korea should remain unaffected from political turmoil between the two Koreas.

Historical Background of Economic Cooperation

The first official joint statement between the two Koreas was released on July 4, 1972, nearly nineteen years after the Korean War ended on July 27, 1953. The "South-North Joint Communiqué" states that "Reunification will take place without reliance on or intervention by foreign nations; it will be achieved by a peaceful means"; that "The two sides shall take measures to stop propaganda broadcasting against the other side, stop military aggression and prevent any military clashes"; and that "The two sides shall institute various exchanges in the economic, social and cultural areas; cooperate in holding inter–Korean Red Cross talks; open a Seoul-Pyongyang hotline; and set up a South-North mediation committee."

Regardless of the cooperative spirit expressed in the 1972 Communiqué, economic cooperation between the two Koreas had not taken place for many more years because of two related reasons: the lack of progress on the political front and several provocative actions carried out by North Korea. On October 9, 1983, for instance, four South Korean cabinet members were killed by North Korean agents in Burma. On November 29, 1987, Korean Air 858 was destroyed by two North Korean agents forty-five minutes away from Bangkok, killing all 115 passengers and crew members aboard. As the Soviet Union was formally dissolved in 1991, ending their economic support to North Korea, the focus of North Korean issues shifted to the development of nuclear weapons. In fact, the current nuclear crisis began during 1989 when Yongbyon's nuclear facility was identified through U.S. satellite photos.

On October 21, 1994, the United States and North Korea concluded four months of negotiations by adopting the "Agreed Framework" in Geneva, which called for North Korea to freeze and eventually eliminate its nuclear facilities, a process that would require dismantling three nuclear reactors, two of which were still under construction. In exchange, North Korea was promised two light-water nuclear reactors (LWRs) and annual shipments of heavy fuel oil during construction of the reactors. The LWRs were arranged for construction through the Korean Peninsula Energy Development Organization (KEDO). On March 9, 1995, KEDO was formed in New York, with the United States, South Korea, and Japan as the organization's original members. On June 1, 2006, the KEDO Executive Board announced that it had formally terminated its plans to build two LWRs in North Korea due to the "continued and extended failure" of North Korea to comply with its relevant obligations under the 1994 Agreed Framework. KEDO was more a political arrangement than an act of economic cooperation. We thus turn our attention to economic cooperation.

Dawn of Economic Cooperation

Although trade between the two Koreas began in the late 1980s, the first meaningful event in inter–Korea economic cooperation occurred on January 13, 1998, when Chung Ju-young, founder of the Hyundai chaebol, traveled to North Korea through China and signed an agreement with North Korea on what is known as the Mt. Kumgang tourism project. Chung's visit to North Korea was made possible by the election of Kim Dae-jung as president of South Korea in December 1997.

During his inaugural speech on February 25, 1998, President Kim Dae-jung announced his "sunshine policy" for dramatic improvement of inter–Korean relations, which led to President Kim winning the Nobel Peace Prize in 2000. On June 16, 1998, Chung Ju-young followed his January visit to North Korea by sending a convoy of fifty trucks loaded with 500 cattle directly across the heavily fortified demilitarized zone (DMZ) that divides the two Koreas. This event is known affectionately as Operation Rawhide.

On August 31, 1998, North Korea launched a three-stage Taepodong-1 rocket with a range of 1,500 to 2,000 kilometers over Japan. Pyongyang announced that the rocket successfully placed a small satellite into orbit, a claim contested and proven to be false by the U.S. Space Command. Admittedly, the U.S. intelligence community was surprised by North Korea's advances in missile-staging technology, and the launching of the long-range missile led to a strain in relations between North Korea and the allies of South Korea.

Importantly, the launching of the long-range missile did not derail negotiations on the Mt. Kumgang tourism project. On October 29, 1998, Hyundai and North Korea's Asia-Pacific Peace Committee (APPC) signed an agreement on the Mt. Kumgang tourism project, and three weeks later, on November 18, the first cruise ship left South Korea for sightseeing at Mt. Kumgang.

From June 13 to 15, 2000, the first inter–Korean summit was held in Pyongyang between Kim Dae-jung of South Korea and Kim Jong-il of North Korea. The June 15 Joint Declaration paved the way for the sunshine policy, with no mention of nuclear weapons. The June 15, 2000, Declaration included a statement that would "promote a balanced development of both economies through the expansion of bilateral economic cooperation." The idea of the Kaesong Industrial Complex (KIC) must have been one of the proposed bilateral cooperation efforts since only about two years later, on November 20, 2002, North Korea established the Kaesong Industrial District Law.[1] In September 2002, the reconnection work of trans–Korea roads began. Also in September 2002, the connection project of inter–Korean railways began.[2]

Significantly, all these developments on the economic front were moving forward even after then President George W. Bush made his rather notorious speech on the Axis of Evil on January 29, 2002. On June 30, 2003, the Phase I development of the KIC project began. During 2004, the reconnection of trans–Korean roads was completed for use in reaching the Kaesong Industrial Complex on the east and Mt. Kumgang on the west. Also during 2004, an inter–Korean maritime agreement was reached, allowing North Korean merchant ships to pass through the Jeju Strait. On December 15, 2004, the first products produced at the KIC were shipped to South Korea.

The political environment has rapidly worsened since 2005. On February 10, 2005, North Korea declared that it had nuclear weapons and pulled itself out of the six-party talks. Following this declaration, the United States began to tighten its financial pressure on North Korea. On September 5, 2005, the United States identified Macao-based Banco Delta Asia as North Korea's main money laundering channel. All U.S. banks, Bank of Tokyo, Mitsubishi, Mizuo, and the Korea Exchange Bank stopped transactions with Banco Delta Asia. On February 16, 2006, Banco Delta Asia gave in to U.S. pressure and stopped all transactions relating to North Korea.

On July 5 (July 4, U.S. time), 2006, North Korea launched seven missiles, of which one was the long-range Taepodong-2 type. Note that the key issue, at least to the United States and Japan, is not missiles, but long-range missiles. On September 14, 2006, Japan banned withdrawals and overseas remittances from accounts owned by organizations and individuals linked to North Korea. This action effectively froze North Korea's assets in Japan. On October 9, 2006, North Korea conducted an underground nuclear test. On October 11, 2006, Japan banned North Korean ships from entering Japanese ports, barring most North Korean nationals from entering Japan, and banning all imports from North Korea.

It is important to note that joint economic projects between the two Koreas continued during this rapidly worsening political environment. In December 2005, the construction of the two inter–Korean railways was completed, although test runs on the connected sections in the east and west coasts were not carried out until May 17, 2007. The newly connected Gyeonggi Line in the west, near the KIC, is 27.3 miles long, while the Donghae Line in the east, toward Mt. Kumgang, is 25.5 miles long.

From October 2 to 4, 2007, the second inter–Korea summit was held between Roh Moo-hyun of South Korea and Kim Jong-il of North Korea. The October 4, 2007, Declaration for Development in Inter-Korean Relations and Peace and Prosperity stressed efforts to continue the June 15, 2000, Declaration between Kim Dae-jung and Kim Jong-il, and pledged to create a special cooperation zone in the West Sea, which turned out to be more a confrontational zone than a cooperative zone. On October 16, 2007, the construction of Phase I development of the KIC was completed.

Lee Myung-bak Inauguration

When Lee Myung-bak was inaugurated as President of South Korea on February 25, 2008, promising more effective results in dealings with North Korea, Kim Dae-Jung's sunshine policy encountered its first major speed trap.[3] President Lee stated during his inauguration speech: "Unification of the two Koreas is a long-cherished desire of the 70 million Korean people. Inter-Korean relations must become more productive than they are now. Our attitude will be pragmatic, not ideological. The core task is to help all Koreans live happily and to prepare the foundation for unification." Unfortunately, North Korea returned to its destructive habits of old.

On July 11, 2008, Park Wang-ja, a South Korean tourist, was shot to death by a North Korean soldier at Mt. Kumgang, allegedly because she strayed away from the allowed path. The next day (July 12), South Korea suspended tours to Mt. Kumgang, pending a joint investigation into the shooting incident. On April 5, 2009, North Korea launched the three-stage Unha-2 rocket, widely believed to be a modified version of its long-range Taepodong-2 missile. This was followed by the launch of a Taepodong-2 on the next day (April 6). Importantly, none of these provocative activities by North Korea affected cooperative relations on economic projects between the two Koreas. Note that the suspension of the Mt. Kumgang project was unrelated to the launching of these missiles.

When the South Korean Navy ship *Cheonan* was sunk in the West Sea on March 26, 2010, with its forty-six sailors killed, inter–Korean relations reached a new low. On May 20, 2010, South Korea announced the findings of a multi-national investigation team that a North Korean torpedo sank the *Cheonan*. Responses to the announcement were quick and harsh.

On May 24, 2010, the South Korea Ministry of Unification announced the following sanctions against North Korea: (a) a complete ban on North Korean ships' passing through the Jeju Strait; (b) suspending all inter–Korean cooperation; (c) freezing all aid projects excluding humanitarian aid for the vulnerable classes, infants and children; (d) banning South Koreans from visiting or investing in the North; (e) not allowing South Korean enterprises to do new business in the Kaesong Industrial Complex; and importantly, (f) continuing production at the Kaesong Industrial Complex while limiting the number of South Koreans residing in the Complex to about 1,000.

One day later, on May 25, North Korea made similar announcements: (a) a total freeze of all inter–Korean relations and cooperation; (b) abrogation of the agreement on non-aggression between the two Koreas; (c) suspending the work of the Panmunjom Red Cross liaison representatives; (d) expulsion of South Korean personnel in the Kaesong Industrial Complex (eight expelled at the time); and (e) a total ban of the passage of South Korean ships and airliners through the territorial waters and air of North Korea. On August 30, 2010, the U.S. State Department announced a new set of sanctions that had little, if any, meaning against or impact on North Korea as a response to the sinking of the South Korean Navy ship.

Again, it is important to note that neither South Korea, nor North Korea, took any measures of closing or even reducing the KIC operations beyond a cosmetic level.

Scope of Inter-Korea Economic Cooperation

In terms of statistical data, economic cooperation between the two Koreas can be interpreted in two ways. In the broad sense, inter–Korea economic cooperation includes trade of all types between the two Koreas that the Korea Ministry of Unification classifies as commercial trade and non-commercial trade. Commercial trade has three components: commission-based processing, economic cooperation projects, and general commercial. The process of commission-based trade takes place when a South Korean company sending raw materials and semi-processed goods to North Korea, where they are processed by low-wage workers. The processed goods are then sent back to South Korea. Economic cooperation projects, which are considered economic cooperation in the narrow sense, refer mainly to imports and exports of products manufactured in the Kaesong Industrial Complex. General commercial trade refers to imports and exports that are not included in the two categories above. Non-commercial trade means economic aid to the North.

The historical scope of economic cooperation between the two Koreas is summarized in Table 1. The flow of goods from North Korea to South Korea began modestly in 1989 with about $18.7 million, but increased steadily, reaching over $934 million in 2009. The flow of goods from South Korea to North Korea began in 1990 with $69,000, but increased steadily, peaking at over $1 billion in 2007. The total amount of goods traded both ways between the two

Koreas has been approaching almost $2 billion each year since 2007. Figures for 2010 are for January through August only. During those eight months, the total amount of goods that moved from North Korea to South Korea was $707 million, while the total amount of goods that moved from South Korea to North Korea was $613 million. When monthly trade figures are added for the entire year of 2010, these amounts are expected to be comparable to those of 2007 to 2009.

The amount of commission-based goods, under the heading of "Process" in Table 1, has increased steadily over the years, involving hundreds of companies. In each of 2008 and 2009, the total amount of commission-based goods that moved from North Korea to South Korea exceeded $250 million, while the total amount of commission-based goods that moved from South Korea to North Korea exceeded $150 million.

The amount of goods produced at the Kaesong Industrial Complex has increased rapidly in recent years, while the amount of trade classified as "Others" which includes general commercial and non-commercial trade had also increased steadily until 2007 but declined in 2008 and 2009. Finally, monthly data for 2010 indicate that the May 24 and 25 announcements by both Koreas on limiting economic cooperation led to a decrease in the flow of processed goods and general commercial trade, but had no adverse impact on the flow of products produced in the Kaesong Industrial Complex.

Chosun Ilbo (a major Korean-language daily newspaper) describes on its Web site, accessed on May 25, 2010, the impact of the May 24, 2010 sanctions announced by South Korea as follows. South Korea imported $245.19 worth of North Korean products during 2009, including $54.23 million of shellfish, $20.97 million of dried fish, and $18.83 million of zinc. North Korea also earned about $31.75 million in processing trade with the South in 2009, which does not include production activities at KIC that are not subject to sanctions. In addition, "North Korea's ships will have to shoulder an extra $1 million in fuel costs a year when they have to detour the Jeju Straits now that passage has been banned. Being unable to transport trade goods between the two Koreas, the North would lose $9 million in annual transport revenues. Pyongyang also has to sustain a loss from suspended assistance. The South Korean government and private organizations provided the North with $68.9 million in assistance in 2009." *Chosun Ilbo* also reports that South Korean businesses and private organizations "handed the North significant quantities of cash under the table. Secret remittance routes are also included in the latest sanctions." Overall, the amount of financial loss to North Korea appears to be approximately $350 million a year.

Two projects merit further comments: Mt. Kumgang and the Kaesong

Table 1. Inter-Korea Trade in Millions of U.S. Dollars

Year	Imports: NK to SK				Exports: SK to NK			
	Total	Process	Kaesong	Others	Total	Process	Kaesong	Others
1989	18.7	—	—	18.7	—	—	—	—
1990	12.3	—	—	12.3	0.1	—	—	0.1
1991	105.7	—	—	105.7	1.2	—	—	1.2
1992	162.9	0.6	—	162.2	5.5	0.2	—	5.3
1993	178.2	3.0	—	175.2	8.4	4.0	—	4.4
1994	176.3	14.3	—	162.0	18.2	11.3	—	6.9
1995	222.9	21.2	—	201.7	64.4	24.7	—	39.7
1996	182.4	36.2	—	146.2	69.6	38.2	—	31.5
1997	193.1	42.9	—	150.2	115.3	36.2	—	79.1
1998	92.3	41.4	—	50.9	129.7	29.6	—	100.1
1999	121.6	53.7	—	67.9	211.8	45.9	—	165.9
2000	152.4	72.0	—	80.4	272.8	57.2	—	215.6
2001	176.2	72.6	—	103.6	226.8	52.3	—	174.4
2002	271.6	102.8	—	168.8	370.2	68.4	—	301.8
2003	289.3	111.6	—	177.6	435.0	73.4	—	361.6
2004	258.0	107.7	0.1	150.2	439.0	68.2	41.6	329.2
2005	340.3	131.2	19.8	189.3	715.5	78.5	156.9	480.0
2006	519.5	159.4	75.9	284.2	830.2	93.6	222.9	513.8
2007	765.3	204.5	101.2	459.6	1032.6	125.4	339.5	567.7
2008	932.3	257.3	290.1	384.8	888.1	151.0	518.3	218.8
2009	934.3	254.0	417.9	262.3	744.8	155.7	522.6	66.5
2010	707.0	0.0	0.0	0.0	612.7	0.0	0.0	0.0
Jan.	89.5	19.4	51.3	18.8	79.9	10.8	64.7	4.4
Feb.	76.4	21.8	43.6	10.9	77.1	14.0	56.7	6.5
March	119.7	32.2	60.9	26.6	82.3	10.6	66.5	5.2
April	104.2	26.6	56.6	21.1	85.8	11.1	70.3	4.3
May	97.2	16.3	58.7	22.2	59.4	7.0	50.7	1.6
June	65.9	6.9	55.0	4.0	56.9	0.5	56.0	0.3
July	72.8	8.6	61.9	2.3	89.2	23.3	65.4	0.5
Aug.	81.4	14.5	65.5	1.4	82.2	15.1	66.6	0.5

Source: Korea Ministry of Unification, *Inter-Korea Trade*, a monthly report on inter–Korean exchanges and cooperation, Aug. 2010, pp. 62 and 72.

Note: Process means commission-based processing trade; Kaesong means trade relating to Kaesong Industrial Complex Project; and Others are "general" commercial trade and "non-commercial" trade.

Industrial Complex. The number of tourists visiting Mt. Kumgang started modestly at 10,554 in 1998, increased to 268,420 in 2004, one year after the visit over the land route was approved, and peaked at 345,006 in 2007 before the project was suspended in 2008 over the shooting death of a South Korean tourist by a North Korean guard. Assuming that the tourism project resumes at 300,000 visitors per year and each visitor spends $500 per visit, the amount of revenue to North Korea may reach $150 million a year. Put differently, this is the amount North Korea may be forgoing while the tourism project remains suspended. In addition, "The contract signed by Chung Ju Yung in 1998 promised the North monthly payments of $12 million through February 2005 for a total of $942 million, regardless of the number of tourists. This was on top of the $308 million paid for the development rights and the $104 million cost of building the facilities."[4] Mt. Kumgang tourism remained suspended as of this writing in December 2010.

Although the Kaesong Industrial Complex is not subject to the May 2010 sanctions by South Korea and North Korea, it is important to know the scope of its operation. KIC began its operation in 2005 with fifteen factories, producing products valued at $15 million. By 2008, the number of plants increased to sixty-eight, and the value of production increased to $251 million. At the end of June 2009, the Korea Ministry of Unification posted on its Web site that about 40,000 North Korean workers and 1,000 South Korean workers worked at 109 factories. Importantly, "In March 2008, the German car parts manufacturer Prettl began the construction of a plant, becoming the first non–Korean company investing in KIC."[5] Further, "two Chinese companies have also signed contracts to start production at the complex."[6] The Kaesong Industrial Complex is becoming a global operation with its economic and political implications extending well beyond the two Koreas.

The minimum monthly salary was raised in 2008 from $57.50 to $60.375, with additional payment for overtime work. Salaries of North Korean workers are not paid directly, but "are transferred to Central Special Direct General Bureau (CSDGB), a cabinet-level administrative organization and constitute a growing source of income for the North Korean government. The CSDGB pays the workers in North Korean Won at the official exchange rate after deducting US$7.50 for social security and other insurances."[7]

It should also be noted that "goods produced in the KIC are defined as products 'Made in North Korea' on which higher import tariffs are imposed when they are exported by South Korea, making many KIC products much more expensive and therefore less competitive on the world market. When negotiating the Free Trade Agreement with the United States (KORUS-FTA), the South Korean government tried to include goods produced in the Kaesong Industrial Complex, but so far, without success."[8]

Should Inter-Korean Economic Cooperation Be Subject to Sanctions?

U.S. sanctions against North Korea are explained in detail elsewhere,[9] while the futility of economic sanctions has been discussed by others.[10] Economic sanctions by South Korea against North Korea have been rare, raising the question of whether projects of economic cooperation between the two Koreas should be subject to current and future sanctions. Before one answers this question, it may be interesting to review two issues: history of sanctions by South Korea against North Korea, and trade relations between North Korea and China.

As discussed, the first meaningful economic cooperation between the two Koreas began in 1998, when Chung Ju-young signed an agreement with North Korea on Mt. Kumgang tourism on January 13, and President Kim Dae-jung announced his "sunshine policy" during his inaugural speech on February 25.

Note that when North Korea launched a long-range missile on August 31, 1998, and thus attracted a harsh political reaction from the allies of South Korea, South Korea did not impose any sanctions of its own and continued negotiations on the Mt. Kumgang tourism project. Note also that when North Korea conducted an underground nuclear test on October 9, 2006, that led to economic sanctions by Japan and the United States, all joint economic projects between the two Koreas, including the Mt. Kumgang tourism and the Kaesong Industrial Complex projects, continued with no interruption. The July 12, 2008, suspension of the Mt. Kumgang tourism project was more a reaction to the shooting death of a South Korean tourist that needed a clarification, than an economic sanction. The first meaningful economic sanctions by South Korea against North Korea were imposed when North Korea was found to be the trigger of the March 26, 2010, sinking of the South Korean Navy ship, *Cheonan*. Even this provocative act by North Korea had no impact on the operation of the Kaesong Industrial Complex. Importantly, both South Korea and North Korea did not take any retaliatory measures that could have affected the operation of the Complex.

Consider Table 2, which compares the volumes of trade before (August 2009) and after (August 2010) the May 2010 sanctions were levied with harsh words by both Koreas against each other. Volumes of commission-based trade, general commercial trade, and non-commercial trade all decreased, but still continued in August 2010. The volume of trade based on economic cooperation increased significantly, lifting the total post-sanction volume ($163.6 million) above the pre-sanction volume ($136.6 million). Economic relations between the two Koreas may have become too close and complex to be ended by turbulence in political relations between the two.

Finally, consider the trade relations between North Korea and China. Excluding 2001, in which North Korea imported a large amount of rice from Japan, North Korea's exports and imports had been increasing steadily since

Table 2. Composition of Inter-Korea Trade in $Millions: Sum of Both Ways

	Aug 2009	Aug 2010
Commercial Trade		
Commission-Based Processing	43.5 (31.9%)	29.6 (18.1%)
Economic Cooperation (Kaesong)	74.4 (54.4%)	132.1 (80.7%)
General Commercial	17.7 (13.0%)	1.4 (0.9%)
Sub-total	135.6 (99.03)	163.1 (99.07)
Non-Commercial Trade	1.0 (0.7%)	0.5 (0.3%)
Total	136.6 (100%)	163.6 (100%)

Source: Summarized from Korea Ministry of Unification, *Inter-Korea Trade*, a monthly report on inter–Korean exchanges & cooperation, Aug. 2010, pages 23–26.

1990 until about 2006. In 2006 and beyond, however, North Korea's trade deficits were greater than North Korea's total exports. The annual amount of North Korea's trade deficit easily exceeded one billion dollars in recent years. Significantly, the share of North Korea's trade with China has increased dramatically since 2001. In 2009, for instance, the share of North Korea's exports to China relative to the total exports of North Korea during the year was 64.7 percent, while the share of North Korea's imports from China relative to the total imports of North Korea during the year was no less than 77.5 percent. It may be an understatement that China is a very important economic partner to North Korea.

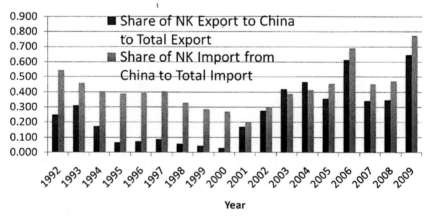

Figure 1. China's Share of NK's Total Trade

Conclusion

The history of economic cooperation between North Korea and South Korea is barely over twenty years old, but has become a complex one involving hundreds of South Korean companies and thousands of different products. Large cooperative projects between the two Koreas began with President Kim Dae-jung's sunshine policy in 1998. The volume of inter–Korea trade began to increase rapidly in 2004, when the products produced at the Kaesong Industrial Complex began to flow between the two Koreas. Against the numerous provocative acts by North Korea, which included test-launching missiles and tests of nuclear bombs, South Korea steadfastly stayed away from imposing any economic sanctions against North Korea until 2010, when North Korea was found guilty of sinking a South Korean Navy ship. Even that event left the Kaesong project unaffected.

Ominously, North Korea's dependence on China as a trading partner has increased dramatically since 2001. In 2009, the share of North Korea's exports to China relative to North Korea's total exports was 64.7 percent, while the share of North Korea's imports from China relative to North Korea's total imports reached 77.5 percent. Consider also that one of the key objectives of South Korea in economic cooperation with North Korea is to inform as many North Koreans as possible of the freedom and higher living standards that South Koreans enjoy.

In view of all these considerations, it appears to be in the best interest of South Korea to not only lift any and all existing economic sanctions against North Korea, but also to expand economic cooperation with North Korea. These efforts will lead to dissemination of greater information among North Koreans regarding the freedom and the high quality of life in the rest of the world, and keep North Korea from depending more on China that leaders in South Korean should find alarming. Admittedly, it will not be easy for political leaders in South Korea not to respond when North Korea carries out provocative acts. Overall, leaders in South Korea have done a good work over the past twenty or so years in continuing inter–Korea economic cooperation without jeopardizing most of these projects against confrontational approaches by all sides involved. Expanding inter–Korea economic cooperation beyond the current state of progression, however, may require new courage and wisdom of future leaders in North Korea as well as South Korea.

Notes

1. The KIC is one of the four special economic zones in North Korea and the only large-scale economic project jointly undertaken by both Korean governments. For details, see Sung Hoon Lim and Kang-Tage Lim, "Special Economic Zones as Survival Strategy of North Korea," *North Korean Review* (Fall 2006): 47–61.
2. Suk Hi Kim and Eul-Chul Lim, "The Kaesong Inter-Korean Industrial Complex: Perspectives and Prospects," *North Korean Review* (Fall 2009): 81–92.

3. Ibid.

4. Kim In Sung and Karin Lee, "Mt. Kumgang and Inter-Korean Relations," *NCNK Issue Brief*, November 19, 2009 (Washington, DC: National Committee on North Korea), p. 1.

5. Sabine Burghart and Rudiger Frank, "Inter-Korean Cooperation 2000–2008: Commercial and Non-Commercial Transactions and Human Exchanges," *Vienna Working Papers on East Asian Economy and Society* 1, no. 1 (2008): 13.

6. Ibid., p. 14.

7. Ibid.

8. Ibid., p. 14.

9. Semoon Chang, "The Saga of U.S. Economic Sanctions on North Korea," *Journal of East Asian Studies* 20 (Fall/Winter, 2006): 109–139; Semoon Chang, "Should U.S. Economic Sanctions on North Korea Be Lifted?" *North Korean Review* 2 (Fall 2006): 36–46; and Karin Lee and Julia Choi, "North Korea: Economic Sanctions and U.S. Department of Treasury Actions, 1955–September 2007," January 18, 2007, National Commission on North Korea, http://www.ncnk.org/resources/news-items/u-s-sanctions-and-other-treasury-department-actions/?searchterm=economic%20sanctions.

10. Marcus Noland, "The (Non) Impact of UN Sanctions on North Korea," *Peterson Institute, Working Paper Series*, W P 08–12, December 2008.

CHAPTER 6

Economic Reform and Alternatives for North Korea
Thomas F. Cargill and *Elliott Parker*

ABSTRACT

This chapter assesses the potential for reform in North Korea, and considers the lessons learned from economic reform and transition in China, the Soviet Union, and Central Europe. We focus in particular on the importance of reforms in the financial regime, and argue that in the absence of a major change in North Korea's environment, such as a crisis caused by reduced economic and/or political support from China, or increased access by the North Korean population to events in the rest of the world, the current situation is likely to continue for many years. North Korea will thus continue to alternate between declining, stagnant or mediocre economic growth. It will also continue to be a source of geo-political instability in the world in general and Asia in particular.[1]

Introduction

North Korea, a.k.a. the Democratic People's Republic of Korea, has existed as a socialist state for over 60 years, only a decade less than the tenure of the Soviet Union. Like the Soviet Union, North Korea has gone from rapid growth to economic stagnation. The Soviet Union and other socialist economies in the face of collapse and/or stagnation adopted market reforms to various degrees and established sustainable growth. This is especially true of China. In contrast, North Korea's economic, financial and political institutions have changed little while other former socialist economies have adopted more open and competitive market structures and frequently more open political institutions. North Korea's economy has been essentially stagnant for the past three decades.

The correlation between economic growth and market reforms during the past is well established, though some continue to debate the causal relationship. Shleifer reviewed various economic and social indicators for the world and concluded that in what he calls the "Age of Friedman" over the last quarter of the twentieth century, "the world economy expanded greatly, the quality of life improved sharply for billions of people, and dire poverty was substantially scaled back."[2] The institutional redesign of the former socialist economies toward more market-oriented structures demonstrated the economic benefits of market reforms. In sharp contrast, almost three decades of economic stagnation in North Korea have led many observers to wonder how much longer the North Korean regime can survive.

Each decade since 1980 has produced predictions of North Korea's imminent collapse, beginning with the rapid economic decline after both the Soviet Union and China dramatically reduced financial support. However, North Korea continued to survive as a closed, socialist and authoritarian regime. In the late 1990s North Korea experienced major famine and economic distress, and again many were predicting collapse. North Korea, however, continued to survive.

The most recent prediction of collapse came in the late 2000s, as North Korea appeared to be on the verge of a second famine and the success of market reforms in the former socialist economies, especially China, was overwhelming. Again, North Korea as a closed, socialist and authoritarian regime continues to survive.

The history of the second half of the twentieth century demonstrated that state-managed economies like North Korea's are not sustainable in the long run, but the long run can be very long. There remain skeptics about the benefits of market reform; however, the theoretical and historical evidence clearly shows state-managed economies are not sustainable in the long run. Reforming the socialist system is necessary to achieve sustained growth but extremely difficult, because it almost always requires some political institutional redesign that reduces authoritarian control.

Reform, however, may create economic distress and undermine political authority. China is one of the few examples of a nation that maintained authoritarian central control while permitting significant market reforms. Even in China's case however, it is not clear whether market reforms will generate political distress in the near future if a growing and prosperous middle class demands greater political freedom. The short-term risk of reform in terms of both economic and political distress during the transition period may appear far too great for a hereditary communist leadership like North Korea.

Authoritarian leadership regimes are not prone to commit suicide. With the benefit of assistance from China, heavy doses of propaganda on an isolated public that portrays the Korean people as a pure people in a sea of corrupt countries, nuclear blackmail aimed at Japan and the West, exports of nuclear and missile technology, counterfeiting operations, and international aid, the North Korean leadership has been able to avoid reforms that might weaken its control over the country.

"Hegel remarks somewhere," Karl Marx wrote, "that all great world-historic facts and personages appear, so to speak, twice. He forgot to add: the first time as tragedy, the second time as farce."[3] The unpredictability and potential danger to the world of North Korea makes it hard to find the humor in "farce," but the state of North Korea's economy does often border on the absurd. North Korea's reforms to date have been tentative and inadequate, and unless significant and risky reforms are implemented, North Korea will one day face even more dramatic economic distress than Russia experienced under Yeltsin.

The authors reviewed North Korea's development and tentative steps toward reform arguing that it was only a matter of time before the distortions of the economy accumulative to such a point that left no choice but to engage in market reforms.[4] Cargill, in the context of health problems of Kim Jong Il and the Kaesong Industrial Complex, suggested there existed some potential for reform.[5] Hindsight suggests instead that this potential for reform may have been vastly overstated. Tensions caused by the sinking of the South Korean warship *Cheonan* in March 2010, the less-than-optimistic United Nations report on North Korean's nuclear and missile proliferation,[6] the November 2010 announcement of a new and highly sophisticated uranium enrichment facility, and a short time later in November 2010 the dramatic shelling of South Korean Yeonpyeong Island are events that make it hard to find any degree of optimism. Ultimately, reform will occur because it will become increasingly difficult to isolate the North Korean population from the reality of the rest of the world and/or the dead weight loss of inefficiencies in the economy will accumulate to a crisis stage and force reform of some degree. That day, however, may be far off.

The remainder of this chapter consists of four sections. First, it discusses the causes, the process and overall record of reform in the former socialist economies to better understand North Korean exceptionalism. Second, it discusses the Chinese transition. The China case is important because any North Korean reform would likely follow the Chinese approach. China has been able to date to achieve major market reforms while maintaining an authoritarian set of political institutions. Third, it focuses on the importance of financial reform in any transition from state-directed to more market oriented economies and even in China this will become an Achilles' heel in the future if financial liberalization is not achieved. Failure to reform the financial system has led to much economic and financial turbulence throughout the world including the market-oriented industrialized economies. In the fourth section, the North Korean case is discussed in the context of socialist reform, the Chinese model and financial liberalization. A short concluding section ends the chapter.

The Record of Socialist Reform

In the twentieth century, less-developed countries that adopted centrally managed socialist systems usually experienced rapid growth, at least initially, as state control over every aspect of the financial sector permitted forced savings and centralized coordination mobilized economic resources. Once the easy gains were achieved, however, growth almost always slowed as incentive problems led to a stagnation of labor productivity and the efficiency of resource allocation became more important. In particular, the lack of financial mechanisms to impose bankruptcy on inefficient firms, or the lack of a market price structure to even meaningfully measure efficiency, made it virtually impossible to reallocate resources away from poor past investments. The Soviet Union had been the model for centralized planning even though in many countries Marxist ideology has not played a major role. North Korea in particular is not and has never been actually a Marxist regime. The Soviet Union provides a classic example of the rise and fall of socialist central planning, however.

By the time the Union of Soviet Socialist Republics was established in 1921 after the Bolshevik Revolution of 1917, the Soviet Union had already experienced the disastrous implementation of War Communism designed to immediately establish Full Communism. War Communism attempted to effectively militarize agriculture and industry, and resulted in a famine costing an estimated five million lives in addition to those millions lost in the First World War and the Russian civil war. The first Soviet effort at reform after the failure of War Communism was Lenin's New Economic Policy in the 1920s. The new policy helped the economy recover but it also led to an ideological debate that ended with Stalin's implementation of agricultural collectivization, state monopoly over industry and trade, and the first of many Five-Year-Plans which established bureaucratic management over the national economy. Stalin also created a totalitarian state to maintain political power and enforce economic planning through a combination of terror and a siege mentality.

Stalin's death in 1953 initiated new reforms to deal with the accumulating inefficiencies of Stalinist central planning. Khrushchev introduced policies to decentralize parts of the economy and encourage agricultural investment, and also permitted a mild political thaw as Stalin's reign of terror was increasingly denounced. These reforms were only marginally effective. A decade later, Brezhnev and Kosygin introduced new incentive reforms while they also recentralized decision-making. Decentralization was not as effective as Khrushchev had expected because the incentive problems in state-owned enterprises meant that autonomy gave managers more freedom to be even more inefficient. The ideology of the Soviet Union against the market left only a return to centralization as a solution. When this failed the Soviet Union attempted more dramatic market reforms under Gorbachev.

The centrally planned economy may be extremely inefficient, but it can be highly effective at marshalling resources in a less-developed economy. Putting the population to work, and forcing a high rate of savings through the state monopoly over trade and banking can initially lead to rapid growth rates. In the long run, however, diminishing returns, the overuse of natural resources, the disincentives of poorly allocated and badly managed labor, and the growing complexity of planning lead to ever-slower growth rates.

Some socialist economies attempted significant economic reforms, ranging from Yugoslavia's labor-managed economy and Hungary's New Economic Mechanism to Gorbachev's Perestroika (the program of economic and political reform in the Soviet Union initiated by Mikhail Gorbachev in 1986). These reforms attempted to introduce a significant amount of both private production incentives and market-based prices, but their success was limited. In the case of Perestroika, for example, the government allowed small private entrepreneurship and replaced state planning targets with negotiated contracts between firms. The result, however, was a diversion of resources away from the state sector and a collapse in state production, a situation often made worse by poor macroeconomic management.

Significant reforms in most cases, however, came only after intense economic and financial distress or in some cases collapse of the regime. Some governments fell due to popular revolts, while others fell after political liberalization attempted to boost their legitimacy through free elections. The new governments found themselves with all the institutions of a centrally managed economy, but without the ideological glue that had held it all together. Some like Poland and the Czech Republic chose rapid "big bang" transitions, with rapid price liberalization and gradual privatization assisted by their proximity to export markets in Western Europe. Others, like Hungary, chose a more gradual process that avoided the sharp recessions seen elsewhere but failed to create conditions for sustained growth, at least not until more dramatic reforms were implemented. However, the economic and political costs were high, and many governments that led these transitions did not remain long in power.

In Russia and other former Soviet republics in Central and Eastern Europe, many of the fundamental problems of the transition process were in the financial sector. First, the banking sector was slow to commercialize, its initial portfolio consisted of state-directed loans to state-owned enterprises, and it lacked the means to evaluate creditworthiness and monitor firm performance. As a result, the financial system relied on the implicit state guarantee to continue to make loans to state firms in order to keep them from shutting down, effectively pouring good money after bad. Second, with perhaps the sole exception of the Czech Republic, governments failed to cope with falling profits from state-owned enterprises facing increased competition and increased expenditures on subsidies and direct provision of public goods. Because private capital markets were virtually nonexistent due to years of repression, governments turned to central banks to finance their budget deficits, with the result that investment became less uncertain in an inflationary macroeconomic environment.

By the 1980s, the Soviet Union was experiencing not only negative rates of return on investment, but there were many sectors of the economy producing negative value-added. The economy was characterized by chronic shortages and poor-quality products, poor motivation and little innovation. Gorbachev's efforts to counteract these problems, and save the socialist economy in the twelfth Five-Year Plan failed. His subsequent efforts to introduce more dramatic reforms effectively dismantled the old system but did not establish a workable alternative. In the 1980s, the Soviet Union was on the verge of collapse because of the accumulation of deadweight loss generated by fifty years of planning in the absence of an incentive structure that could rationalize the allocation of resources. Inflation was high in spite of being officially repressed, growth was negative in spite of continued high rates of investment, and while reforms were proposed and debated, they were rarely implemented. The fall of the Berlin Wall in 1989 and the collapse of the Soviet Union in 1991 signaled the end of Marxist socialism in Eastern Europe.

This history repeated itself in the socialist economies of Central and Eastern Europe. Though the Soviet Union had repressed most efforts at economic reform, except for those in Yugoslavia that tried to create a labor-managed economy, nonetheless different efforts had been made in East Germany, Poland, and Hungary. Once the Brezhnev Doctrine[7] was withdrawn, dramatic reforms were implemented, though not in time to save the socialist economies.

Economic decline accompanied political collapse, though some of these nations were better able to negotiate the restructuring territory better than others.

Jeong (2009) uses a principal-components approach to model the difficulty of reform and transition for the successor states to the Soviet Union and the formerly socialist economies of central and Eastern Europe.[8] The longer the economy was socialist, the higher the economy's initial income, the more inflation was repressed, the more dependent on trade with other socialist economies, the more closed the economy to other trade, and the greater the amount of industrial distortion, the more severe the economic decline once reform or transition begins.

The path of economic reform in these transition situations highlights several key policies.[9] Price liberalization is crucial to finding scarcity-based prices that clear markets and improve the incentive to produce, but it needs to be combined with macroeconomic stabilization. Because a socialist government, either current or former, usually lacks access to developed capital markets, declining revenues from state-owned firms and the increased need for a social safety net generates budget deficits that usually tempt the state to abuse monetary siegnorage. Privatization of state-owned firms is usually included, along with allowing foreign trade and investment on a level-playing-field basis.

While privatization of state-owned firms is usually included as a necessary step to improve production incentives, it has proven much less successful than many had hoped. Institutional redesign is difficult for any country, but especially difficult in a society that has failed to include any incentives to efficiently allocate resources. Instead, most new growth comes from new firms, and most of the state firms eventually go out of business. Parker explained this in Schumpeterian terms, as the lack of creative destruction through competitive selection leads to a rapid accumulation of both capital and inefficiency over time.[10] Cargill and Parker, focusing on the difference between state-directed and market-directed financial regimes, modeled this process to demonstrate that the gradual accumulation of inefficiencies makes the transition to a more competitive financial regime very costly.[11] The more time goes by in running an economy without competitive pressures, the greater the transition costs.

It is remarkable North Korea has avoided the institutional changes that other socialist economies have experienced after the rise and fall of state-directed planning. Like most state-directed economies the North Korean economy advanced in the beginning, but as inefficiencies accumulated economic growth declined or stagnated. Unlike most state-directed economics, however, North Korea has resisted institutional redesign.

The Chinese Exception

Of the centrally planned socialist economies, only China was really able to achieve significant reforms without economic decline. This success, however, emerged from crisis. China had suffered a disaster of monumental scale during the Great Leap Forward from 1958 to 1961 (an event that some have referred to as the Great Leap Backwards), as Mao turned Marx's historical materialism upside down. The Cultural Revolution that followed, once Mao regained the power that the Great Leap had cost him, led to great hardship and economic stagnation that lasted until his death in 1976.

After Deng Xiaoping pushed for a more pragmatic approach to reform, China's performance was helped by its particular reform path, by the fact that China was still largely a rural economy, and by the continued political legitimacy of its government. Unlike in Gorbachev's Soviet Union, China did not begin reform in the industrial sector but first focused on the agriculture sector, and China did not begin to dismantle the centrally-managed economy until it had already become largely irrelevant. In addition, there have been few changes in the structure of the authoritarian Chinese government.

After Deng's supporters gained the upper hand in 1978, China began with agricultural decollectivization, as production management was turned over to individual households and both rural and urban markets were created for the distribution of food. Agricultural productivity boomed, and living standards in both rural and urban areas improved. Rural surplus labor was unintentionally released for other pursuits, and rural enterprises were allowed entry into sectors once the sole domain of state-owned monopolies.

China followed a pragmatic political approach, and also began reform with an Open Door policy that not only created Special Economic Zones for foreign investment but also encouraged joint ventures, improved export incentives, and tolerated tourism. Chinese students began to study abroad in large numbers, and while some stayed abroad others returned with new ideas and expectations. In a decade, China went from a closed economy to one in which both exports and imports made up a significant portion of economic activity, and in its second decade of reform that trade and foreign investment became the primary driver of economic growth.

Once these first reforms had taken hold, China also reformed its financial and industrial sectors. Unfortunately, China found that its traditional state-owned enterprises were difficult to reform, and giving enterprise managers autonomy over access to loans from state-owned banks led to overinvestment and a serious non-performing loan problem. However, the use of a dual-track system allowed for the gradual emergence of a new economy without dismantling the old one. The dual-track system also increased arbitrage opportunities for firm managers, opportunities that could only be checked by a strong state. In spite of this increased corruption, China's state firms were thus able to "grow out of the plan."[12]

Chinese state-owned enterprises had nonetheless accumulated significant inefficiencies over the decades, and the gradual transition to a quasi-competitive market was inconsistent with these firms remaining as the cornerstone of the economy. Instead, the most rapid growth was seen in the nontraditional sector, such as in the township and village enterprises and the foreign-invested firms, in part because these firms were new and the more efficient ones grew fastest by attracting more capital.

So it was not until state firms were pushed into new management arrangements, a greater variety of ownership forms was allowed (including wholly owned foreign firms and privately owned Chinese firms), and the most inefficient firms began to be shut down that Chinese firms became somewhat more efficient in their use of capital. Instead, much of Chinese growth came from a high savings rate and the shift of labor from low-productivity agriculture to light industry.

The Chinese Communist Party called this acceleration of reform the "Socialist Market Economy." After Deng's Xiaoping's death in 1997, Jiang Zemin announced a policy of "release the small, retain the large," in which smaller state firms were shut down or privatized, while larger and more profitable firms were restructured along the lines of South Korea's Chaebol conglomerates. Chinese state banks gradually became more commercially oriented, as the state tried to separate its lending policy interventions from profit-based banking.

China was able to gradually transform itself into a rapidly growing market-based global economy with the Chinese Communist Party still firmly in charge. It did so after the economic collapse of the Great Leap Forward, and after the stagnation resulting from the Cultural Revolution. It kept its authoritarian structure in place as market reforms were gradually introduced, and it followed a pragmatic approach that engaged the rest of the world and created alternatives before the old system was dismantled. China thus became the model for other socialist economies to follow, though few have done so successfully. Vietnam's Doi Moi reforms perhaps came the closest to matching China's success.[13] Any real reform that may commence in North Korea will most likely follow China's model.

Financial Liberalization in Socialist Economies

Financial liberalization in the non-socialist economies first manifested itself as market and governmental innovations in both domestic and international financial institutions. For example, the collapse of the Bretton Woods fixed exchange rate system in 1973 was a key turning point in the shift from state-directed to market-directed financial regimes. The transition most frequently emerged in the financial sector with interest rate liberalization, increased asset diversification powers for financial institutions, and development of money and capital markets. The transition then spread to the real sector and is now manifested by a broad liberalization of a broad range of public and private institutions.[14]

Many of the former Soviet Bloc economies and a number of Asian economies have witnessed significant structural change in terms of how far they have shifted from state-directed regimes. Japan and South Korea, for example, have gone from economies that regulated virtually all interest rates, engaged in varying degrees of credit allocation, restricted the inflow and outflow of capital and foreign direct investment, and possessed corporate sectors with no meaningful corporate governance or transparency, to economies that now permit market forces to play a significant role in both real and financial transactions.

China presents an even more dramatic example of change. The Chinese economy was far more rigidly controlled and exhibited far more economic and financial distress at the start of the transition than either Japan or South Korea. In addition, China lacks a democratically elected government while Japan and South Korea have functioning democratic governments. While China continues to be ruled by a Communist government, one now certainly more Leninist than Marxist, China's economic and financial institutions are undergoing major reform as market forces are permitted to play increasing roles.

The transformation in most economies has been associated with increased economic growth, increased standard of living, and increased world integration. At the same time the process has not been smooth and some economies have experienced financial and economic distress. The Asian Financial Crisis that began in 1997 led to currency flight, failures of financial institutions, and declining output in a number of Asian economies, including South Korea. China was little affected as it had only begun to liberalize its financial sector and continued to maintain an airlock system on its foreign currency market. Similarly, the Great Recession in the United States (2007–2009) has had financial repercussions worldwide, even in many countries where the financial sector did not engage in risky lending behavior.

The North Korean Reform Experience

Like the Soviet Stalinist economy from which it came, North Korea implemented a centrally planned economy that forced savings from a poor population for industrial investment. Like the Soviet Union after the Russian civil war, and like China after its revolution, North Korea after the Korean War adopted a siege mentality that enabled it to justify its policies in order to protect itself from a hostile outside world. While actual Soviet policy allowed only minimal access to the outside world, official Soviet doctrine was international in scope. By contrast, North Korea preached cultural exceptionalism and a more insular form of self-reliance called Juche, which combined aspects of Maoism and Confucianism with an intense personality cult centered on Kim Il Sung (and later Kim Jong Il). In many ways, the North Korean cultural exceptionalism was drawn from that preached by Japan during its colonial period.

In the two decades after the Korean War, North Korea grew rapidly, keeping pace with South Korea even after the latter became more export-oriented under General Park Chung Hee (September 30, 1917–October 26, 1979; president of South Korea, 1961–1979). Though its terrain was relatively mountainous, North Korea was the beneficiary of some remaining capital investment from the Japanese occupation, while South Korea was relatively more agricultural and relatively more devastated by the war. North Korea's planned economy also invested significantly in heavy industry, and also received significant outside assistance from China and the Soviet Union. Military spending rose to a third of national income by the late 1960s, and this diversion of economic resources helped to contribute to slowing economic growth in North Korea, even as South Korea boomed from an export-led growth strategy.

Few statistics have been officially reported since the 1960s, and much of what information is available is based on scattered official statistics of problematic quality, anecdotal evidence, and educated guesses. It is generally accepted North Korea grew faster than South Korea both before and after the Korean War, and some observers suggest it may have reached growth rates of as high as 12 percent per year. According to Cho, North Korean economic growth was positive through the mid-1970s.[15] By the 1970s, however, the North Korea's economy began to stagnate, and South Korea surpassed the North.

Estimates from the Organization for Economic Co-operation and Development (OECD), the Bank of Korea, and elsewhere suggest that per-capita income growth stagnated from 1973 to 1991, and then plummeted afterwards. Cho attributes North Korea's decline in output to both the accumulation of inefficiencies of the command system and the withdrawal of assistance from the Soviet Bloc economies as they began to shift from state to market-directed regimes. While the North Koreans preached self-reliance to an almost religious extent, it was nonetheless more dependent on trade than observers might expect. In 1990, its trade ratio was 20 percent of GDP, and imports outweighed exports by a 3:2 ratio.[16]

With the collapse of Soviet support after 1991, the Bank of Korea estimates that the gross domestic product (GDP) fell by a third by 1998. By 1998, imports had declined by over two-thirds, and though GDP also declined steeply, the trade ratio fell to 11 percent. Food shortages became chronic, particularly during the famine of 1995–98, and the country was unable to feed itself. North Korea had inadequate domestic sources of energy, particularly with the rapid decline in domestic coal production. Shortages of raw materials, particularly metal, steel, cement, and fertilizer, became widespread, hampering the full employment of industrial capacity. In spite of the famine, which North Koreans referred to as the "arduous march" and cost them roughly half a million lives, the population still grew by almost 10 percent during the 1990s. As a result, per-capita GDP was thus almost 40 percent lower in 1998 than in 1990.

In the late 1990s there was a growing consensus that North Korea was on the verge of collapse. While this may have been an exaggeration, macroeconomic performance was poor in the 1990s, budget deficits were growing, and reports of famine in rural areas were widespread. In response, North Korea commenced a variety of economic reforms in July 2002.[17] The July 1 reforms included increased administrative prices and incomes, revisions in the distribution system, enhancing the merit system, decentralizing the planning process, expanding corporate sector autonomy, and establishing trust banks. Some of these reforms, particularly the price reforms discussed below, may best be described as an official acknowledgement of an already-existing reality.[18] There were also announcements that firms would be allowed more control over the disposition of their production, once quotas were met, and this opened up the possibility of a future dual-track system for production within and beyond the plan.

North Korean prices were administratively set by the state on the basis of "necessary social labor expenditure," not by relative scarcity in markets. Shortages were exacerbated during the famine of 1995–98, and prices rose dramatically for commodities and farmers' markets outside of direct state control.[19] Though no official price indices were reported, repressed inflation was finally addressed in the reforms of 2002, when official increases in prices, wages, and the official exchange rate rose by 2,000–6,000 percent. Nonetheless, prices continue to be largely controlled by the state.

These efforts were not the first time North Korea had attempted reform. A joint venture law was enacted in 1984, the Rason Special Economic Zone was created in Rajin-Sonbong in 1991, and another was created in Sinuiju

City in 2002. While Russian and Chinese firms have bid for access to these areas, they have nonetheless failed to live up to their promise. Outside of "politically motivated investments" that Rosenberger and Babson argued lacked "basic economic and commercial logic," foreign investors have not found these economic opportunities to be inviting.[20] Some of these have reported that North Korean officials make them pay discriminately higher wages and input prices, and as a recent example from the Kumgangsan Tourist Region demonstrates, they are quick to threaten nationalization of foreign assets when political disputes arise.

The economy of North Korea could be separated into three distinct sectors after the reforms, a formal sector which was in decline due to the failure of central planning and the state-owned enterprises, a predominantly agricultural private sector that was growing as rural markets were allowed and over-quota production from cooperatives was marketized, and a relatively independent military sector that continued to demand a large portion of national resources.[21]

After the reforms, North Korea did appear to return to growth. The Bank of Korea estimates that North Korean GDP grew by more than 20 percent over the past decade, more than enough to keep pace with a population that grew by less than 7 percent. However, per-capita output in 2009 remained 30 percent below the 1999 level,[22] and increasingly large portions of GDP were being diverted to industrial investment and military expenditures under North Korea's Songun "military first" policy.

Though the legitimacy of the political structure is dependent on the status quo, the possibility of North Korea returning to its early days of rapid growth is virtually nonexistent. Nonetheless, as Kornai points out, the classical socialist economy is viable in the medium run as a coherent, closed system.[23] Many of the reforms that North Korea has engaged in so far are largely in the category of what Kornai calls the "'perfection' of control." By leaving alone the monopoly of control at the top and the property relations of nationalized firms and collectivized agriculture, the state's efforts to improve incentives and efficiency through bureaucratic reorganization, decentralization, adjustment in official prices, and simplification of planning indicators are only able to provide temporary relief at best.

Since these reforms began, North Korea has had a regular series of conflicts with South Korea, Japan, and the United States. Qiao argues that these conflicts are intentional, and driven by domestic North Korean politics.[24] In the absence of conflict, capital inflows from the South threaten to undermine the regime's absolute control, and domestic pressures for reform begin to build. By creating international conflicts, the government can reassert its siege mentality and appeal to nationalism, temporarily halting capital inflows and silencing voices for increased reform. In response to the argument that North Korea ultimately desires a relationship with the United States, Myers retorts by asking how North Korea "could possibility justify its existence after giving up the confrontational anti–Americanism that constitutes its last remaining source of legitimacy" if it did so.[25]

The economic reforms of the last decade were perhaps a small step in the right direction, but failed to do what will be needed for sustained growth. But even the anemic growth of the last two decades is now threatened by growing tensions with South Korea, which has supplied a significant amount of food aid and trade at concessionary prices. South Korea may now cut off or dramatically reduce economic support including support of the Kaesong Industrial Complex, which has been financed entirely by South Korea and is a source of dollars to North Korea. Reduced economic support, especially a reduced or abandoned Kaesong Industrial Complex would be another serious blow to the North Korean economy. Projects like the Kaesong Industrial Complex illustrate the benefits that even small reforms by North Korea could generate and yet, North Korea continues to resist reform because of its desire to maintain the current power structure.

There are four possible outcomes. First, the North Korean economy could collapse from the accumulation of inefficiencies. Much like the albatross in Coleridge's *Rime of the Ancient Mariner* (a symbol of good luck to the sailors), the dead weight loss of inefficiencies could force the North Korean economic ship to a complete stop and force dramatically and unpredictable reform. Second, the legitimacy of the North Korean government could decline as the government's control over information about the outside world weakens. The collapse of the Soviet Union had perhaps as much to do with access to information about the rest of the world as it did with of the accumulation of inefficiencies in the economy. While this access to information is inevitable, there is no way to predict how this would then unfold. Third, the quality of leadership at the top might wane as power is shifted to less-talented individuals, and with it public support of the leadership. Like the reduced ability to control information, there is no way to predict how this would unfold and bring about reform. Finally, China may be able to force reform, though to date China has been reluctant to use its economic, financial and political support to do so.

The best prospects for reform are likely a combination of one and four, but any prediction is hazardous. According to Noland, former U.S. vice president Walter Mondale once said that "anyone who claimed to be an expert on North Korea was either a liar or a fool."[26] Hence, these observations are offered with that thought in mind.

Conclusion

What makes economic reform in a socialist economy successful? China has demonstrated that a pragmatic approach is possible as economic outcomes in China appear to dominate ideological preferences in many ways. In spite of occasional political tensions, China has also been able to maintain reasonably good international commercial relations and has allowed its society to gradually become increasingly globalized. The maintenance of a sound currency backed by significant foreign exchange reserves has provided implicit insurance for foreign investors.[27]

China also benefited from fortunate sequencing of reforms, a result of China's pragmatic and gradual approach. As Parker and Wendel pointed out, more often than not China followed reforms with more reforms, instead of retrenchment, as the reforms led to inevitable problems.[28] Finally, China strived to maintain political control during economic reform, and gradually created a viable alternative before dismantling the old system.

North Korea may retain firm political control, but it has failed to meet the other conditions for successful reform. According to Jeong, the reforms implemented over the past decade may still help to reduce the potential income decline should the regime ever collapse and the economy begins a transition, but those costs will still be enormous.[29]

At some point in the future, the inefficiencies of the system will accumulate and generate an even more serious crisis, but it appears that North Korea has not yet reached that point. In fact, there is some evidence economic conditions have improved in the last few years. While it is debatable whether the recent increase in output signals sustained recovery, there is a reasonable basis to conclude that reforms introduced in 2002 may be responsible for improvement in economic conditions.

While North Korea is not on the verge of collapse, it is only a matter of time until a more serious economic and financial crisis occurs, unless the regime makes a more significant commitment to reduce the degree of state direction over real and financial resources. The choice it has to face now is whether to allow these reforms or to delay them until the regime eventually collapses. The problem, or course, is that real reform will threaten the regime's control over the North Korean people.

Notes

1. This chapter is an extension of Thomas F. Cargill and Elliott Parke, "Economic and Financial Reform: Alternatives for North Korea," *North Korean Review* (Fall 2005): 5–21.

2. A. Shleifer, "The Age of Milton Friedman," *Journal of Economic Literature* 47, no. 1, (2009): 126.

3. K. Marx, *The Eighteenth Brumaire of Louis Bonaparte*, 1852. http://www.marxists.org/archive/marx/works/1852/18th-brumaire/ch01.htm.

4. T.F. Cargill and E. Parker, "Economic and Financial Reform: Alternatives for North Korea," *North Korean Review* 1, no. 1 (2005): 5–22; and Bernhard Seliger, "The July 2002 Reforms in North Korea: Liberman-Style Reforms or Road to Transformation," *North Korean Review* 1, no. 1 (Fall 2005): 52–62

5. T.F. Cargill, "A Perspective on Institutional Change in North Korea," *North Korean Review* 5, no. 1 (2009): 90–104.

6. United Nations Security Council, *Report of the Panel of Experts Established Pursuant to Resolution 1875 (2009)*, submitted May 12, 2010, http://www.fas.org/irp/eprint/scr1874.pdf.

7. The doctrine expounded by Leonid Brezhnev in November 1968 affirming the right of the Soviet Union to intervene in the affairs of Communist countries to strengthen Communism.

8. H.-G. Jeong, *What Can North Korea Learn from Transition Economies' Reform Process?* Korea Institute for International Economic Policy, Working Paper 09–04, 2009.

9. J. Kornai, *The Road to a Free Economy* (New York: W.W. Norton, 1990).

10. E. Parker, "Schumpeterian Creative Destruction and the Growth of Chinese Enterprises," *China Economic Review* 6, no. 2 (1995): 201–223.

11. T.F., Cargill and E. Parker, "Asian Finance and the Role of Bankruptcy: A Model of the Transition Costs of Financial Liberalization," *Journal of Asian Economics* 13, no. 3 (2002): 297–318.

12. B. Naughton, *Growing Out of the Plan: Chinese Economic Reform, 1978–1993* (New York: Cambridge University Press, 1995).

13. Doi Moi, which literally means change and newness, is the Vietnamese Communist Party's term for reform and renovation in the economy.

14. T.F. Cargill and T. Sakamoto, *Japan Since 1980* (New York: Cambridge University Press, 2008), pp. 55–68.

15. M.-C. Cho, "Current Status of the North Korean Economy," in C.Y. Ahn, ed., *North Korea Development Report 2002/2003* (Seoul: Korea Institute for International Economic Policy, 2003), p. 34.

16. Ibid.

17. C.Y. Ahn and J.B. Ro, "Overview," in C.Y. Ahn, ed., *North Korea Development Report 2002/2003* (Seoul: Korea Institute for International Economic Policy, 2003), p. 21.

18. Y.-S. Lee and D.R. Yoon, *The Structure of North Korea's Political Economy: Changes and Effects*, Korea Institute for International Economic Policy, Discussion Paper 04–03, 2004.

19. S. S. Park, "The Monetary and Price Management System," in C.Y. Ahn, ed., *North Korea Development Report 2002/2003* (Seoul: Korea Institute for International Economic Policy, 2003), p. 384.

20. L. Rosenberger and B. Babson, "North Korea," working paper, ch. 17, 2001. http://www.pacom.mil/publications/apeu02/17NKorea12f.pdf.

21. Lee and Yoon, *op. cit.*

22. Bank of Korea, "Gross Domestic Product of North Korea in 2009," working paper, 2010.

23. J. Kornai, *The Socialist System: The Political Economy of Communism* (Princeton, NJ: Princeton University Press, 1992).

24. Y. Qiao, "North Korea Market Opening and the Response of the International Community," In Y.-C. Cho and J. Kim, *Changes in North Korea and Policy Responses of the*

International Community Toward North Korea, Korea Institute for International Economic Policy, 2009.

25. B.R. Myers, *The Cleanest Race* (Brooklyn, NY: Melville House, 2010), p. 164.

26. M. Noland, "Famine and Reform in North Korea," Institute for International Economics, WP 03–5, 2003.

27. T.F. Cargill, F. Guerrero and E. Parker, "Policy Traps and the Linkage Between China's Financial and Foreign Exchange Systems," in K.H. Zhang, ed., *China as the World Factory* (New York: Routledge, 2006).

28. E. Parker and J. Wendel, "Reform of China's State-Owned Sector: Parallels with the U.S. Regulatory Experience," in J.G. Wen and D. Xu, eds., *The Reformability of China's State Sector* (River Edge, NJ: World Scientific, 1997), pp. 281–299.

29. Jeong, *op. cit.*

CHAPTER 7

China–North Korea Relations
Dick K. Nanto and Mark E. Manyin

Abstract

This chapter provides a brief survey of China–North Korea relations, assesses China's objectives and actions, and raises policy issues for the United States. It finds that while Beijing maintains its military alliance and continues its substantial trade and economic assistance to Pyongyang, in recent years many Chinese and North Korean interests and goals have grown increasingly incompatible. In China, more and more officials and scholars appear to regard North Korea as more of a burden than a benefit. However, Beijing's shared interest with Pyongyang in preserving North Korean stability generally has trumped these other considerations.

Introduction

The People's Republic of China (PRC) plays a key role in U.S. policy toward North Korea, officially known as the Democratic People's Republic of Korea (DPRK). The PRC is North Korea's closest ally, largest provider of food, fuel, and industrial machinery, and arguably the country most able to wield influence in Pyongyang. This close bilateral relationship is of interest to U.S. policymakers because China plays a pivotal role in the success of U.S. efforts to halt the DPRK's nuclear weapons and ballistic missile programs, to prevent nuclear proliferation, to enforce economic sanctions, to keep the peace on the Korean Peninsula, and to ensure that North Korean refugees that cross into China receive humane treatment. As North Korea's main trading partner and benefactor, China can play the role as an intermediary or may even exercise leverage with Pyongyang in times of crisis, particularly following a military provocation by North Korea when the United States or South Korea have little direct communication with DPRK leaders. China's actions also are key in reforming the DPRK's dysfunctional economy and meeting the basic human needs of the North Korean people. China hosts the Six Party Talks on denuclearization, is able to provide credible advice to Pyongyang on issues such as economic reform, and plays an important role on the United Nations Security Council and other international organizations that deal with the DPRK. In general, the Obama Administration—as was true of the Bush Administration—has emphasized common interests rather than differences in its policy toward China regarding North Korea.

Although China is prominent in U.S. policy toward North Korea, North Korea is only one of numerous items on the Sino-U.S. agenda. In deciding whether to criticize China when its actions toward North Korea are at odds with U.S. interests, Obama Administration officials must weigh the possible spillover into these other areas, some of which appear to have a higher priority to the White House than North Korea. China has become a major player on the world stage, and cooperation with China increasingly is becoming essential in tackling a variety of global issues. China is now the second largest economy in the world after the United States and in 2010 surpassed Japan. Together, the United States and China account for more than half of global energy imports and emit over 30 percent of global greenhouse gases. The U.S. trade deficit and reliance on capital inflows are unlikely to be resolved without cooperation from China, since it has an annual surplus of more than $200 billion in merchandise trade with the United States and holds $880 billion in U.S. Treasury securities. This intersection of interests on the world stage influences how the United States and China deal with the DPRK.

In other respects, conflicts of interests between the United States and China also drive relations between the two countries and spill over into each country's relations with North Korea. U.S. relations with China are increasingly becoming strained over issues such as U.S.–South Korean naval exercises near China's exclusive economic zone, the undervaluation of the Chinese currency, Chinese territorial claims, U.S. sales of weapons to Taiwan, China's indigenous innovation policy, Chinese cyber-attacks on American computer systems, tighter regulation of foreign businesses in China, and competition for influence in Asia.

China's primary interest of stability on the Korean peninsula is often at odds with U.S. interest in denuclearization and the provision of basic human rights for the North Korean people. In 2010, Beijing and Pyongyang were going through a period of fairly amicable diplomatic and economic relations following the negative response by Beijing to the DPRK's nuclear and missile tests in 2009 and China's support of new United Nations Security Council sanctions directed at North Korea. China's enforcement of the U.N. sanctions, however, is still unclear. China has implemented some aspects of the sanctions that relate directly to North Korea's ballistic missile and nuclear programs, but Beijing has been less strict on controlling exports of dual use products. Some observers also have charged that Beijing has not made a concerted effort to stop suspicious air traffic between North Korea and Iran.[1] Chinese shipments of banned luxury goods to the DPRK continue to flow almost unabated.

North Korea has entered a phase in its strategic planning that poses particular challenges to both China and the United States. While Pyongyang's goals and tactics remain somewhat murky, the DPRK has entered into a particularly delicate time with a confluence of forces pulling the Pyongyang government in different directions. The measures by Kim Jong-il to ensure a smooth succession by his son Kim Jong-un requires a purity of ideology and credibility with the leaders of the Korean People's Army. Yet a smooth succession requires that sufficient food be available for the non-elite in society and that members of the Kim regime support the dynastic succession. This support was being engendered partly with luxury and other goods distributed to their families. However, U.N. and U.S. sanctions arising from the North Korean nuclear and ballistic missile programs have banned shipments of luxury goods to North Korea, and trade with South Korea, Japan, and the United States has virtually stopped.

The world view of the Kim regime also seems highly distorted. Pyongyang sees the world, particularly the United States, as increasingly hostile. Its belligerent rhetoric often leads to military provocations. As part of its national goals, the DPRK is seeking to become recognized as a nuclear power and is trying to convince the world to "learn to live in peace" with such a nuclear-armed North Korea." The country also has embarked on a program to become a strong and prosperous nation by 2012, the one hundredth anniversary of the birth of the country's founder, even though such a goal is almost impossible to achieve without more trade and investment from other countries.

North Korea follows what appears to be a carefully choreographed cycle of provocations and bluster, followed by a charm offensive and requests for aid, and then a return to provocations. In 2010, it entered into the provocation phase by precipitating three events that are directly counter to Chinese national interests. In March 2010, North Korea was found to have torpedoed a South Korean naval ship, the *Cheonan*, killing nearly 50 crew members. In November 2010, Pyongyang revealed the existence of a sophisticated complex of centrifuges to enrich uranium, a program that was long denied, and then followed that with the shelling of South Korea's Yeonpyeong Island, killing at least four South Koreans.

The provocations phase usually is followed by a diplomatic offensive in which the DPRK engages in negotiations that give the appearance of progress but in reality buy time for Pyongyang to further refine its offensive nuclear capabilities while ostensibly seeking cooperation and a warming of relations. The diplomatic offensive often results in deliveries of economic and humanitarian assistance.[2] In late 2009, under such an offensive, North Korea released two American journalists and a South Korean captive; restarted high-level diplomatic exchanges with the United States, South Korea, and China; hinted that it may return to the Six Party Talks; and proposed to conclude a peace treaty to replace the armistice that ended the Korean War.

China's North Korea Policy

U.S. government officials generally praise the PRC for its role as an active member in multilateral efforts to address and halt North Korea's nuclear weapons program. But the exact nature of China's security concerns, its political objectives, and the extent of its influence on North Korean actions has remained elusive to many observers of PRC–North Korean relations. Much of the reportage on PRC–North Korea interaction has appeared contradictory. On the one hand, PRC officials often put the lion's share of the responsibility on the United States to be "flexible" and "patient" with North Korea. On the other hand, China has declared North Korea to be in breach of U.N. nuclear safeguards and has been willing to be critical of North Korean pronouncements and actions that it finds unacceptable.[3] China voted for U.N. Security Council Resolutions 1718 (2006) and 1874 (2009) imposing sanctions on the DPRK following its missile and nuclear tests.

Anecdotal evidence, however, suggests that some PRC officials have grown increasingly perturbed at North Korean intransigence on the nuclear issue. Beijing has permitted harsh criticisms of North Korea in authoritative journals and newspapers that would not have been permitted in the past. Chinese pundits have been allowed to write contemptuously of the DPRK and how its actions have threatened Chinese interests.[4] In 2010, some newspapers reported that a view has been gaining traction in Beijing that China could accept Korean unification under Seoul's control. Such a view seems to be coming from the younger generation of Chinese Communist party leaders, in particular those not associated with the military.[5]

However, senior PRC officials continue to visit Pyongyang and receive warm welcomes, even though in 2010, Kim Jong-il returned from China with no additional promises of economic assistance. Beijing has stressed that a nuclear-free Korean peninsula is one of its priorities, but it also has supported North Korea as it has built, started, stopped, and restarted its nuclear plant.[6] In the international effort to pressure North Korea to abandon its nuclear weapons program, PRC officials are presumed to have substantial leverage with North Korea; yet Beijing was unable to prevent Pyongyang from conducting its first test of a nuclear weapon on October 9, 2006,[7] nor its second test on May 25, 2009.[8] China also has been unable or unwilling to curtail North Korea's uranium enrichment program.

As for concerns over proliferation of weapons of mass destruction, Beijing generally discounts the threat of nuclear proliferation by the DPRK to non-state terrorist groups. China also seems less concerned about nuclear cooperation between the DPRK and countries friendly to China such as Iran and Myanmar/Burma.

For years, the U.S. policy debate has been dogged by diametrically opposed opinions about exactly what China's real security concerns and political objectives are on the North Korean nuclear issue. These continuing internal U.S. disagreements helped to paralyze much of the U.S. policy process with respect to the DPRK during most of the George W. Bush Administration. According to one view, espoused by many in the U.S. government, China was doing a credible job with North Korea and had been a helpful host and interlocutor for the United States in the whole process of the Six Party Talks involving the United States, the PRC, Japan, Russia, and North and South Korea. These proponents held that Americans can count on the sincerity of PRC leaders when they say that Beijing's principal priority is a non-nuclear Korean peninsula.[9] In spite of the military alliance and political roots that the PRC shares with North Korea, these proponents maintain that PRC officials have grown weary and frustrated with the unpredictability and intransigence of their erratic neighbor. Furthermore, some say, China may have less leverage with Pyongyang than many suggest and risks losing what little leverage it does have if it reduces or terminates its substantial food and energy assistance to North Korea.

The chief rival to this viewpoint holds that China is being duplicitous on the North Korea question and insincere in its statements supporting a freeze or dismantlement of North Korea's nuclear weapons program.[10] According to this view, Beijing actually has substantial leverage with Pyongyang but elects not to use it in order to ensure that the North Korean issue continues to complicate U.S. regional strategy and undermine the U.S. position in Asia. This is the reason that China appears casually tolerant of North Korea's erratic and unpredictable behavior, why Beijing rarely criticizes North Korea for its provocations, and why Beijing has sided so often with the North Korean position in the Six Party Talks. Furthermore, these proponents suggest that Beijing and Pyongyang actually may be coordinating their policies on North Korea's nuclear weapons program, including the timing of North Korea's more provocative pronouncements and actions, in an effort to keep the United States off balance.

Beijing's first priority on the Korean peninsula appears to be stability both in the Kim Jong-il regime and in the country as a whole. For Beijing, diplomacy, or the prospect thereof, is the preferred solution to every provocation by the DPRK. As long as the United States, South Korea, and others are talking to the DPRK, they are unlikely to take harsher actions against Pyongyang. In addition, any deliveries of economic and humanitarian aid to North Korea that result from the talks can only help to ensure stability. For example, after the shelling of Yeonpyeong Island, China did not condemn the action but called for the countries participating in the suspended Six Party Talks to convene what it described as emergency consultations in Beijing.[11]

A significant issue for U.S. policy has been the plight of tens of thousands of North Koreans who have been crossing back and forth over the North Korea–China border since the North Korean famine of the 1990s. Estimates of North Koreans living in China range from 30,000 to more than 100,000. Despite being a party to relevant United Nations refugee conventions, China has not allowed U.N. agencies, in particular UNHCR (United Nations High Commissioner for Refugees), the UN Refugee Agency, or non-governmental organizations to have access to North Koreans who are residing in China. Beijing views these individuals as economic migrants (rather than political refugees) who cross the border illegally, primarily in search of food.[12] The Chinese government also has periodically deported North Korean border crossers or allowed North Korean authorities to seize North Koreans in China. Those who are repatriated may face punishment ranging from a few months of "labor correction" to execution. A number of reports also document the difficult conditions faced by North Koreans who remain in China.

Development of China's North Korea Policy

North Korea exists because of the division of the Korean peninsula into south and north occupation zones (the former administered by the United States and the latter by the Soviet Union) in August 1945 at the end of World War II. Initially meant to be temporary, Cold War politics resulted in the division being solidified in 1948 with the establishment of the Republic of Korea (South Korea) and the Democratic People's Republic of Korea (North

Korea). Each country remained under the influence of its original occupying power. When North Korea invaded the South in June 1950, the United Nations and the United States came to South Korea's defense. The intervention of PRC military forces late in 1950 on behalf of North Korea marked the beginning of what later became, in July 1961, the formal PRC-DPRK military alliance—the Treaty of Friendship, Cooperation, and Mutual Assistance—which committed either party to come to the aid of the other if attacked.[13]

In addition to their mutual defense alliance, the PRC and DPRK in these early years were bonded by their shared Leninist-socialist ideologies, by their wartime military cooperation, and by years of PRC reconstruction efforts and assistance to Pyongyang. PRC leaders saw North Korea as a crucial buffer state between the PRC border and American military forces stationed in South Korea. In addition, both Pyongyang and Beijing shared what one analyst has called the frustration of "divided nation ideologies"—the separation of North Korea from South Korea on the Korean Peninsula, and what Chinese leaders viewed as the separation of the PRC on the mainland from Taiwan.[14] The shared interests and identities between the two governments were enough to assure cordial relations for decades. But these mutual affinities began to diverge in the early 1980s when the PRC initiated economic reforms and market mechanisms under Deng Xiaoping, and in 1992 when Beijing established full diplomatic ties with South Korea. Despite these differences and ebbs and flows in the relationship, official ties (measured, for instance, by the number of high-level bilateral meetings) improved and economic flows increased in the 2000s, to the point where by 2009 China had re-emerged as North Korea's dominant economic partner, if not its lifeline.[15]

While Beijing still maintains its military alliance and continues its substantial economic assistance to Pyongyang, in recent years many PRC and North Korean interests and goals appear to have grown increasingly incompatible. North Korea has remained insular, highly ideological, and committed to what many find to be a virtually suicidal economic policy direction. China, on the other hand, has rejected its past excesses of ideological zeal to become a pragmatic, competitive, market-driven economy that increasingly is a major economic and political player in the international system. However, from Beijing's perspective, its shared interest with Pyongyang in preserving North Korean stability generally has trumped these other considerations. The growing tensions between Beijing's shared interests with Pyongyang and its increasing differences with that government have created a complex and murky picture for U.S. policymakers who have sought to convince Beijing to be more coercive with Pyongyang and more cooperative with Washington in attempting to shut down North Korea's nuclear weapons program.

PRC Policy Objectives

PRC leaders have conflicting political and strategic motivations governing their North Korea policy. On the side of the ledger supporting China's continued close relations with Pyongyang are: shared socialist political ideologies; the human and capital investment China has made in North Korea; Beijing's credibility as a patron and ally; increased economic ties; Beijing's desire for a "buffer" against South Korea; and the potentially catastrophic consequences for China's economy and social structure if something goes terribly wrong in North Korea, with which China shares an 850 mile border. On the opposite side of the ledger are: Beijing's presumed frustration at dealing with North Korean brinkmanship and unpredictability; the financial drain China incurs by continuing to prop up its bankrupt ally's economy; the prospect that North Korea's nuclear status will provoke a nuclear arms race in Asia; and the potential for Beijing's military involvement in any conflict provoked by Pyongyang. Chinese leaders appear to have to continually re-calibrate and re-balance these competing goals as events unfold on the Korean peninsula. At its very core, though, Beijing appears to have a number of fundamental policy objectives that do not change.

Assuring Stability and the "Status Quo" on the Korean Peninsula

The political, economic, and security consequences for China of a destabilized North Korea are serious enough for China to justify maintaining stability on the Korean peninsula as a primary policy goal. However unpredictable and annoying the North Korean government may be to Beijing, any conceivable scenario other than maintaining the status quo could seriously damage PRC interests. Another collapse of North Korea's economy (such as occurred in the 1990s) would severely tax the economic resources of the Chinese central government and, depending on how it dealt with the flood of refugees across its border with the DPRK, could shine a world spotlight on how China treats the refugees and open Beijing to increased criticism from the world community. Armed conflict between North and South Korea likewise would be disruptive to PRC economic and social interests, in addition to risking conflict between the United States and PRC militaries on behalf of their allies. Beijing would face a different set of challenges should North Korean political upheaval mirror the demise of East Germany, in which North and South Korea would unite under the latter's terms. The PRC could then have a nuclear armed and democratic U.S. ally, and possibly U.S. troops and military facilities, directly on its border without the benefit of an intervening buffer state.

Within this context, Beijing's continuing economic assistance to North Korea can be easier to explain. Rather than a deliberate attempt to sustain North Korea's nuclear weapons program or undermine an ultimate resolution to the Six Party Talks, as some have suggested, China's food and energy assistance can be seen as an insurance premium that Beijing remits regularly to avoid paying the higher economic, political, and national security costs of a North Korean collapse, a war on the peninsula, or the subsuming of the North into the South.

Maximizing PRC Influence

Beijing's second overarching policy goal appears to be a concerted effort to maximize its influence on the Korean peninsula as well as its leverage in Asia and with all the relevant parties in the Six Party Talks. In the case of North Korea, however, no one knows what kind of leverage Beijing actually has with Pyongyang. It may be that PRC leaders are uncertain as well, given North Korea's penchant for the unexpected and its demonstrated willingness at times to reject Chinese overtures, carrot and stick alike. If Chinese leaders are, in fact, unsure of the extent of their own leverage, they appear unwilling to be more assertive in testing what those limits might be.

In the calculation of PRC leaders, then, Beijing's food and energy aid to Pyongyang achieves several objectives. It not only helps to stabilize the erratic regime, but furthers China's economic influence over North Korea and potentially helps to encourage North Korea to reform its own economy. Such aid also maximizes PRC leverage by raising the costs of misbehavior while suggesting that rewards are possible for good behavior. In other bilateral relationships, Chinese leaders have learned the value of economic interdependence. Beijing appears to have grown more confident that its own giant economy has the power not only to confer economic benefits but to narrow the range of options available to its smaller economic partners. In addition to food and energy assistance, Beijing may calculate that its willingness to provide investment and economic benefits across the Sino-DPRK border will bring North Korean interests more in line with those of China.

Reconvening the Six Party Talks

The PRC also is generally thought to see collateral benefit in its continued involvement with the other players in the Six Party Talks, especially with the United States. For this, Beijing's interests appear to be served by having the Six Party Talks reconvene and continue—one of the hopes expressed by China and the United States in the U.S.-China Joint Statement issued during President Obama's visit to China in November 2009.[16] Continuation of the Six

Party Talks process allows Beijing to expand on its mediating role and offers it the potential of being an original crafter of a key international agreement.

Finally, continuation of the process burnishes Beijing's credentials with South Korea and gives Beijing leverage with the U.S. Government as well as a wealth of opportunities for bilateral discussions and senior-level meetings with U.S. and other policymakers. China also insisted on language in U.N. Resolution 1874 that allowed for sanctions to be lifted if the DPRK returned to the negotiating table.[17]

Assuring China's Regional Security Interests/Territorial Integrity

Another policy goal for Beijing is the assurance of regional stability and China's own territorial integrity. Leaders in Beijing are aware that a nuclear armed North Korea could lead to decisions by Japan, South Korea, and possibly Taiwan and other Asian neighbors to develop their own nuclear deterrents and ballistic missile capabilities.[18] China may also fear that the North Korean nuclear program could spur a significant Japanese conventional rearmament.[19] In keeping with Beijing's own domestic policy priorities, its emphasis on social stability, and its ambition for regional dominance, it can be argued that nothing is more to be avoided than the proliferation around China's periphery of nuclear-armed governments more capable of defending their own national interests when those conflict with China's.

Beijing probably anticipates that the U.S. response to more robust security programs in the region would include an accelerated missile defense program for U.S. friends and allies. Such an enhanced missile defense capability would undermine the effectiveness of Beijing's missile deployment threat opposite the Taiwan coast, aimed at keeping Taiwan from acting on its independence aspirations. North Korea is thus linked to China's primary core interest of assuring its "territorial integrity." Beijing also realizes that the U.S. focus on the North Korean military threat generates a hook that keeps U.S. forces tied down on the Korean peninsula and looking north toward the DPRK rather than looking south and showing more concern over possible hostilities across the Taiwan Strait.

North Korean Policy Objectives

The Kim Jong-il government's over-riding policy concerns appear to be security and regime preservation, with a current focus on generational leadership succession. To achieve these ends, the government devotes considerable energy toward acquiring the resources necessary to provide a reasonably high quality of life for the country's elite even at the cost of providing for the country's other citizens. The government's short-term goals include a smooth succession for Kim Jong-un and preparations for the 100th anniversary of the birth of Kim Il-sung, the founder of the DPRK, in 2012. By then the country intends to become a recognized military and economic power and a "great, prosperous, and powerful country."

Pyongyang feels it has already attained the status of a politically, ideologically, and militarily powerful state, but it seeks to be recognized by the world as a nuclear weapon state. Although the DPRK has tested two nuclear weapons, its ballistic missile delivery system is still under development. For Pyongyang, nuclear weapons and missiles along with artillery aimed at South Korea are the keys to its security. Its conventional military forces lack modern equipment, technology, fuel, and experience, although they still are capable of inflicting a huge amount of damage on South Korea. Without nuclear weapons, however, the country would be considered a "basket case" hold-over country from the Cold War, surrounded by nuclear powers, and able to garner about as much world attention as Myanmar or Laos. DPRK leaders also recognize that putting the military first and transferring resources from the civilian to military side of the economy can only last so long unless there is robust growth in civilian production. Hence the goal of becoming an "economically powerful state" is crucial both to supply the army and to fulfill a lifelong "cherished desire" of Kim Il-sung, the founder of the country.

Sino-DPRK Interaction

As geopolitical realities generally dictate, China is more important to the DPRK than the DPRK is to China. Chinese leader Mao Zedong once described the Sino–DPRK relationship to be as close as "lips and teeth," but in many ways North Korea has become more of a thorn in the side of China than a reliable ally. In recent years, China also has had to respond to the same DPRK policy cycle of provocations, diplomacy, aid deliveries, and back to provocations as have other countries of the world. China, however, is usually not the direct target of the DPRK's provocative actions (such as testing ballistic missiles or nuclear bombs) and threats. Such actions generally are aimed at the United States, South Korea, or Japan. Beijing, though, has to face the fact that Pyongyang regularly has ignored its advice not to proceed with provocative actions, which, once taken, leave China to fend off hostile reactions by other countries in order to maintain stability on the peninsula.

North Korea's core interest of regime preservation overlaps with China's interest in preserving stability on the peninsula. Since the late 1990s, as long as North Korea has been able to convince Beijing's senior leadership that regime stability is synonymous with North Korea's overall stability, the Kim government has been able to count on a minimum level of China's economic and diplomatic support. Indeed, North Korean leaders appear to have used this shared interest to neutralize its growing economic dependence on China, as the greater North Korea's dependency, the more fearful Chinese leaders may be that a sharp withdrawal of PRC economic support could destabilize North Korea.

China also often has cooperated with North Korea along their border region to ensure that the number and activities of North Korean border-crossers do not spiral out of control. In November 2003, China reportedly transferred responsibility for securing its border with North Korea from the police to its army.[20] Many of China's two million ethnic Koreans live along this border, and it is a favorite crossing point for refugees from North Korea.

Diplomatic Relations

From North Korea's perspective, its relationship with China has long been fraught with ambivalence. While for nearly two decades China has been Pyongyang's most reliable source of economic and diplomatic backing, China's periodic willingness to go along with sanctions efforts in the U.N. Security Council and the fluctuations in Chinese assistance undoubtedly have made North Korea wary of becoming overly dependent on Beijing, or on any other outside power. During the Cold War, for instance, then-leader Kim Il-sung adeptly used the Soviet-Chinese rivalry to extract considerable economic assistance from Moscow and Beijing. When Chinese support waned in the mid–1990s, North Korea opportunistically turned to other outsiders, including Taiwan, for aid, particularly as it was wracked by a devastating famine.

For the decade prior to 2008, left-of-center governments in Seoul under what was called the "Sunshine Policy," provided considerable economic assistance and diplomatic support for Pyongyang. Since the mid–1990s, North Korea has episodically reached out to the United States as an important source of food aid and energy assistance. Japan also was moving toward normalizing relations with the DPRK and providing North Korea with a large cash settlement until the issue of Japanese citizens abducted by the North Korean intelligence service derailed the talks in late 2004 and halted bilateral aid and trade. Indeed, since late 2008 the degree to which China has emerged as North Korea's dominant trade and aid partner is remarkable.

For China, the DPRK's nuclear program has added a new dimension to bilateral relations and to the strategic situation in the region. When the DPRK tested a ballistic missile and its second nuclear weapon in April-May 2009, many believe it crossed a threshold with China. Until that time, Pyongyang apparently had convinced Beijing that it was pursuing its nuclear activity primarily as a bargaining chip in negotiations with the United States and other countries. Following the May nuclear test and subsequent statements by North Korean leaders, it became apparent that not only had Pyongyang been deceitful in its assurances to Beijing but that the DPRK never intended to relinquish its nuclear weapon programs and its goal was to become a recognized nuclear weapon state. Suddenly, China's attitude toward the DPRK shifted and two of Beijing's goals with respect to the DPRK came into sharper focus—denuclearization and stability on the Korean peninsula. Denuclearization likely would not occur, and sanctions resulting from the nuclear activity potentially could destabilize the North Korean economy.

China's role in hosting the Six Party Talks creates a delicate balancing act for Beijing with respect to its relations with the DPRK. Although denuclearization of the Korean peninsula would be desirable for China, Beijing fully recognizes Pyongyang's security situation and perception that it is completely surrounded by nuclear powers or countries under the U.S. nuclear umbrella and that South Korea, Japan, and the United States are "hostile" powers. Aside from the Six Party Talks, however, Beijing appears to be focusing on its primary interests of stability and regime preservation in Pyongyang and preferring that the United States and other parties in the talks take the lead on denuclearization.

As an example of the mixture of interests and actions by Beijing, when China supported U.N. Resolution 1874 condemning the DPRK's nuclear test, Beijing insisted on certain provisions to protect its fundamental interests of peace and stability on the Korean peninsula and preventing the creation of a unified North and South Korea that might destroy its buffer zone with South Korea or bring a less friendly, U.S. ally up to its border. In voting in favor of Resolution 1874, the Chinese representative Zhang Yesui stressed that the sovereignty, territorial integrity and legitimate security concerns and development interests of the DPRK should be respected and that after its return to the Nuclear Non-Proliferation Treaty, the DPRK would enjoy the right to the peaceful use of nuclear energy as a State party. The Chinese representative also said that the U.N. Security Council's actions should not adversely impact the country's development or humanitarian assistance to it, and that as indicated in the text of the resolution, if the DPRK complied with the relevant provisions, the Council would review the appropriateness of suspending or lifting the measures. He also emphasized that under no circumstances should there be use of force or threat of use of force.[21]

As the resolution led to a tightening of sanctions and to some high-profile interdictions or attempts to interdict shipments of suspected cargo bound to or from the DPRK, Pyongyang went on a diplomatic offensive not only with countries of the West but with China. On October 4, 2009, the sixtieth anniversary of diplomatic relations between China and the DPRK, Chinese Premier Wen Jiabao made a "goodwill trip" to Pyongyang, the first by a Chinese Premier in eighteen years. He was accompanied by a large delegation of high ranking officials. Both countries vowed to support each other and signed several documents including an agreement on economic and technological cooperation.[22] Wen also offered to expand and strengthen economic cooperation and exchange, and the two sides reached a consensus to proceed with construction of a new bridge over the Yalu (Amnok) River between their two countries (funded by China and estimated to cost over $150 million).[23] In addition, Wen reportedly offered an economic cooperation package worth another $50 million.[24]

In 2010, Kim Jong-il visited China for the fifth and sixth times. Kim had gone to China in 2000, 2001, 2004, and 2006,[25] so more than three years had passed since his last visit.

On November 23, 2009, Chinese Defense Minister Liang Guanglie visited Pyongyang, the first defense chief to visit since 2006.[26] The main objective of Minister Liang's DPRK visit reportedly was to bring "closer friendly exchanges between the Chinese and DPRK armed forces and promote exchanges and cooperation between the people and armies of the two countries." Denuclearization was not an announced goal of the visit.[27] On November 17, North Korean General Kim Jong-gak, the first vice director of the General Political Bureau and an influential leader in the North Korean Army, visited Beijing. These military exchanges reversed the split between the armies of the two countries after military-to-military ties were virtually severed in the late 1950s when Kim Il-sung conducted a mass purge of the so-called pro–Chinese "Yanan faction" in the North Korean military. After the May 2009 nuclear test, it became apparent that the influence of the military on DPRK policy had grown, and China apparently felt the need to re-establish communication channels with the Korean People's Army.[28]

Economic Relations

China, with its huge economy and rapid rate of growth, is the lifeline that keeps the DPRK economy alive. China not only provides needed food, equipment, and consumer goods, but it stands as a model of how a backwards, command-type economy can develop without compromising its socialist ideals. For several years, Beijing has been trying to induce the DPRK to undertake economic reforms similar to those pursued by China over the past quarter century. The rise of markets and other "reforms" that have occurred in North Korea, however, have resulted primarily from a "bottom up" process and from necessity as the central government faltered on its ability to deliver food and living essentials through its distribution system. Inflows of consumer goods from China and an increasing number of cooperative industrial projects, primarily in the Northern Korean provinces, have created a market-based means of generating income and distributing goods to families.

In November 2009, a Chinese-language website reported that China is planning a major new development zone called the Tonghua-Dandong Economic Zone, along the North Korean border aimed at boosting trade. This zone is to include the rebuilt bridge, a new port, a duty-free zone, warehouses, and international transit facilities. It is to cover about 350 km or most of the Western half of the Sino–DPRK border.[29]

North Korea's leaders have displayed mixed reactions to this Chinese penetration into their economy and the concomitant spread of private markets. These market activities not only carry negative strategic ramifications (challenges to North Korea's philosophy of self reliance and to North Korean socialism), but, more importantly, such Chinese-style capitalism and influx of consumer goods could have a potentially corrosive effect upon the level of control the Kim regime has over the lives of individuals.

In late 2009, the DPRK government carried out a currency reform that actually amounted to a confiscation of wealth by the central government and an attack on Chinese-style markets. Much of the wealth that became worthless had been accumulated by "illegal" merchants and traders through their activity on private markets. Under the currency reform, the government issued new currency denominated in amounts one-hundredth of those on the old currency. Introduced ostensibly to control inflation, the catch was that the amount that households could exchange was limited initially to about $40 (later raised to about $200). Holdings of foreign exchange also were prohibited, so the currency reform effectively became a device to confiscate wealth, much of it earned by buying goods in China and selling them in North Korean markets.[30] This reform amounted to a rebuke, not only of wealthy North Korean merchants, but of China since the PRC had been encouraging market-oriented reforms similar to its own. The currency reform, however, was such a disaster that the government official in charge reportedly was shot.

Although China is the DPRK's largest trading partner, the DPRK plays a relatively minor role in China's trade. In 2009, North Korea ranked 82nd among China's export markets—smaller than Kenya, Sri Lanka, or Peru. As a source of imports, North Korea ranked 77th—below Gabon, Yemen, or Ukraine.

As shown in Table 1, Sino–DPRK trade has been rising steadily. While such trade is dwarfed by China's trade with countries such as South Korea (total bilateral trade of $156 billion in 2009), both imports from and exports to the DPRK have increased significantly over the past decade. In 2009, despite the depressing effect of the global financial crisis, DPRK exports to China increased to $793 million, although Chinese exports to the DPRK slowed slightly to $1,888 million. The bilateral trade is highly imbalanced with China's surplus exceeding $1 billion in 2009.

Table 1. China's Merchandise Trade with the DPRK, 1995–2009
($ in millions)

Year	China's Imports	China's Exports	Total Trade	China's Balance
1995	63.609	486.037	549.646	422.428
2000	37.214	450.839	488.053	413.625
2005	496.511	1,084.723	1,581.234	588.212
2006	467.718	1,231.886	1,699.604	764.168
2007	581.521	1,392.453	1,973.974	810.932
2008	754.045	2,033.233	2,787.278	1,279.188
2009	793.026	1,887.741	2,680.767	1,094.715

Source: China, Ministry of Commerce (excludes Hong Kong and Macau).

Table 2. Estimated North Korean Trade by Selected Trading Partner
($ in millions)

North Korean Exports			North Korean Imports		
Destination	2008	2009	Source	2008	2009
World	3,052.3	2,235.0	World	5,196.6	3,488.2
South Korea	932.3	934.3	China	2,033.2	1,887.7
China	754.0	793.0	South Korea	888.0	744.8
Others	1,366.0	507.7	Others	2,275.4	855.7

Sources: Congressional Research Service. Underlying data from United Nations COMTRADE database.

As shown in Table 2, in 2009 North Korea exported an estimated total of $2,235 million in merchandise (down from $3,052 million in 2008) while importing $3,488 million (down from $5,197 million in 2008). This created an apparent merchandise trade deficit of $1,253 million (down from $2,144 million in 2008) with $1,095 million of that with China.[31] China provides more than half of North Korea's imports. On the export side, South Korea was the largest buyer of North Korean products, and China was second. However, if exports to and imports from South Korea of raw materials, components, and products assembled in the Kaesong Industrial Complex, just across the border in North Korea, are not counted, the vast majority of North Korean trade is with China. Economic sanctions imposed by Japan and the United States have reduced their respective trade with the DPRK to almost nothing except for intermittent humanitarian aid.

In 2009, China's major imports from North Korea included mineral fuels (coal), ores, woven apparel, iron and steel, fish and seafood, and salt/sulfur/earth/stone. China's major exports to North Korea included mineral fuels and oil, machinery, electrical machinery, vehicles, knit apparel, plastic, and iron and steel.

A recent development has been North Korea's increase in exports of primary products (such as fish, shellfish and agro-forest products) as well as mineral products (such as base metallic minerals). Pyongyang reportedly has imported aquaculture technology (mainly from China) to increase production of cultivated fish and agricultural equipment to increase output of grains and livestock. It also has imported equipment for its coal and mineral mines. Much of the coal and mineral exports have resulted from partnering with Chinese firms through which the Chinese side provides modern equipment in exchange for a supply of the product being mined or manufactured.

China is a major source for North Korean imports of petroleum. According to Chinese data, in 2009, exports to the DPRK of mineral fuel oil totaled $327 million and accounted for 17 percent of all Chinese exports to the DPRK. China, however, does not appear to be selling this oil to North Korea at concessionary prices. In 2008, the average price for Chinese exports of crude oil to North Korea was $0.78 per kilogram, while it was $0.71 for such exports to the United States, $0.66 for South Korea, $0.81 for Japan, and $0.50 for Thailand.[32]

China's economic assistance to North Korea accounts for about half of all Chinese foreign aid. Beijing provides the aid directly to Pyongyang, thereby enabling it to bypass the United Nations. China is, therefore, able to use its assistance to pursue its own political goals independently of the goals of other countries. It is widely believed that some Chinese food aid is taken by the DPRK military. This allows the World Food Program's food aid to be targeted at the general population without risk that the military-first policy or regime stability would be undermined by foreign aid policies of other countries.[33]

China is the largest foreign direct investor in North Korea (not counting South Korean investment in the Kaesong Industrial Complex). In 2007, the total foreign direct investment (FDI) into the DPRK reported to the United Nations amounted to $67 million (excludes investment from South Korea).

Of this, China supplied $18.4 million. In 2008, of a total of $44 million, China supplied $41.2 million. Chinese companies have made major investments aimed at developing mineral resources located in the northern region of the DPRK. This is part of a Chinese strategy of stabilizing the border region with the DPRK, lessening the pressure on North Koreans to migrate to China, and raising the general standard of living in the DPRK.

China and Economic Sanctions

Following North Korea's second nuclear test in May 2009, China issued a strong statement of condemnation and in June 2009 backed U.N. Security Council Resolution 1874 that provided for additional sanctions on the DPRK. This included an arms embargo with the exception of exports to the DPRK of small arms and light weapons and their related materiel; an embargo on items related to nuclear, ballistic missiles and other weapons of mass destruction programs[34]; and a ban on the export of luxury goods to the DPRK. It also included a travel ban and/or an assets freeze on designated North Korean persons and entities.

The PRC, however, constitutes a large gap in the circle of countries that have approved the U.N. resolutions and are expected to implement them. China takes a minimalist approach to implementing these sanctions. North Korea continues to use air and land routes through China with little risk of inspection, and luxury goods from China and from other countries through China continue to flow almost unabated to Pyongyang. In addition, North Korea uses front companies in China to procure items under sanction.[35]

China did cancel a joint venture with North Korea to produce vanadium (used to toughen steel alloys used in missile casings) and has intercepted a shipment of 70 kg of vanadium hidden in a truckload of fruit crossing the border into North Korea.[36] China reportedly also has called a halt to the work by a Chinese investment company to build facilities for a copper mine in Hyesan, North Korea. An estimated 400,000 tons of copper are deposited there. In November 2006, the Chinese firm had signed an agreement with (North) Korea Mining Development Trading Corporation to develop the mine. This trading corporation was included in the designations in UNSC Resolution 1874.[37]

As for arms shipments, data on China's exports of arms to North Korea are generally not available. However, countries do report their trade in small arms and ammunition with the DPRK. China's exports of small arms and ammunition to North Korea reached $3.5 million in 1996 and $2.85 million in 1999, but they were fairly insignificant until 2009 when such sales jumped to $4.32 million. In 2009, China was the only reported exporter of small arms to North Korea.

In exports of luxury goods, China claims that the ban is not enforceable because the United Nations resolution did not specify precisely what goods are involved. The definition of a luxury good does vary by country, but certain items would seem obvious for inclusion. For example, in July 2010, Radio Free Asia reported that Kim Jong-il had provided 160 luxury cars (made in China) to directors of provincial committees of the Korean Workers Party and to municipal committee secretaries (higher level officials already had vehicles).[38] Such cars would be included on a list of luxury goods by most any country.

Using the U.S. and U.K. definitions of luxury goods, in 2009, countries that report trade to the United Nations exported $212.2 million in luxury goods to North Korea. China led the way, with exports of luxury goods of $136.1 million (mostly tobacco, computers and cars). Brazil exported $36 million (mostly tobacco and precious stones), Singapore $29 million (mostly tobacco), and Russia $4 million (mostly cars, some beef and computers but no alcoholic beverages). Western visitors to Pyongyang in September 2010 reported that there seemed to be no scarcity of luxury goods in markets there. Most of the luxury goods seemed to be from China, but those from Japan also were plentiful. Clearly, China has not been enforcing the U.N. sanctions on luxury goods. Clearly, China holds the key to implementing sanctions on the DPRK, and it arguably could devote more resources to detecting and stopping North Korean violations of U.N. Security Council Resolutions.

Notes

1. U.S. Department of State, Bureau of Public Affairs, "Background Briefing on North Korea," July 15, 2009.

2. Kim Myong Chol, "North Korea Begins 'Plan C,'" *Asia Times*, October 14, 2009, online edition. Zhang Liangui, "There Is a Dangerous Component in the 'Warm Winter' of the DPRK Nuclear Issue," *Huanqiu Shibao* (in Chinese), December 9, 2009, p. 14, translated by Open Source Center as "PRC's Zang Liangui Views DPRK's 'Plan C' for Nuclear Status," Document Number CPP20091230710002.

3. Attributed to PRC U.N. Ambassador Wang Guangya, "Annan Says Six Party Talks in North Korea's Interest," *Voice of America*, press release, February 15, 2005.

4. Jonathan D. Pollack, "North Korea's Nuclear Adventurism Tests China's Patience," *Yale Global Online*, October 23, 2009.

5. Christian Oliver and Geoff Dyer, "China Could Accept Korean Unification," *Financial Times*, November 30, 2010, FT.com.

6. See Congressional Research Service Report RL31555, *China and Proliferation of Weapons of Mass Destruction and Missiles: Policy Issues*, by Shirley A. Kan.

7. Anthony Faiola and Dafna Linzer, "N. Korea Pledges Nuclear Test; Need Cited

to Deter Threat from U.S., but No Date Is Set," *The Washington Post*, October 4, 2006, p. A1; and Joseph Kahn, "North's Test Seen as Failure for Korea Policy China Followed," *New York Times*, October 9, 2006, p. 6.

8. Evan Ramstad, Jay Solomon, and Peter Spiegel, "Korean Blast Draws Outrage," *The Wall Street Journal*, May 26, 2009, Internet edition.

9. China has repeatedly held to its general view on the importance of denuclearization, although some find meaningful the varying apparent strengths of its assertions. In one press conference, Foreign Ministry spokesperson Kong Quan stressed that "the Chinese side's persistence on the denuclearization of the Korean Peninsula and on maintaining peace and stability on the Korean Peninsula is resolute and unwavering." Translated in *FBIS*, CPP20050217000174, February 17, 2005. At another press conference four days later, the same spokesperson described China's position "that we stick to the goal of a nuclear free Peninsula." Translated in *FBIS*, CPP20050223000101.

10. John Tkacik, "Does Beijing Approve of North Korea's Nuclear Ambitions?" *Backgrounder No. 1832*, the Heritage Foundation, March 15, 2005.

11. Ian Johnson and Helene Cooper, "China Seeks Talks to Ease Korean Tension," *The New York Times*, November 28, 2010, Internet edition.

12. The international instruments that provide protection to refugees include the 1951 United Nations Convention Relating to the Status of Refugees (Refugee Convention) and the 1967 Protocol to that Convention. Parties to the Refugee Convention have an obligation to abide by the principle of "non-refoulement," which means that "No contracting State shall expel or return ("refouler") a refugee in any manner whatsoever to the frontiers of territories where his life or freedom would be threatened on account of his race, religion, nationality, membership of a particular social group or political opinion."

13. The Korean War effectively came to an end when an armistice agreement was signed on July 27, 1953. The South Korean government refused to sign the armistice, which has not been replaced with a formal peace treaty or comprehensive peace agreement.

14. Andrew Scobell, "China and North Korea: From Comrades-in-arms to Allies at Arm's Length," Strategic Studies Institute, U.S. Army War College, March 2004, p. 2.

15. For a review of Sino-North Korea relations in the 1990s and 2000s, see Scott Snyder, *China's Rise and the Two Koreas* (Boulder, CO: Lynne Rienner, 2009), chapter 5.

16. President Obama made his first visit to China from November 15 to 18, 2009. The U.S.-China Joint Statement was issued on November 17, 2009. http://www.whitehouse.gov/the-press-office/us-china-joint-statement.

17. China also has insisted on ambiguity in parts of U.N. sanction resolutions and have used that ambiguity to escape criticism for not implementing the resolutions.

18. Danielle Demetriou, "Japan Should Develop Nuclear Weapons to Counter North Korea Threat," *The Telegraph*, April 20, 2009. Internet edition.

19. For more on the prospects for and debate over Japan developing nuclear weapons, see Congressional Research Service report RL34487, *Japan's Nuclear Future: Policy Debate, Prospects, and U.S. Interests*, by Emma Chanlett-Avery and Mary Beth Nikitin.

20. James Foley, "China Steps Up Security on North Korean Border," *Jane's Intelligence Review*, November 1, 2003.

21. UN Security Council Statement, SC/9679, June 12, 2009.

22. Signed at the ceremony were the "Protocol on the Adjustment of Treaties Between the Governments of the DPRK and China" and the "Agreement on Economic and Technological Cooperation Between the Governments of the DPRK and China," exchange documents on economic assistance and other agreed documents in the field of economy, an accord on exchange and cooperation between educational organs of the

two countries, a memorandum of understanding (MOU) on exchange and cooperation in the field of software industry and a protocol on common inspection of export and import goods between the state quality control organs of the two countries, a MOU on tour of the DPRK sponsored by the tourist organizations of China and an accord on strengthening the cooperation in protecting wild animals. *Agreement and Agreed Documents Signed between DPRK, Chinese Government,* October 4, 2009, Korea Central News Agency of the DPRK.

23. Korea Central News Agency of DPRK, "Talks Held between DPRK and Chinese Premiers," October 4, 2009.

24. "China Brings Lavish Gifts to N. Korea," *The Chosun Ilbo*, English edition, October 7, 2009, Internet edition.

25. "Unification Minister Seeks Central Role in Ties with North Korea," *The Chosun Ilbo*, English edition, January 9, 2010, Internet edition.

26. Associated Press, "China's Defense Minister Travels to North Korea," *The China Post*, November 23, 2009.

27. Yuan Liu Yantang and Sun Xiali, "Military Diplomacy Creates a Peaceful Periphery" (carried in Open Source as "PRC Experts Examine China's Military Diplomacy With DPRK, Japan, Thailand," *Liaowang*, November 30, 2009, in Chinese, translated by Open Source, Document CPP20091209710009.

28. "Chinese Defense Minister Pledges Loyalty in North Korea," November 24, 2009, *Chosun Ilbo*, English edition.

29. Michael Rank, "China Approves Tumen Border Development Zone," *North Korean Economy Watch*, November 23, 2009, archive for the "Tonghua-Dandong Economic Zone" Category.

30. For details, see Stephan Haggard and Marcus Noland, *The Winter of Their Discontent: Pyongyang Attacks the Market*, Peterson Institute for International Economics, Policy Brief Number PB10-1, Washington, DC, January 2010.

31. The South Korea Trade-Investment Promotion Agency (KOTRA) has estimated that in 2008, North Korea exported $1,130 million while importing $2,685 million for a trade deficit of $1,555 million. The KOTRA data, however, exclude data for about 60 developing countries and do not include South Korean trade with the DPRK.

32. Average price calculated by World Trade Atlas using Chinese trade statistics.

33. Bradley O. Babson, *Towards a Peaceful Resolution with North Korea: Crafting a New International Engagement Framework*. Paper presented at a conference sponsored by the American Enterprise Institute, Korea Economic Institute, and Korea Institute for International Economic Policy, Washington, DC, February 12–13, 2004.

34. A list of items under embargo can be found at http://www.un.org/sc/committees/1718/xportimport_list.shtml.

35. David Albright and Paul Brannan, "Taking Stock: North Korea's Uranium Enrichment Program," the Institute for Science and International Security, October 8, 2010.

36. "China Foils Smuggling of Missile-Use Material to North Korea," *The Chosun Ilbo*, July 25, 2009, Internet edition.

37. "N. Korea Mining Project Buckles Under UN Sanctions," *The Chosun Ilbo*, July 30, 2009, Internet edition.

38. Tae Hong Kim, "Kim Jong Il Showers Loyals with Cars," *The Daily NK*, July 30, 2010.

CHAPTER 8

North Korea's "Collapse" Pathways and the Role of the Energy Sector

Peter Hayes and *David von Hippel*

Abstract

Although the authors deem a collapse of North Korea's central government authority unlikely and certainly undesirable, the likely effects of collapse on the North Korean people and those of its neighbor nations make necessary analysis of its impacts. Focusing on North Korea's crucial energy sector, this chapter posits four potential "collapse" pathways for the North Korean government. Each of these pathways is analyzed for its implications for the provision of energy services in North Korea. A conclusion summarizes the lessons provided by collapse pathways for near-term initiatives by the international community to assist the North Korean energy sector.

Introduction[1]

The prospect for the DPRK (Democratic People's Republic of Korea) and its leadership is bleak. Kim Jong-il's health is poor, and though a succession has been announced, the successful transfer of power from father to son is of unknown probability. There is little chance that the economic poverty of almost all North Koreans will improve. The external powers, especially the United States, will continue to squeeze the DPRK with sanctions. Hyperinflation is on the cards in the aftermath of the failed currency redenomination. External aid will be minimal so long as the nuclear weapons issue remains unresolved.

This dismal future does not mean the DPRK is about to collapse. The "collapsists" have been arguing since the end of the Cold War that the DPRK "is about to collapse." Indeed, one notable expert, Aidan Foster-Carter, issued his latest prediction in this vein on November 15, 2009, saying that the DPRK could "fall at any moment"[2]—a claim no more persuasive than his earlier one, made in 1992![3] Many scenarios, including a persistent, slow recovery and gradual modernization of the DPRK, are possible.[4] Serial collapsists have the advantage that their prognostications can be neither confirmed nor denied—they are making what Karl Popper termed "unfalsifiable" statements. The continued survival against all apparent odds of the DPRK is not regarded as refutation of the collapsist prediction. Nor apparently does it pose a longevity worthy of investigation and explanation. Apparently, the only option is to wait for the predicted outcome, at which time the prediction has a *post–ad hoc* character, of truth after the fact. Thus, we should tread warily when it comes to claims about the prospective nature of collapse in the DPRK.

There is a reason, we suggest, that the DPRK has outlasted every other statist, personalized regime since the end of the Cold War. The DPRK is different, it is unique, and it represents a sample of one. It is hard to conduct authentic social science with a sample of one, especially from a distance. Moreover, this sample of one is intimately connected with and arguably inextricably linked with the status of U.S. policies toward the DPRK. The DPRK and the U.S. national security state were born in war with each other; they have remained at war for nearly six decades; they are at war today. In our view, one cannot analyze the prospects for change in the DPRK without simultaneously analyzing the rates and types of change in U.S. foreign and military policy.

Rather than outright collapse in the next decade, far more likely is either a "slow burn," by which we mean continuing slow degradation of the economy and consequent adaptation at local levels to tighter scarcity constraints; or a very slow recovery nurtured by economic reforms, buttressed by external support from and trade with China, and large-scale labor exports; or a faster recovery based on rapprochement with the ROK (Republic of Korea, or South Korea) and the integration of DPRK state-owned enterprises with the ROK's chaebols.

We estimate that the non-collapse pathways dominate, covering roughly 95 percent or more of the overall spectrum of policy possibilities; and that the primary question is what support and reconstruction policies are available to avoid outright collapse, the outcome that is most likely to lead to loss of control of fissile material, nuclear warheads, people (including those with nuclear weapons knowledge), and escalation to war via civil war or cross–DMZ war. Many, perhaps most, of the policy responses needed to avoid collapse are the same as will be needed in the case of outright collapse.[5] The main difference in the post-collapse pathways—which perhaps provides an obvious lesson in the economics of policy choice—is the greater scale and speed, and therefore the cost needed to reestablish stability rather than to merely maintain it.

The biggest single qualitative difference between the non-collapse and collapse pathways will be in the post-collapse military dimension. Obviously, the highest-velocity policy response in the case of the DPRK's collapse will be moves by the ROK military to occupy and control key leadership posts, military bases, critical infrastructure, and transport chokepoints. How long this intervention would last is impossible to know in advance, but it could be held in place for many months or even years, depending on the degree to which local populations comply with the legitimacy of the occupying forces, rather than rebel against perceived injustices inflicted during the takeover. This particular policy response has its own energy implications, both in its execution, and in its implications for energy-sector reconstruction and immediate humanitarian assistance to the population of the DPRK. We will not cover, however, the military-energy aspects of establishing post-collapse control of the DPRK in this chapter, although we will review the implications for postwar reconstruction of how a war might be fought with the DPRK.

In spite of these caveats and our best judgment that collapse is unlikely, it is conceivable and therefore should be addressed. Indeed, we have observed situations in the DPRK where the fabric of rural life was literally coming apart, and the demands on individuals and social units appeared beyond human endurance. By collapse, however, we have a specific meaning in mind in this essay, namely the complete breakdown of central government in Pyongyang. Given the number of interacting internal and external variables that affect the probability of collapse of the DPRK in the long term, that probability is simply unknowable. Thus, we will concentrate largely on the short to medium term in our analysis.

Whether precipitated by war, coup, or simply continuing slow economic decline, it is incumbent on the international community to help to provide services and support to stabilize North Korea in the unlikely event of outright collapse. Fortunately, many of the measures that would be needed are the same as should be undertaken in the non-collapse pathways. Among the many likely needs of the North Korean population following a collapse—food, clean water, heath care, and economic development among them—the need to promptly provide the population with reliable and demonstrably improving access to energy services (heat, light, mechanized transportation, and so on) will be a key to stabilizing the country, meeting other post-collapse needs, and readying the North for eventual smooth (one hopes) integration with South

Korea. In this chapter, we begin, in a largely qualitative way, an exploration of the implications for the energy sector of North Korea of various DPRK "collapse" pathways, and for the approaches that South Korea and other interested parties will need to take to rebuild and redevelop that sector, and in planning for the same eventuality.

Background: The DPRK's Energy Sector since 1990, and Nautilus Analytical Approaches

When the Soviet Union was dissolved in 1990, the DPRK lost not only its major supplier of crude oil and of parts for its power plants and factories, but also the markets for the bulk of the goods that its factories were designed to produce. The rapid economic and resource contraction, compounded by a series of floods and droughts that affected both agriculture and energy production, plus economic isolation resulting from the international reaction to the DPRK's nuclear weapons program, resulted in a downward economic spiral of reduced energy availability and reduced industrial energy demand, as the country's infrastructure fell into disrepair and markets dried up. By 2000, the DPRK's use of coal and production of electricity had fallen to almost a quarter of its 1990 levels, and overall energy end use had fallen to less than 40 percent of what it had been a decade before. Since this period, the DPRK's energy sector has been sustained primarily by an annual half-million tons of crude oil from China, modest imports of refined oil products, Korean tenacity and ingenuity that have kept some of its coal mines and aging power and coal production infrastructure running, and the substitution of wood and other biomass for subsistence energy use. Much of the DPRK's major energy and industrial infrastructure dates to the 1950s, 1960s, and 1970s, with some, including major hydroelectric plants, dating to the 1920s Japanese occupation era.

Since 2000, there have been modest improvements in the DPRK's economy and energy sector, with some power plant repairs, new small hydroelectric facilities, and new mining activity underwritten, in large part, by Chinese investment. Still, shortages of power, district heat, and coal persist, with blackouts even in Pyongyang, and much more tenuous power supply in other areas. In effect, the North Korean electricity system, though it is nominally a nationwide transmission and distribution grid, is a patchwork of a few regional and some local grids, centered around major and smaller power plants. Most of the large thermal (almost all coal-fired) power plants and heating plants are only partially in operation due to damage of various kinds to one or more boilers/generating units, and/or to transformers, substations, or other parts of the transmission and distribution system. This means that even if large amounts of fuel or electricity were suddenly to be available to the DPRK, distribution of that energy would be problematic.

The combination of erosion in its energy system and industrial infrastructure, together with similar erosion in its transport infrastructure in many areas and lack of investment capital, means that the DPRK will not be able to reconstitute—or, perhaps more accurately, redevelop—its energy system and economy in general without outside help. Rebuilding power plants—most of which were built with major components imported from the U.S.S.R. or elsewhere—could not be done, at least for many years, using materials "made from scratch" in the DPRK, because the industrial infrastructure to make the required power plant components is either no longer operating or, in fact, was never present in the DPRK. Similarly, decades of relative isolation have left the DPRK substantially without the capabilities in metallurgy, electronics, and other fields that would allow it to develop new industries offering export markets to bring in hard currency. This means that the DPRK cannot redevelop its infrastructure sufficiently to develop a sustainable, peaceful economy without outside help.

Even for the DPRK's economy to remain at its current "subsistence" level, help from other nations has been required. As noted above, the DPRK receives sufficient crude oil from China to keep one of its two oil refineries running, though at well below full capacity. This oil is paid for at market prices, but the DPRK runs an annual trade deficit with China. China could provide more crude oil to the DPRK, and has done so in the past (in some years during the 1990s), but the fairly constant flow of oil from China to the DPRK for the past decade or so suggests that China has determined the amount of oil that the DPRK's economy needs to receive to fuel basic economic functions, and is providing that amount. This suggests to us that although China is willing to provide fuel to keep the DPRK's economy from failing, it is unwilling, until the DPRK can afford the additional imports on its own, to provide sufficient assistance to actually redevelop the DPRK's economy.

Hard data on virtually anything regarding the DPRK is hard to come by, and the energy sector is no exception. Given that some understanding of the DPRK's energy sector has been (and still is) needed in order to allow the international community to effectively engage with the DPRK on energy issues, we have worked since 1994 to assemble and update a description and quantitative estimate of activity in the DPRK's energy sector. Our approach in doing so has been to obtain as much information as possible about the DPRK's economy and energy sector from media sources, visitors to the DPRK, and other sources as available; use this available information, together with comparative analysis of energy supply and demand in other nations over time, to assemble a coherent and consistent picture of the DPRK's energy sector;[6] and think about possible future paths for the DPRK's energy sector/economy, the changes that might bring those paths about, and their implications for DPRK energy end-use and infrastructure.

Figure 1 shows our estimates of the evolution of the DPRK's energy demand by fuel. Note that the 2008 estimates shown in this figure are preliminary only, as we are in the process of updating our DPRK energy-sector analysis.[7]

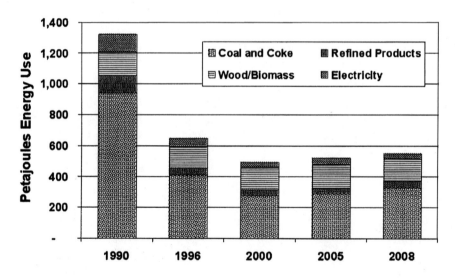

Figure 1. Estimated DPRK Energy End-Use by Fuel, 1990–2008

Starting from the estimates of historical energy supply and demand assembled as above, we prepared future scenarios of energy-sector development for the DPRK, using the Long-range Energy Alternatives Planning (or LEAP) energy/environment software tool.[8] In our earlier work, as shown in Figure 2, we compared a "Redevelopment" path, implying significant opening of the DPRK's economy to outside investment and assistance, but without significant emphasis on energy efficiency improvement, with a "Sustainable Development" path emphasizing energy efficiency and (to a lesser extent) renewable energy, and a "Regional Alternative" path also including the DPRK's participation in several types of regional energy infrastructure (e.g., gas pipelines and elec-

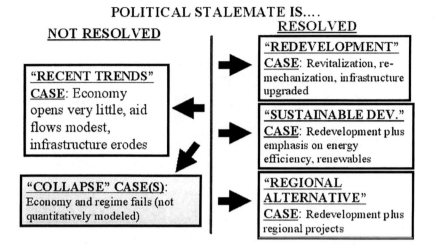

Figure 2. DPRK Energy Paths Considered Quantitatively to Date

tricity trading). An additional path modeled, the "Recent Trends" path, assumed that a substantial solution to the DPRK nuclear issue was not forthcoming, and recent trends in the DPRK's economy continued. Under the "Redevelopment" path, one notable result is a decline of biomass fuels use in the future, and the increased use of electricity, and later, gas, as these fuels become more available to North Korean consumers.

As a general indicator of path results to date, Figure 3 compares final electricity use by path. The "sustainable development case" (diagonal stripes) is set up to provide the same energy services as the "redevelopment case" (dots), but with much more aggressive use of energy efficiency, which significantly reduces overall electricity demand. The "Recent Trends" case shown here is probably closest to the "Slow Collapse" path discussed later in this chapter. Figure 4 shows the significant reduction in greenhouse gas emissions achieved in the sustainable development case and the regional alternative case relative to the redevelopment case. The dashed line with squares shows the greenhouse gas emissions benefits of redevelopment approaches that emphasize energy efficiency and regional cooperation early on. In the "Recent Trends" case, a gradual economic improvement occurs, but without much assistance from outside, and as a result without much improvement in energy efficiency. The "Recent Trends" path also assumes that military energy use—which, as of 2005, was less than 9 percent of the DPRK's total energy use, but slightly over a third of the DPRK's use of petroleum products and over half of all diesel oil and gasoline use—will continue indefinitely at near-current levels,

Figure 3. DPRK Total Final Electricity Use by Path

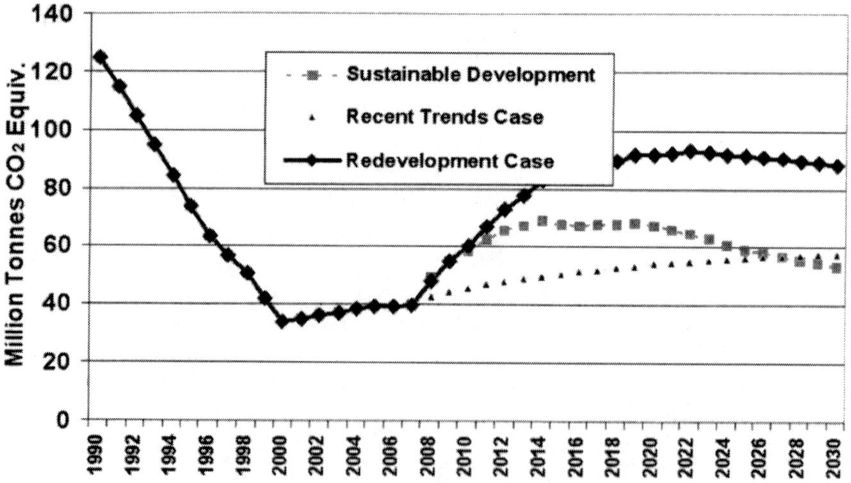

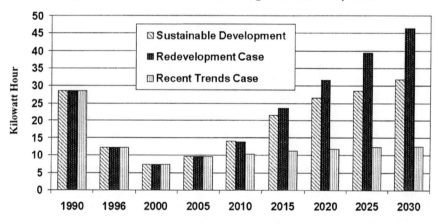

Figure 4. The Global Warming Potential by Case

while in the other paths, as a "peace dividend," a substantial shrinking of the DPRK military occurs, with a reduction in the DPRK military's energy use of over 50 percent (e.g., in the "Redevelopment" path) as a result.

The net costs of reductions in energy use in moving between the "Redevelopment" path and the "Sustainable Development" or the closely related "Regional Alternative" path may be relatively small or even negative. Redevelopment with greater energy efficiency costs more on the demand side, but saves money overall by reducing supply-side and resource costs. These results of our earlier work showed negative net costs (i.e., net savings) for the "Sustainable Development" and "Regional Alternative" paths, relative to the

"Redevelopment" path, even assuming future oil prices much lower than today's levels. We are continuing to update these analyses, but expect that revised results will show the same general trends, reinforcing the conclusion that the least expensive way to redevelop the DPRK will be as an energy-efficient economy, and underscoring the benefits of a focus on energy-efficiency-related cooperation and assistance options as emphasized below and in our previous work.

Two light-water nuclear reactors (LWRs) were being constructed on the east coast of the DPRK near Kumho, under the auspices of the Korean Peninsula Energy Development Organization (KEDO), up to 2003.[9] Although the construction of these reactors has since been suspended, reaching an agreement on resuming the LWR project has remained a political priority of the DPRK. As a consequence, the two LWRs were assumed to be installed and are included in all of the cases shown in Figures 3 and 4 except the "Recent Trends" path. In these analyses, the first 1 gigawatt (GW) LWR unit was assumed to start generating electricity in 2013. If we were repeating the analysis today, we would assume that the LWRs would not be on line until 2018 or so, at the earliest, if they were included in the pathways at all.

Potential "Collapse" Pathways

Analytical Approach and Listing of Pathways Considered

Our general approach to the analysis of potential pathways of regime collapse in the DPRK is as follows. First, we define several significantly different, illustrative regime collapse pathways. We make no predictions about the relative likelihood of any of these paths, and freely admit that the four paths we illustrate have been chosen out of a universe of many possible options. The second step in the analysis is to think about the impacts of regime collapse, for each path, on the DPRK's energy sector, and, by extension on energy and related infrastructure that supports the DPRK's economy. Third, we consider how the ROK, the United States, and the rest of the global community might, or would, need to respond to energy needs following each different type of collapse. Finally, we identify "robust" planning approaches that, if pursued now or quite soon, would prove useful in the event of any type of collapse pathway.

Our four possible paths of regime collapse are described briefly below, and in more detail in the section that follows:

- War: A brief but very destructive war occurs between the DPRK and the ROK and its allies—precipitated by a military incident that escalates rapidly—and leads to essentially immediate unification.
- Regime Implosion Leading to a New Authoritarian Regime: A death or other event leads to regime replacement in the DPRK, with the new regime being modernizing, but leaning toward China and Russia for economic support, and away from the ROK and its Western allies.
- Regime Change by Palace Coup Leading to a ROK-Installed Regime: While not immediately leading to unification, this collapse path would lead to modernization that in turn would lead to at first *de facto* economic unification, then, somewhat later, political unification with the ROK.
- Slow Collapse Leading to Regime Change through Internal Conflict: In this path, the Kim family and/or other leaders continue the current (largely) isolationist policies, which leads eventually—though perhaps not for many years—to the collapse of the DPRK state, with the ROK and its allies obliged to "pick up the pieces."

The "War" Path

This path of regime collapse assumes that a shooting war between the DPRK and the ROK, once set off by a military incident of some kind, escalates quickly. Given the proximity of the DPRK's artillery to the ROK border, we assume that this path results in considerable destruction in the northern ROK, and also in considerable destruction in many areas of the DPRK, especially in areas associated with military installations, but perhaps sparing areas near the DPRK's northern borders. Based on previous work, our rough estimate is that the DPRK would not be able to sustain a conflict for very long (probably for weeks, or at most, a month or two) due to the lack of fuel supplies. This assumes that China does not somehow step up fuel deliveries to the DPRK, which seems unlikely if the DPRK is seen as the aggressor in the conflict.

We assume that war leads to ROK administration of the DPRK. We further assume that the ROK's administration of the DPRK is managed in such a way that significant dissatisfaction with the administration on the part of the North Korean population is avoided. This is a crucial assumption, as an insurgency related to popular local dissatisfaction with ROK administration of the DPRK would set the DPRK's rebuilding and redevelopment back years, as has been the case following the U.S. wars in Iraq and Afghanistan. Would the DPRK's population welcome ROK/U.S. victors with open arms? Iraq/Afghanistan provide cautionary tales, but an analysis of that particular issue, though it has potentially significant ramifications for the types of energy infrastructure improvements that will be possible/effective, is beyond the scope of this chapter. Clearly, however, one of the lessons of Iraq is that the degree to which the administration quickly ramps up the provision to the populace of the essentials of life—food, clean water, health care, electricity, waste treatment, jobs—will play a huge role in how well the populace adapts to its new government.

How the war was prosecuted by the ROK/U.S. side would have a significant bearing on the tasks needed to reconstruct the energy system. For example, would the ROK/U.S. alliance choose to destroy power plants wholesale, or just render plants relatively temporarily unusable with surgical strikes on key, relatively easily replaceable components? Would it destroy the DPRK's operating refinery, or just cut the supply lines for refined products? Would it destroy coal mines, or just cut power to them, and rail lines from them?

We assume that, given that ROK/U.S. air power superiority would provide control of the skies within days, the ROK/U.S. military command could be prevailed upon to knock out the energy infrastructure surgically. War planners would probably deem it necessary to knock out the electricity grid to deny power to munitions and armaments factories, and other military installations. Doing so by wholesale destruction of the transmission and distribution (T&D) grid and major power plants, however, would make it much harder to redevelop the DPRK's energy sector in a timely fashion, and would probably be unnecessary. Targeting and destroying, for example, substations at power plants, which are already in very poor shape, would knock the power plants off line indefinitely, and be much easier to fix than would major damage to the power plants themselves. It seems unlikely that ROK/U.S. forces would try to destroy or permanently disable the DPRK's one major operating (northwest) refinery, as it is so close to China, but they might seek to bomb major rail and road links that would be used to provide fuel to the front, and possibly sink or disable some coastal tankers used to transport petroleum products, and/or target petroleum fuel depots. Disrupting the provision of power to DPRK coal mines would knock most coal production off line, but again, targeting rail links would be inflicting damage that would be relatively easy to fix (once the war ended), but still effective in reducing the DPRK's supply of fuel to the front lines during the war. Probably some war damage would be sustained in the DPRK's seaports, especially those that host submarines or Special Forces that use naval craft. Due to concerns about humanitarian impacts, plus effects on ROK water resources (rivers that flow across or near the DPRK/ROK border) and on China (for rivers in the northern part of the DPRK), we assume that ROK/U.S. forces would avoid damaging hydroelectric facilities, at least the dams, but might, again, choose to knock hydropower stations off line (except probably, the several Supung and other power stations shared by the DPRK and China that are located along northern border rivers) by destroying key substations.

The descriptions of the "War" path above, and the analysis of its energy implications provided below, assume that Russia and especially China stay out of the conflict. If they do not stay on the sidelines, at least in a military sense, the ROK/DPRK conflict becomes a very different and much more dangerous altercation, to say the least, with possible global consequences.

The "Regime Implosion Leading to New Authoritarian Regime" Path

In the second path considered here, a new regime takes over from the Kim family as a result of the death of Kim Jong-il or his successor, or as a result of some internal coup. The new regime is authoritarian but modernizing, and is dominated by military and technocratic elements. Despite its modernizing elements, the new regime continues to spurn the ROK and the West. Rather, the modernizing approach implies much higher than recent rates of investment (from non–ROK, non–Western sources), and as a result the energy infrastructure is rebuilt/redeveloped in close cooperation with China and Russia. For the most part, international governmental organizations and international financial institutions are also excluded by the new regime from the DPRK's modernization process.

The elites of the new regime serve themselves by modernizing the DPRK's economy enough to modestly improve the lot of the general population, but do so in the process of establishing businesses that mostly emphasize export of the DPRK's mineral and labor resources, with China and Russia as major partners. The elites of the regime operate the export companies, and thereby install themselves as a Korean equivalent of the Russian oligarchs of the 1990s. The ROK remains locked out of the DPRK's economy in the short and medium term, but may in the longer term obtain regional network integration by paying rent to the DPRK government for energy infrastructure and transport corridors through the DPRK to resources in Russia and markets in China and beyond.

The "Regime Change by Palace Coup Leading to ROK-Installed Regime" Path

In this path, following, for example, an act by Kim Jong-il or his successor that it considers the "last straw," a group of cosmopolitan younger DPRK diplomats and technocrats backed by young officers in the KPA (Korean People's Army) takes power, and immediately establishes links with the ROK, the United States, and their allies. The result, initially, is an authoritarian regime that is sympathetic to the ROK and the West. The regime slowly, perhaps very slowly, installs elements of democracy in the DPRK, but focuses first on economic reforms. These economic reforms place emphasis on planning a DPRK economy that complements the ROK economy. For example, initially, the reforms would likely emphasize development of the DPRK's mineral resource base to help provide raw materials for ROK industry, and would utilize cheap labor in the DPRK to compete in industries (e.g., textiles and basic electronics) that have been moving out of ROK to lower-cost suppliers such as China and India. To fund these economic reforms, significant investment would be drawn from the ROK, and probably from the United States and elsewhere as well.

As with the China- and Russia-leaning elite in the "Regime Implosion Leading to New Authoritarian Regime" path, the new, ROK-leaning regime elites seek to serve themselves, but do so possibly by setting up ROK-style chaebol that they control, and that interface with/draw investment from analogs in the South. Such a regime might be amenable to large-scale virtual exports of DPRK labor via the internet, for example, for Korean-language records processing for the insurance, medical, and telecommunications industries.

The "Slow Collapse Leading to Eventual Reunification" Path

In this variant of "Regime Implosion," either Kim Jong-il or a successor from the Kim clique maintains control, or another regime (perhaps run by a "regent" governing the country in the name of a successor to Kim) takes power. In either case, however, there is a failure to modernize or open the DPRK significantly to the outside world. Aided by continued isolation, the national regime's control over the country becomes progressively less effective due to continued erosion of energy and other infrastructure, and its inability to provide food and other essentials for the population as a whole.

As this erosion continued, possible situations between national control and total collapse of authority might include the effective fragmentation of the DPRK into "fiefdoms" run by powerful party or military leaders, perhaps supported individually by national neighbors or large foreign investors such as Chinese companies.

We assume that this scenario would lead to eventual reunification of the DPRK with the ROK. Control of information coming into North Korea would break down as the power of the central authority to impose order waned,[10] which, coupled with continued decline in living standards, would lead eventually to disillusionment on the part of the majority of the population, internal conflict, civil disorder, and possibly even civil war in the DPRK. A civil war situation might be difficult to conceive of, given the lack of significant ethnic or religious divides in the DPRK, but a possible mechanism could occur in a "fiefdom" situation, where rival warlords began to struggle for territory or power. Overall, the process of decline under this path might be very slow, taking years or even decades to play out, but would likely end with a rapid collapse at the end stage that required urgent intervention by the ROK or China.

Implications of Collapse Pathways for the DPRK's Energy Sector and for Provision of Energy Services in the DPRK

Each of the four "collapse" pathways outlined above has its own implications for how the DPRK's energy sector would be affected. As such, each of the pathways implies different ways in which those in the international community with the wherewithal to help might provide or plan to provide energy services to the DPRK's population and economy in response to, or to soften the effects of, regime collapse. What follows are our initial thoughts on the energy-sector and energy-assistance implications of each of the paths described above.

The "War" Path

Major military conflict between the DPRK and the ROK (and its allies) would eliminate considerable energy and industrial infrastructure in the DPRK, though much of it is already failing and/or obsolete. If a "surgical" military approach was used, the minimum short-term requirements to supply basic energy services to the DPRK and to start to build a peaceful DPRK economy would likely be to:

- Replace virtually all substation equipment, including both equipment that was war-damaged and equipment that had simply become inoperable over time, as most substation transformers and related equipment are reportedly in poor condition.
- Establish emergency electricity generation, initially fueled with diesel oil or possibly liquefied petroleum gas (LPG, a mixture of propane and butane). This generation might take the form of power barges in coastal areas or where river transport is possible, and package diesel or portable combined heat and power plants in inland areas.
- Try to get major coal-fired power stations restarted, and restart or sta-

bilize output from coal mines to supply them, while undertaking temporary transmission repairs sufficient to get electricity onto the local or regional grid on a semi-reliable basis.
- Ramp up petroleum products production in ROK refineries in order to substitute for whatever DPRK fuel production/transport capacity was destroyed in the war, with additional fuel provided to supply emergency generation facilities. The ROK's present refining capacity is sufficiently large to easily supply the ROK and the DPRK together—though possibly not both states at ROK per-capita levels of consumption. Given the status of the DPRK's fuels demand infrastructure, however, the DPRK would not reach ROK levels of consumption for many years. As such, overall refined products supplies might not be a problem in a suddenly reunified Korea, but the infrastructure to move supplies to where they were needed in the North—port facilities, rail facilities, and roads—would need upgrading even if they were not damaged by war.
- Try to get major hydroelectric facilities restarted, including required transmission repairs and/or repairs to dams.
- Provide critical power and fuel for agriculture. The urgency of doing so would, of course, depend on the season in which the conflict occurred, but planning for supporting the DPRK's agriculture as much as possible would be a priority in any circumstance in order to reduce the quantity of food aid that would inevitably be required.

If a surgical military approach was *not* used by the ROK and its allies, supplying basic services and economy-building in the DPRK would be more difficult. For example, immediate replacement of most power plants would be needed, meaning more "triage" solutions to restart parts of energy facilities, however possible, and more provision of emergency generation. Significant emergency civil engineering work would be also needed to shore up damaged infrastructure, repair ports, rail facilities, and roads so that emergency supplies of refined products could be brought in.

A key complication of the "War" path is that it would be necessary to rebuild/develop the DPRK at the same time as the considerable damage to the ROK infrastructure was being repaired. This complication argues for the need for countries beyond the ROK and the United States to take a very active role in DPRK reconstruction, as a great deal of ROK rebuilding effort would necessarily be domestically focused. The need to support/rebuild both South and North Korea would make coordination, even in the midst of postwar chaos, even more necessary if citizens both south and north of the 38th parallel were to get the necessary services in a timely manner. All of these factors underline the need for detailed and coordinated pre-crisis planning.[11]

In any postwar path, there would be a need to quickly ramp up capacity-building for energy, environment-related, and other occupations. Capacity-building would be needed in part because trained people would be needed for reconstruction and redevelopment, but also because the North Korean population would need gainful, useful, peaceful employment. This is especially true for those officials and technicians associated with sensitive industries (e.g., military industries and nuclear weapons programs) in today's DPRK. A key focus of early capacity-building efforts should be on providing skills and technologies that encourage the growth of local economies that are capable, to a large degree, of providing essentials such as food and energy services for them. As concrete example, training should be provided for redeployment of scientists and technicians working at the Yongbyon nuclear weapons complex and military missile development/production programs, so as to make sure their skills are directed toward productive and peaceful activities, rather than being diverted to serving threatening states or organizations.

In the medium and longer term, several types of actions will be needed under a collapse via the "War" path:

- Planning for and setting out to build an integrated ROK/DPRK grid, probably starting with extending the ROK grid into areas in the southern part of the (current) DPRK, and building local/regional grids in other areas for eventual hook-up to the national grid.
- Making sure that damaged energy demand infrastructure is replaced with the most energy-efficient devices available, so as to lessen the requirements for new or rebuilt energy supply infrastructure.
- Making sure that energy-efficient devices are chosen for all of the new housing, commercial, and industrial developments that would be built as the North's economy and living standards started to catch up with those of the South.
- Evaluating which industrial facilities would need to be developed (or in rare cases, rebuilt), and planning for evolving supply systems for fuels (such as electricity, gas, heat) to serve the "evolving economy"— which would mean, for example, putting supply systems where people would be located in the future (i.e., not necessarily planning to put facilities where people happen to be located in the short term, while they are still employed in the planned economy and survival-level cottage industries), factoring in elements such as re-mechanization of agriculture and shifts in economic composition toward the serv-

ices sectors, and away from heavy industry, and probably toward cities and away from the countryside.
- Working with the Russians to reconstruct—or, more likely, construct anew—the Sonbong refinery, related port facilities, and the combined heat and power facilities associated with and serving the refinery and the local area.
- Working with the Russians to bring gas supplies and gas transmission and distribution infrastructure into and through the DPRK to the ROK, and/or develop new liquefied natural gas (LNG) import, storage, and regasification facilities somewhere near the 38th parallel. LNG facilities would likely be shared to serve both the North and South.

The "Regime Implosion Leading to New Authoritarian Regime" Path

In this path, the technocratic regime would presumably assess the country's energy needs, and attempt to focus internally on energy infrastructure redevelopment, taking advantage of largely Chinese and Russian technical help. Energy infrastructure development would be focused on serving raw materials export industries, and as such might be focused on areas in the north and west of the DPRK, leading to somewhat geographically and sectorally unbalanced energy systems. For example, if the regime was focused on maximizing income from raw materials and labor exports, it might give limited attention to improving energy supplies to and infrastructure in urban areas (outside of areas where elites live) or to rural areas (outside of where minerals are found).

The ROK and the West would be expected to have limited short- and medium-term influence under this path. The main options the ROK and the West might have to influence the DPRK's energy sector would be to try to work through the Russians and Chinese to provide capacity-building, and thus affect patterns of change in DPRK energy infrastructure at the margin, and also to look for opportunities for joint ventures with Russians on regional infrastructure (e.g., in electricity and gas networks, and on oil refining). Working through the Chinese and Russians, however, might be complicated by the bottom-line focus of Chinese and Russian trading companies operating in the DPRK, which might leave little room for modifications in approach that would help an eventually reunified Korea. In general, the ROK and the West could offer capacity-building on energy and related topics as a lever to start opening the DPRK economy to other influences, but how those overtures might be received by the new DPRK regime, under this path, is hard to predict.

In the longer term, assuming an eventual gradual or sudden opening of the regime, the ROK/West would need to focus on providing energy infrastructure in areas and populations left underserved by export-oriented infrastructure.

The "Regime Change by Palace Coup Leading to ROK-Installed Regime" Path

The implications for the energy sector under this path are similar in many ways to those under the "surgical strike" variant of the "War" path, but with less DPRK destruction/dislocation to deal with, and without the need to rebuild infrastructure in the ROK.

- As such, short-term needs under this path would include:
- Making a full assessment of the status of the North Korean electricity grid (T&D and generation) and other major energy and related infrastructure, including mines, refineries, rail facilities, and ports.
- Replacing virtually all electrical substation equipment, starting with failed and failing units.
- Establishing emergency electricity generation, initially with diesel or possibly LPG-power barges in coastal areas, and package diesel or combined heat and power plants in inland areas, focusing where power supply is particularly inadequate, in order to build social stability in those areas and stem out-migration.
- Where possible, applying quick repairs to keep the best of the major coal-fired power stations going for a few years while the national power grid is being replaced.
- Looking for ways to upgrade existing hydroelectric facilities to improve their safety of operation, efficiency, and generation capacity.
- Ramping up ROK refined products production to supply currently unmet demand for transport fuels in the DPRK, plus diesel fuel needs for temporary generation.
- Providing critical power, fuel, and equipment for farming.

In the medium and longer term, one priority under this path would be to assess coal supply infrastructure to determine if any existing mines would be cost-effective to operate in the longer term; and to shut down and abandon North Korean mines with a poor prognosis—possibly as a result of a damaged mining infrastructure that would be too difficult to repair, unsafe mining conditions, a poor resource base, or simply poor mine economics. Even under this path, it would not make sense to abandon mines immediately as the regime changes, given the importance of coal to the existing infrastructure and the importance of the coal industry as an employer, but the coal-mining sector would have to be reviewed soberly, and shrunk if needed in favor of importing coal from major international low-cost producers if the assessment so indicated. A second major priority would be to evaluate which industrial facilities needed to be developed, based in large part on demand for DPRK-located facilities as indicated by the willingness of private-sector actors to invest. In addition, in the medium and longer term, plans would need to be developed for evolving supply systems for fuels (electricity, gas, heat, and refined products) to serve the evolving Northern economy.

Again in the medium and longer term, under the path leading to an ROK-friendly regime, a key requirement would be to establish markets for fuels, and the regulatory authorities to oversee them, with an eye toward merging markets and regulatory authorities in a unified Korea. For markets, the DPRK could in fact lead the ROK into the world of "smart grids" and smart electricity meters. This could include, for example, widespread use of time-of-demand pricing, local generation, and renewable generation. Demand for electricity in North Korea under this path could be expected to increase rapidly, accompanied by an opportunity (not to be missed) to build a very modern, very high-efficiency supply and demand-side electricity sector. Hand-in-hand with this effort should go development of progressively tighter building energy efficiency regulations, and the development of human capacity to enforce these and other regulations, and to design and construct high-efficiency buildings.

As with other paths, it would be desirable to work with Russia, and possibly with China and other nations, to explore and extend regional electricity and gas grids, and to partner on a new Sonbong refinery.

Last, but certainly not least, this path would provide both the opportunity and need to do aggressive capacity-building on a vast host of topics, starting as soon as possible. This would mean sending the best North Korean students to the ROK, the United States, and elsewhere for study, and providing them with incentives to return to work in North Korea; but also—just as, if not more, importantly—building up North Korean educational institutions at all levels.

The "Slow Collapse Leading to Eventual Reunification" Path

In this path, the energy infrastructure would continue to slowly decay, following the general pattern—albeit occasionally partially reversed by occasional isolated repair projects and new developments—of the last two decades. As the infrastructure decayed, it would continue to become more inefficient over time, and also lose capacity (e.g., electricity generation capacity, transport capacity, heat production capacity, and so on) as the performance of individual units continued to decline, and as units failed altogether. In this path, scavenging for metals to sell for scrap might take an increasing toll on important energy infrastructure systems, and other infrastructure as well.

In this "Slow Collapse" path, the DPRK's efforts to keep infrastructure running would continue, but would run up against diminishing returns due to a lack of replacement parts and of outside expertise that could only be acquired with scarce foreign exchange dollars. Exceptions to the pattern of decaying infrastructure might be infrastructure that was required to support export ventures with outside investors—for example, Chinese companies—where the outside investors had a vested interest in making sure that key infrastructure was operable.

From the perspective of the ROK and its allies, actions to usefully help to address DPRK energy-sector and related needs in the short-to-medium term would be limited. So long as a central regime hostile to the outside remained in power in North Korea, little could be done but to take advantage of the (likely) rare opportunities that would occur for engagement and capacity-building. As the central regime lost power, there might be more opportunities for small, local engagement projects addressing energy-sector needs, but such projects would be difficult and potentially hazardous to carry out, and might more likely be the province of non-national groups such as non-governmental or international organizations. If an era of "fiefdoms" occurred during the slow collapse, arranging any type of regional project, such as gas pipelines or rail interconnections would be very difficult due to shifts in who was in charge or in power in areas transited by proposed infrastructure at any given time.

In the longer term, when the collapse of the state was complete, with or without an interim "fiefdom" era, the types of measures required of the ROK and its partners following reunification-by-default would be the same as in the "Regime Change by Palace Coup" path, but with a significant difference. Continued degradation of energy infrastructure, leading (in part) to extreme scarcity and suppressed demand, would be likely to make eventual reconstruction/redevelopment and recovery of North Korea a progressively larger and larger long-term issue for the ROK, with growing complexity and expense.

Also in the longer term, relative to a more immediate collapse, the "Slow Collapse" path implies that full assessments of the DPRK's energy and related infrastructure would not be possible for some time. As a result, the countries and organizations that would need to step in to provide energy services and rebuild energy infrastructure under a collapse scenario would not be able to fully assess the slowly deteriorating situation until actual collapse occurred, at which point needs (for food, water, electricity, waste treatment, health care, jobs, and other essentials) would likely be more urgent than they would have been had collapse occurred sooner.

The lack of access to the DPRK for a full energy-sector assessment means that planning for energy-sector support, and increasingly, as time passes, redevelopment, would need to continue to be informed by fragmentary information. This underlines the need for the international community to (a) coordinate and share information on the DPRK whenever possible, (b) use that information to formulate and regularly update plans for energy-sector triage and rebuilding under a collapse scenario, even if collapse is long in coming, and (c) provide resources to consistently support both (a) and (b). Gathering data and analyzing the energy-sector information would require coordination by all interested parties. Considerable persistence and patience would also be required of those in the ROK and the international community who had to prepare for DPRK regime collapse in keeping energy-sector assistance and contingency plans updated, and remaining in readiness to effectively activate plans when needed.

Lessons from Collapse Pathways for Near-Term Initiatives and Planning Efforts

Our initial consideration of the energy-sector implications of potential DPRK regime collapse pathways suggests that there are a number of possible initiatives that the ROK, the United States, and the broader international community can undertake to be ready to assist in the event of a DPRK regime collapse:

- Do capacity-building on lots of topics whenever possible. It is cheap, useful, and necessary in any path, and has many ancillary benefits. Required capacity-building topics include technical training in electricity generation, energy efficiency, oil refining, renewable energy, environmental remediation, waste treatment, reforestation, and other similar disciplines. In addition, training would be needed in running commercial enterprises, including economic analysis, building and operating regulatory and legal systems, and many other organizational topics. Ancillary benefits of capacity-building include engagement at the individual and organizational level, opening minds to new ways of thinking, increasing the availability of competence and personal connections for application at key movements of transition, as well as the availability of in-country trainers to rapidly expand training as needed.

- Plan now for the inevitable wholesale rebuilding of the transmission and distribution system. An initial step might be to stockpile key components, such as transformers and substation switchgear, for rapid installation as needed.
- Assess the ROK's current refining capacity versus the petroleum products needs of a reunified Korea. Start talking with the Russians about the possibility of rebuilding and expanding the Sonbong refinery so as to be ready to rapidly start a refinery project when conditions permit.
- In order to reduce the burden on the energy supply infrastructure, ensure the provision of high-efficiency energy demand (and supply) devices when rebuilding the DPRK's economy—rather than, for example, marketing secondhand appliances, industrial motors, power plants, automobiles, and other devices to the DPRK—so as to make sure that the DPRK has a better chance of catching up with technology in the South, yielding better outcomes from social, resource conservation, environmental, and economic/infrastructure integration perspectives.
- Think through how markets for energy goods can be established so as to spur private-sector investments.
- Plan integrated energy infrastructure/economic development demonstration projects and try to get some integrated projects implemented even before collapse.
- Network with other interested parties to provide the best assessment possible of the DPRK's energy-sector status and needs, and collaborate on concrete plans so as to be able to swiftly and effectively address those needs when an opening occurs.

Finally, medium- and long-term regional energy projects such as a regional electric grid tie-lines and/or regional gas pipelines should be implemented in ways that provide China and Russia with some leverage over the reconstruction agenda should the DPRK collapse. This leverage might be needed, in part, to ensure that the ROK handed over all fissile material and nuclear weapons-related hardware and knowledge to the IAEA and/or to nuclear weapons states in the scenario where such hardware and knowledge was obtained/inherited by the ROK from DPRK sources, after the collapse of the DPRK. Meanwhile, policy-makers should focus on measures needed to stabilize the DPRK to avoid collapse in the short and medium term.

Notes

1. This chapter was originally prepared as part of The Korea Project, co-organized by the Korean Studies Institute at the University of Southern California and the Office of the Korea Chair at the Center for Strategic and International Studies, Washington, D.C., and presented at the "The Korea Project: Planning for the Long Term" conference, held in Los Angeles, on August 20–21, 2010. Originally published online by the Korean Studies Institute.
2. Bryan Kay, "Is Collapse of NK Regime Imminent?" *Korea Times*, November 15, 2009, http://www.koreatimes.co.kr/www/news/nation/2010/08/120_55550.html.
3. Aidan Foster-Carter, "The Gradualist Pipe-Dream: Prospects and Pathways for Korean Reunification," in *Asian Flashpoint: Security and the Korean Peninsula*, ed. A. Mack (Canberra: Allen and Unwin, 1993), pp. 159–175.
4. J. Witt, *Four Scenarios for a Nuclear DPRK*, U.S.-Korea Institute, Working Paper 10-01, February 2010, http://uskoreainstitute.org/bin/s/g/USKI_WP10-01_Wit.pdf.
5. We have outlined in detail appropriate policy options for this goal in, for example, D.F. von Hippel and P. Hayes (2009), "DPRK Energy Sector Development Priorities: Options and Preferences," in the Asian Energy Security Special Issue of *Energy Policy*, http://dx.doi.org/10.1016/j.enpol.2009.11.068; D.F. von Hippel and P. Hayes, *Fueling DPRK Energy Futures and Energy Security: 2005 Energy Balance, Engagement Options, and Future Paths* (Nautilus Institute Report, 2007, http://www.nautilus.org/fora/security/07042DPRKEnergyBalance.pdf); D.F. von Hippel and P. Hayes, "Energy Security for North Korea," *Science* 316 (2007): 1288–1289; D.F. von Hippel, P. Hayes, J.H. Williams, C. Greacen, M. Sagrillo, and T. Savage, "International Energy Assistance Needs and Options for the Democratic People's Republic of Korea (DPRK)," *Energy Policy* 36, Issue 2 (February 2008): 541–552; and D.F. von Hippel and P. Hayes, *DPRK Energy Sector Assistance to Accompany Progress in Denuclearization Discussions: Options and Considerations*, produced as part of the project "Improving Regional Security and Denuclearizing the Korean Peninsula: U.S. Policy Interests and Options," organized by Joel Wit of Columbia University's Weatherhead Institute for East Asia and the U.S.-Korea Institute at the Johns Hopkins University School of Advanced International Studies, Washington, D.C., available at http://www.nautilus.org/DPRKPolicy/vonHippel.pdf.
6. See D.F. von Hippel and P. Hayes, *Fueling DPRK Energy Futures and Energy Security*, for details on the 1990 through 2005 estimates provided in these figures, and for related information. Note that an update to this analysis is under way.
7. Figure 1, as well as in Figures 3 and 4, are based on data collected by the authors and projections prepared by the authors. See the document referenced in note 6 for references to the underlying sources of data used to inform earlier versions of the estimates and projections described in these figures.
8. The LEAP software tool is developed and maintained by Stockholm Environment Institute-United States. For information about the LEAP tool, see http://www.energycommunity.org/.
9. Korean Peninsula Development Organization, *Korean Peninsula Development Organization Annual Report 2003*, December 31, 2003, http://www.kedo.org/annual_reports.asp.
10. Some would say that, due to the advent of cell phone usage in the Chinese border region and in Pyongyang, the control of information in the DPRK is already breaking down.
11. We assume that at least some significant planning for the collapse of the DPRK has been undertaken by ROK government agencies, but if these plans have been reported in the public literature, we have not yet seen them.

CHAPTER 9

Rethinking Special Economic Zones as a Survival Strategy for North Korea

Sung-Hoon Lim

ABSTRACT

This chapter focuses on the challenge of developing North Korean Special Economic Zones (SEZs) successfully in terms of their ability to utilize and exploit both the competitive capabilities and the market forces of the adjacent South Korean economy. To successfully develop all the North Korean SEZs, the North Korean government should develop the four SEZs sequentially. After developing the Kaesong and Mt. Kumgang SEZs, the capital and skills accumulated from these SEZs should be applied to the Sinuiju SEZ. In particular, the North Korean government, which lacks economic resources and skills, should use the "choose and focus" or "sequential development" strategy. This chapter paper concludes that the route to success for North Korean SEZs lies potentially in not only utilizing the market competitiveness of South Korea more effectively, but also in attracting greater levels of investment from South Korean private companies.

Introduction

Two of the four North Korean SEZs are located in areas bordering China and Russia, and the other two are near South Korea. There is, however, a substantial difference between the two groups of SEZs in terms of performance and development. Though the two SEZs located in the northern region of North Korea (Sinuiju and Rajin-Sunbong SEZ) have shown sluggish performance, the two in the southern region (Kaesong and Mt Kumgang SEZ) have shown notable progress.

The first SEZ, the Rajin-Sunbong SEZ (1991) was expected to induce $4.7 billion in foreign investment by 2010. Despite that expectation, less than $100 million has been induced, and operation of the SEZ has nearly been suspended. As for the Sinuiju SEZ—an international complex focusing on trade, tourism, new technology, manufacturing, finance, commerce, and amusement—the same situation was repeated. After Sinuiju Governor Yang Bin was arrested in China, the North Korean government has been unable to find a suitable replacement, slowing the progress of the SEZ project.[1] The North Korean government had shown strong willingness to develop the SEZ by giving it the absolute right of self-governance. But it appears that Pyongyang has withdrawn that plan.[2]

On the other hand, the two cooperative SEZs, the Kaesong and Mt. Kumgang SEZs, have made substantial progress since they were designated. The Mt. Kumgang SEZ generates profits by attracting tourists to resorts near Mt. Kumgang. Hyundai Asan Corporation signed a lease (through 2052) with the North for a plot of land in the area. Since then, South Korean firms have invested approximately 359.2 billion won (US$1=1,134 won), including 226.3 billion won from Hyundai Asan Corporation, in a golf course, hot spring spa, hotel, and sushi restaurant in the SEZ. In addition, the South Korean government invested 60 billion won in opening a meeting hall for separated families in the SEZ in 2008.[3]

Before the Mt. Kumgang SEZ was closed in 2008,[4] the North Korean government had raised its cash revenues by $30 million annually (approximately $500 million in accumulated amounts) as a reward for its tourism license issuance to South Korean partners.[5] As for the North Korean government, it earns additional profits from tourist admission fees. As of October 2010, there were 121 companies and 43,100 North Korean employees in the Kaesong SEZ. The accumulated output is $1.02 billion, and goods amounting to approximately $150 million were exported from January 2005 to October 2010.[6] The growth of the Kaesong SEZ is expected to continue until it reaches 2,000 companies, 350,000 employees, and $16 billion in annual output.[7] Wages paid to North Korean employees since the establishment of the Kaesong SEZ have reached $116.4 million in accumulated amounts from December 2004 to July 2010. The total amount of wages continued to rise to $26.86 million in 2008, $38.31 million in 2009, and $27.08 million from January to July 2010. The average monthly wage of North Korean employees in the Kaesong SEZ is $80.3, which is 70 to 100 times more than the ordinary amount for North Korean workers.[8]

Studies have been conducted on the benefits of SEZs in achieving rapid economic growth in North Korea.[9] Arguments in favor of SEZ development generally point to the positive role that SEZs can play in at least four ways: (1) overcoming a common problem experienced by less-developed countries, the lack of resources required to make large-scale investments in all regions within a country simultaneously; (2) experimentation-based learning and trade-based learning; (3) attracting direct foreign investment and promoting export growth and employment generation; and (4) facilitating economic liberalization, including trade, financial, and institutional liberalization.[10] The South-North cooperative SEZs pushed forward by North Korea possess a more important policy implication than the said benefits. The revenue of $70 million derived from the two cooperative SEZs is the reason why North Korea desires reopening the Mt. Kumgang SEZ, even after a number of provocations by North Korea in 2010, and why Pyongyang does not close the Kaesong SEZ. With the collapse of the Soviet Union and Eastern European bloc economies in 1991, South Korea became the obvious alternative source of assistance for North Korean SEZs.

In view of the present economic situation, this chapter will address possible routes to success for the North Korean SEZs. The first section provides an analysis of complicated features of the SEZs; the second section offers an examination of short-term and long-term development strategies; and the concluding section contains a discussion of the most appropriate way to achieve success for the SEZs through close economic cooperation between the two Koreas, with consideration of the eventual establishment of a future commonwealth.

The Concept and Developmental Logic of a North Korean SEZ

The Concept of the SEZ in North Korea

According to the North Korean *Dictionary of Economics*, the "Special Economic Zone (Open Zone for Foreigners)" is defined as follows:

> China, in 1979, announced some parts of four cities as special economic zones. The purpose of establishing special economic zones was to induce foreign capital, technology, and management skills, as well as increase foreign trade and foreign currency holdings, to accelerate economic development. The Chinese special economic zone is different from the "industrial district" in capitalist countries. While capitalist countries develop capitalist economies by inducing foreign capital in the industrial district, in the Chinese special economic zone, various economic systems coexist on condition that a socialist economy predominates. Foreign capitalists have the right to possess the means of production, a part of or whole rights of management, the right to employ and

discharge workers, and particular privileges and special favors regulated by the Chinese government. Foreign capitalists, however, have to undertake economic activity in the special economic zone under the supervision and direction of the socialist country.[11]

In the same dictionary, the so-called "industrial district" in capitalist countries is defined in the following terms:

> The origin of the industrial district was the Manchester Industrial District in Britain in the late nineteenth century, and this model was diffused all around the world after World War I. In capitalist countries, an industrial district is established under the name of urban and regional development for the pursuit of profits by the "monopolistic capitalist." In colonized countries, the establishment of the "industrial district" became a link to realize the new colonial industrial policies of the modern imperial monopolists. There are many industrial districts in South Korea these days. The imperialist countries, the U.S. and Japan, made South Korea into a military base and a colonized production base for export commodities. The multinational corporations of the U.S. and Japan working in South Korean industrial districts are more invasive and rapacious than the imperialists of the "leased territories" in China in the late nineteenth century. Although the imperialists in the leased territories had the privilege of living in their own special area, they did not set barbed-wire entanglements around the leased territory in order to prohibit the passage of Chinese. The multinational enterprises (MNEs) of the U.S. and Japan in South Korea set barbed-wire entanglements around the large industrial district and control the passage of workers and visitors, exploiting South Korean workers in the district. MNEs privileges of production, distribution, and trade reached all around the nation and had the prerogative of residence by which they construct and live in palatial mansions. The MNEs of the U.S. and Japan obtained South Korean nationality and rights equal to South Korean corporations, as well as extra privileges that even comprador capitalists cannot get. These MNEs have the right to invest 100 percent of capital and reinvest double the amount of the original investment. In addition, they send huge profits earned through exploitation of South Korean workers to their home country without any restrictions. Thus, the industrial district in South Korea operates for the imperialistic exploitation of the MNEs of the U.S. and Japan and is used as a military base and as a colonized production base for export commodities.[12]

Dictionary of Economics was published in 1985 and might not exactly represent the current official opinion of the North Korean authorities. In the mid–1980s, while North Korea expressed dislike for the special economic zones established by capitalists, it tried to understand the special economic zone model as pursued by the Chinese government. This indicates a significant change of attitude in North Korea from its position in the 1970s. In the *Dictionary of Economics* published in 1975, there was no discussion regarding special economic zones or industrial districts at all.

The first special economic zone project began in December 1991 with the government decision to establish a "Free Economy and Trade Zone" at Rajin-Sunbong in northeastern North Korea. The North Korean government began this project after it realized that the earlier North Korean Joint Investment and Management Law designed to induce foreign capital was not working, while the SEZs in China were successful. Pyongyang, however, was not fully prepared to effectively open the Rajin-Sunbong area. The government expected that it would be easy to induce foreign investment capital by just opening the area. That dream was dashed amid little foreign investment. The sole consolation was the understanding that the Rajin-Sunbong experiment was only a first trial opening, and future successful experiments remained possible.[13]

In 2002, the North Korean government designated Sinuiju a special administration zone under an independent governor, with its own right of legislation, administration, and judiciary. Observers can make at least two inferences from these actions. First, the North Korean government still regards the SEZ as an important channel to obtain foreign capital and to solve current economic difficulties. Second, the official concept of the SEZ has changed since the 1985 *Dictionary of Economics*, the definitions of which convey the more defensive idea that "Sinuiju is open to foreign capitalists, and foreign MNEs will strengthen their exploitation of this area to make it a colonized production base for export commodities."

The Developmental Logic Behind the New North Korean SEZs

Why, after the Rajin-Sunbong experiment, did the North Korean government designate Sinuiju a special administration district, Kaesong a special industrial district, and Mt. Kumgang a special tourism district? The answer is that the North Korean government wanted to demonstrate its willingness to open up, to induce foreign investment, and bring in foreign capital and technology. These efforts would lead to national economic growth, as well as provide learning and testing grounds for economic reform measures.

The first aspect of the North Korean government strategy has been to demonstrate its intention to increase foreign investment. North Korea recognizes the importance of providing evidence to foreign investors of its strong desire to consistently reform and open the country to international commerce. The current North Korean economic system is quite different from the international norm, and many North Korean laws and regulations are in need of reform. Recent actions by the North Korean government have, in fact, demonstrated a great deal of willingness to open up to foreign countries. Notably, Pyongyang announced the "7.1 Reformation of the Economic Management

System" policy on 1 July 2002 and established the "Special Administration District" in Sinuiju that September. Shortly afterwards, in October, Kaesong was designated as a special industrial district, and Mt. Kumgang as a special tourism zone. These acts of reform and openness were intended to increase the level of economic support and cooperation of foreigners by projecting an image of peaceful coexistence and an open-door policy. North Korea has used the phrase "peaceful coexistence" in its official media.

As a second component of its strategy, the North Korean government plans to achieve economic growth by attracting capital from abroad. This is the primary goal of its external economic policy. This policy has changed through the years. During the 1950s and 1960s, North Korea depended on fraternal "socialist" countries, giving priority to the Soviet Union. In the 1970s, North Korea did make an effort to induce the import of large-scale capital and technology from Western capitalist countries. But its inefficient economic system, with a focus on loans and export promotion, combined with the international oil instability of the times, caused a significant accumulation of external debt. Thus, in the 1980s and 1990s, the North Korean government altered its policy to focus on new ways of inducing foreign investment. This policy was not successful at the time, because its scope remained too narrow. The collapse of the Soviet-led COMECON trading bloc, followed by ten years of economic recession, contributed to continued economic stagnation. Additional changes and a new vision were clearly required. Consequently, in the twenty-first century, the North Korean government expects the SEZs to be a channel to induce foreign capital for national economic growth.

As a third component of its strategy, Pyongyang intends to propel economic growth through the nationwide expansion of advanced technology and expertise introduced by the SEZs. The first step toward this part of the North Korean economic growth strategy is to open a particular SEZ and induce state-of-the-art foreign technology, facilities, and management skill. The second step is to expand such technology into specified national industries, leading to a more advanced national economic structure. At the same time, the national industrial sector outside the SEZs is intentionally "protected" from the market-adapted process, continuing instead to develop at a slower pace toward basic industrialization. Thus, North Korea expects to import advanced industrial expertise, protect its currently weak national industry, and achieve economic growth through the correlation of industries.

The North Korean government expects the SEZs to play the role of a testing ground for economic reform and as a vehicle for the learning of advanced industry. The government plans to induce the import of advanced economic management systems to the SEZs, testing free market and competition systems. Many elements of the July 1 Reform had already been executed in the Rajin-Sunbong economic and trade zone. The North Korean government implemented several reform policies to develop the Rajin-Sunbong area in June 1997, such as the harmonization of currency matters, readjustment of the exchange rate, granting permission for the private management of restaurants and lodgings, enforcement of self-supporting accounting systems, and the establishment of a free market. These were impressively innovative reforms at the time, although they were later minimized through government interference and control.

Strategies for Developing North Korean SEZs

How to Succeed in the Development of North Korean SEZs

Considering the North Korean SEZ foreign investment climate and available economic resources, a sequential development strategy is required. A simultaneous approach for all SEZs is not likely to succeed. The sequential concept is also valid for affecting the step-by-step transfer of South Korean market competitiveness into SEZs. The substantial task of initiating this approach is based on the connection of a railroad between the two Koreas.

This railroad connection serves a two-fold role: It is a direct link from South Korea to China and Russia, and its presence decreases the cost of physical distribution. It plays a more significant role than these logistical measures, however. A railroad connection can be the channel of South Korean competitive power to North Korea, to serve as the main route for the development of SEZs and eventually form a basis for South-North Korean economic unification. Furthermore, a railroad connection would reduce the cost and difficulty of national unification.

There are two railroad sections in South Korea. The eastside railroad connects the South Korean railroad from Mt. Kumgang, Tongcheon/Wonsan (Hamheung), and Rajin-Sunbong (Cheongjin) to the Trans-Manchurian Railroad (TMR) and Trans-Siberian Railroad (TSR). The Westside railroad connects the South Korean railroad from Kaesong, Nampo (Pyongyang), and Sinuiju to the Trans-Mongolian Railroad (TMGR) and Trans-China Railroad (TCR). Along these two main railroads, electric and communication networks and social overhead capital are planned and will be expanded to other areas of North Korea. These two railroads and roads connecting Seoul to North Korean SEZs will be the transportation axis of the North Korean economic development plan.

To ensure success, a step-by-step developmental approach on North Korean SEZs is more practicable than a simultaneous approach. Applying the lessons from many successful practices in other SEZs, such as the Shanghai SEZ and Shenzhen SEZ in China, international investment funds tend to pursue large markets comprising high populations and high real incomes.[14] There is, however, no comparable market with high purchasing power in North Korea. Therefore, the North Korean SEZ policy has to be set up on the basis of the South Korean market, which has the required purchasing power. The competitive power of North Korea should be constructed on the basis of South Korean competitiveness. The following development strategy flows from this premise.

The Mt. Kumgang SEZ and the Kaesong SEZ, where investment from South Korea is possible, will be the first target for development. The Mt. Kumgang SEZ will focus on tourism and primary industry. The industrial capacity can then be extended to Wonsan, and the industrial competitiveness developed in Wonsan can be managed in Pyongyang, the North Korean capital. Simultaneously, the linkage development to Rajin-Sunbong can be propelled forward. This is one option for the developmental path: the Eastward Expansion Line.

At the same time, the development of the North Korean manufacturing industry begins with the Kaesong SEZ. The cluster linking Kaesong (with Haeju) and the Seoul metropolitan area is planned at the base for the manufacturing industry that will eventually be extended to Pyongyang and the Sinuiju SEZ. The commodities manufactured in the Kaesong SEZ with the support of South Korean competitiveness can be provided to the Sinuiju SEZ for international trade development. This path, Seoul-Kaesong-Pyongyang-Sinuiju, is another developmental option: the Westward Expansion Line. Pyongyang easily connects to Wonsan by highway and railroad, which will support the development of the Eastward and Westward Expansion Lines.

A Fifth SEZ for the Success of Current SEZs

To ensure the success of the four existing SEZs, an additionally designated special zone with a pivotal role is necessary.[15] That would be a Nampo SEZ (or Pyongyang-Nampo SEZ), which is connected with an export-bonded area of South Korea and located in the nexus of light industry, electricity, and logistics. Nampo is now the center of air, land, and sea distribution and infrastructure, with a well developed industrial base. It is located nearby Pyongyang, which has a population of approximately 3 million people. To secure the consumer market and labor force, no other location in North Korea is more attractive than Nampo. A Nampo SEZ, or Pyongyang-Nampo SEZ, would be the pivot of the North Korean SEZs, and it would be a connecting passageway for all regional clusters.

The proposed SEZ would also have the advantage of attracting Chinese investment. Generally, 8 percent of customs tariffs are imposed on Chinese products when they are imported into South Korea; however, when Chinese firms export products manufactured in Nampo to South Korea, customs tariffs would be exempted, according to the South-North Entrance Code. A Nampo SEZ, or Pyongyang-Nampo SEZ would have the additional advantage of assuaging the country-of-origin effect among South Korean consumers, who have certain repulsions to Chinese goods. If Kaesong is a manufacturing complex that targets the Korean consumer market, Pyongyang would be the optimal place as a bridgehead for the North Korean consumer market and overseas export market.

In order to accelerate the designation process of a fifth SEZ, there is greater need to connect the Kaesong SEZ with the South Korean market. If the Kaesong SEZ is expanded, Kaepoong, which is located on the southwest side of Kaesong, would be influential because of its spare space. Kaepoong belongs to North Korea, but it is close to the South Korean territory of Kanghwa Island. If a suspension bridge is constructed between Kaepoong and Kanghwa Island, the distance between the Kaesong SEZ and Incheon Airport, not to mention Gimpo Airport, would take only about 30 minutes by truck. Competitiveness would be enhanced when the Kaesong SEZ and Nampo-Pyongyang complex are connected with the South Korean market and overseas export market. This way, North Korea will be able to complete a base of logistics, tourism, and export near the border. A center of transit distribution, border trade, and tourism will be the result if Kaesong and Kaepoong are connected with South Korea, Sinuiju and Hweryong with China, Rajin-Sunbong with Russia, and Pyongyang in the middle.

Tailoring Strategies for North Korean SEZs

In the short term, the Kaesong SEZ needs to be developed as a South Korean manufacturing-centered SEZ, while in the long term, it must be developed as a production base for multinational enterprises (MNEs) seeking a path into the Northeast Asian market. In the early stages, it is important to push ahead with the first step of development by utilizing South Korean companies (especially small and medium-sized companies) to exploit the advantage of short distance to the South Korean market. The Kaesong SEZ has the benefit of convenient conditions for physical distribution, because it is located near Seoul. It is important to find a development strategy that makes the best use of proximity, while avoiding the problems of limited space in an overcrowded metropolitan area. Furthermore, it is important to make the Kaesong SEZ part of the growth triangle that includes Seoul and Incheon in South Korea. In this triangle, Seoul can take the role of banking and services; Incheon can take the role of physical distribution and trade; and Kaesong can take the role of manufacturing commodities. In the long term, the Kaesong SEZ could play an important role in linking the economic cooperation belt in the Yellow Sea rim. The Kaesong SEZ would link the metropolitan area— including Incheon to Pyongyang and Nampo—as well as link the east coast of China and west coast of the Korean peninsula.

During each development stage, the strategically targeted industry will vary. The industries that can best maximize low-cost North Korean labor should be targeted in the startup stage. Industries appropriate for this stage include labor-intensive light industry that does not require skilled labor, such as bags, clothing, footwear, personal accessories, textiles, and toy industries. In the next stage, industries that need basic-skilled workers, such as assembly, automobiles, electronics, electronic accessories, and machine industries can be targeted. The best strategy is to initially develop partial processing plants or to manufacture simple commodities and then move on to large-scale manufacturing factories and assembly plants. The South Korean government has proposed recommended projects for each developmental stage. The first stage reflects labor-intensive light industries. Technology-intensive industries such as electronics, electricity, and machinery are designated for the second stage, and high-tech industries such as IT and bio are slated for the third stage. Almost all industry categories, except for heavy and chemical industries, are included in this project.

The Mt. Kumgang SEZ is a service-centered zone in which the focus is on tourism. Mt. Kumgang and attractive natural resources nearby present added value. As an institutional investor, Hyundai Asan Corporation has been generating profits by constructing golf clubs, hotels, hot spring facilities, and resorts among other projects, corresponding to the first three business models. Hyundai Asan Corporation is currently planning to establish a light industry complex, ocean museum, sports facilities, and theme park.

The Mt. Kumgang SEZ also provides business opportunities for the agricultural industry, a primary industry. There is an agricultural complex in Onjeongri, which is near Mt. Kumgang. Organic vegetables cultivated in the complex are sold to tourists or in nearby South Korean areas. In contrast to the Kaesong SEZ, the top and middle management staff of the Mt. Kumgang agricultural complex are all North Korean. Besides agriculture, processing plants for marine products and investment in marine product harvesting also represent attractive business opportunities. The substantial business range of the Mt. Kumgang tourism zone includes Wonsan, which is a city where marine product processing and light industries were developed before the U.S.-Soviet division of the Korean peninsula in 1945.

Unlike the Kaesong SEZ, the Mt. Kumgang SEZ is not a specialized location for manufacturing. Therefore, it would be difficult to attract manufacturing investment there. Nevertheless, industries utilizing low-cost labor and marine resources may likely succeed. From a managerial perspective, the Mt. Kumgang SEZ is more flexible than the Kaesong SEZ. The business model of the Kaesong SEZ depends on North Korean labor. On the other hand, the Mt. Kumgang SEZ has a structure that values middle management creativeness.[16]

A primary characteristic of the Sinuiju SEZ is that of internationalization. While the Kaesong SEZ and Mt. Kumgang SEZ are designed to achieve North Korean industrial capability via joint ownership of an industrial base with South Korean industry, the Sinuiju SEZ can be utilized as a primary channel for entering the international market. Physical distribution, high value-added processing, and trade must all be points of focus. A Shanghai-style synthetic SEZ could be considered for Sinuiju, although this would have to be a later strategy. First, North Korean industrial capability must be thoroughly developed. The Sinuiju SEZ could develop its full capacity as a channel to the international market. Sinuiju is only 1 km from the Chinese city of Dandung. In many ways, however, the two cities are totally different. While Dandung is developing rapidly, Sinuiju proceeds slowly. A primary reason is that physical distribution has been a one-way street: from Dandung to Sinuiju. If physical distribution is more reciprocal, Sinuiju can be developed faster. This particular change may lead to greater competitiveness in North Korean industry.

As for the Rajin-Sunbong SEZ, it shares many similarities with the Sinuiju SEZ. Both are located on the frontier, far from the center of North Korea, and are connected to Russia and China by railroad. Moreover, both regions have been providing a non-visa system for foreigners. The similarities imply that the Rajin-Sunbong SEZ is able to develop favorable industries such as export processing, international trade, transportation, and tourism. Distribution industries and trade will find the Rajin-Sunbong SEZ more favorable, though. Whereas the Rajin-Sunbong region possesses three port facilities (Rajin, Sunbong, and Chungjin port), Sinuiju uses the nearby Chinese port of Dandung because there is no existing North Korean port in the area. Thus, the Rajin-Sunbong SEZ may be able to use the said advantages to successfully promote its programs.

North Korea may also begin to acquire competitiveness through the Kaesong SEZ. When the competitiveness of South Korean industry migrates to Sinuiju through Kaesong and Pyongyang, mutual distribution between Sinuiju and Dandung will be realized. Dandung can be developed from the presence of the North Korean market, and Sinuiju can be developed with the help of South Korean competitiveness.

It is difficult to induce foreign investment into the Rajin-Sunbong SEZ, because its development has been slow and it has suffered from a negative image. Recently, however, Russia and China have expressed interest in this region. If Russia and China increase their investment into the Rajin-Sunbong SEZ, its role as a base for physical distribution will be expanded. After the establishment of a connecting railroad, this SEZ can also be the base for entering the maritime provinces of Siberia and the northeastern provinces of China.

It is also important to develop industry in the fields of chemistry, cement, and steel, which meet the characteristics and needs of the region. Crucial to inducing foreign investment is the need to harness human resources and expand the physical distribution network. The next step will have to be the establishment of a policy to develop processing and manufacturing commodities for trade and set up region-appropriate industries. The most important step to improve the competitiveness of the Rajin-Sunbong SEZ will be the connection of a railroad (Seoul to Wonsan) that creates a link with the South Korean physical distribution network. Table 1 illustrates main features of the four North Korean SEZs.

Challenges of Developing Cooperative SEZs

A major obstacle to the promotion of the South-North Cooperative SEZ is the existence of political risks. As explained earlier, the cooperative SEZ strategy is clearly a win-win strategy (at least from the economic perspective). Nonetheless, because of the Korean War, which is not officially over, there is continuing military tension between the two Koreas, and the two cooperative SEZs near the demilitarized zone (DMZ) are constantly subject to rhetoric calling for their suspension or abolishment. Unfortunately, the Mt. Kumgang SEZ has been closed since the July 11, 2008, after the shooting death of a South Korean tourist in a prohibited zone. By contrast, despite several crises, the Kaesong SEZ has never been suspended. Even when the North conducted two underground nuclear tests on October 9, 2006, and May 25, 2009, the two Korean governments did not suspend operations at Kaesong. The SEZ also continued operating during naval incidents in the Yellow Sea, such as the sinking of the South Korean patrol boat *Cheonan* on March 26, 2010, and the North Korean shelling of the South Korean island of Yeonpyeong on November 23, 2010.

Table 1. Features and Situations of North Korean SEZs

Section	Kaesong SEZ	Mt. Kumgang SEZ	Rajin-Sunbong SEZ	Sinuiju SEZ
Area and Size (sq. km.)	• Kaesong city • 66.1	• Mt. Kumgang (to be extended to Wonsan) • 100	• Rajin city and Sunbong city • 746	• Sinuiji city • 132
Location	• Southern area bordering South Korea	• Southeastern area bordering South Korea	• North tip of North Korea bordering China and Russia	• Northwestern area bordering China
Immigration	• Non-visa entrance system but invitation letter required	• Same as Kaesong SEZ	• Same as Kaesong SEZ	• Non-visa entrance system
Corporate income tax	• 10%–14% • Full exemption for 5 years in the manufacturing industry; up to 50% reduction in subsequent 3 years	• Exemption on generated profits	• 14% • Full exemption for 3 years in the manufacturing industry; up to 50% reduction in subsequent 2 years	• Similar to Rajin-Sunbong
Tariff	• Tariff exemption between the two Koreas	• Same as Kaesong SEZ	• Tariff exemption in the processing of export-oriented products	• Similar to Rajin-Sunbong
Legal status	• Controlled by Kaesong Industrial District Management Committee	• Controlled under Mt. Kumgang International Tourism Corporation (North Korea) and Hyundai Asan Corporation	• Controlled by Rajin-Sunbong City People's Committee	• Self-controlled in terms of legislation, administration, and the judicial system • Self-regulation and guaranteed independence

Section	Kaesong SEZ	Mt. Kumgang SEZ	Rajin-Sunbong SEZ	Sinuiju SEZ
Harbor	• Nampo port • Incheon port (South Korea)	• Wonsan and Kosong ports • Sokcho port (South Korea	• Rajin, Sunbong, and Cungjin ports	• No international harbor (using Chinese Dandung port)
Industry	• Light industry-oriented (cosmetics, footwear, paper, textiles, etc.)	• Tourism, agriculture, and marine product processing	• Heavy industry-oriented (chemicals, steel, shipbuilding, etc.)	• Light industry-oriented (cosmetics, footwear, paper, textiles, etc.)
Currency	• USD	• Same as Kaesong SEZ	• North Korean won (foreign currency use or circulation not permitted	• USD, Chinese yuan, and others
Principal investors	• South Korean small- and medium-sized enterprises • Developers: Hyundai Asan Corporation; Korea Land and Housing Corporation	• Hyundai Asan Corporation; Korea National Tourism Organization	• Chinese investors	• Chinese, Japanese, and Russian investors

Other barriers to the development of the cooperative SEZs have been economic sanctions against North Korea by the United States and United Nations. North Korea was added to the U.S. State Department list of state sponsors of terrorism in January 1988, two months after the bombing of a South Korean commercial airliner. As Washington is required by law to veto membership and financial assistance to states supporting terrorism, North Korea has been unable to seek assistance from the International Monetary Fund or the World Bank, among other organizations.[17] In addition, North Korea has been affected by the Trading with the Enemy Act of the U.S., which imposes restrictions on foreign exchange transactions. These restrictions were removed by President Bush and the U.S. Congress in October 2008, the same month North Korea was delisted from the terror sponsor list, but approximately forty U.S.-supported economic sanctions remain. For example, since 1974, the United States has applied higher official duty rates (see Column 2 of Table 1) on North Korean products than on products from countries under the U.S. normal trade relations (NTR) duty rate. The duty rates in Column 2 are at least two to ten times higher than the NTR duty rate. This creates a rules-of-origin issue for Kaesong. Products "made in Kaesong" or "made in DPRK" currently do not have competitive prices in comparison with similar products from other developing economies, such as China, India, and Vietnam. Even if a product were not directly restricted, it would be difficult to be exported to markets other than the South Korean market.

In Annex 22-B of the Korea-U.S. Free Trade Agreement (also known as KORUS FTA), which is still in effect, country of origin designation of Kaesong SEZ-produced goods can be marked as "made in South Korea." Still, there are many procedures to follow before goods from the Kaesong SEZ can be marked accordingly. Terms specifying approval conditions by the Committee on Outward Processing Zones (OPZ) can be extremely strict,[18] and even if something is approved by the OPZ, it has to pass through the U.S. Congress.[19]

North Korean Survival Strategy and Korean Unification

North Korea implemented economic reform measures on July 1, 2002, but they were insufficient to activate its market. Although North Korea reinforced market mechanisms, there was a dearth of consumers with adequate purchasing power for active transactions.[20] The unexpected deficiency in the consumer market contracted foreign investment and caused North Korea to become hesitant in instituting additional economic reform measures. Overall, despite economic changes, an inactivated market hindered North Korea in accumulating investment capital. This experience demonstrated to the North Korean government the importance of securing outside help for long-term economic projects. Following most transitional economies (e.g., China, Eastern Europe, and Russia), North Korea decided to secure foreign capital. North Korea announced the establishment of three additional SEZs to induce foreign direct investment. The Sinuiju SEZ was established to induce Chinese capital, and the Kaesong and Mt. Kumgang SEZs were established to induce South Korean capital. The North Korean government believes that these open SEZs will facilitate the inflow of foreign capital, thereby activating its markets. Furthermore, Pyongyang believes the inflow of capital, technology, and advanced human resource programs from foreign companies will develop its industries.

The gross national income (GNI) of North Korea is less than 3 percent of the South Korean GNI, and its gross domestic product (GDP) is less than 6 percent of the South Korean GDP.[21] The dollar value of the South Korean annual GDP expansion equals the entire North Korean economy. Experts and institutions have estimated the cost of eventual Korean unification to be between $50 billion and $1.7 trillion.[22] The unification of the two Koreas may lead to great confusion throughout the peninsula without economic and political preparation. Consequently, the cooperative SEZs are more than a simple combination of production factors (i.e., North Korean labor plus South Korean capital) from the two Koreas.

The success of North Korean SEZs would lower future unification costs. If the two Koreas were to reunite, production factors of both parties would move quickly toward the most efficient production system. The longer it takes to overcome inefficiency and confusion arising from the different economic systems, the higher unification costs will be. Because of the divergences in the economic structures of the two Koreas, economic principals (e.g., firms and managers) may require more time and investment to identify a stable and profitable business model. The way to reduce unification costs is to narrow the gap between the economic systems. A proven business model would be beneficial in terms of reducing the amount of time required to integrate the systems. Such a model may be found in the cooperative SEZs, that is, the Kaesong SEZ and the Mt. Kumgang SEZ. Both locations offer unique opportunities for trial runs testing the integration of the two economic systems ahead of unification. The business models derived from these cooperative efforts are expected to substantially reduce the costs of eventual unification.

U.S. support for economic development in North Korea would also help advance the process of gradual economic integration of North Korea and South Korea, with the potential for significant long-term economic benefits to Koreans on both sides of the DMZ.[23] More interaction between the United States and North Korea would contribute positively to whatever path the two Koreas find for reconciliation. Cooperation in economic development should not be simply viewed as a "carrot" to reward North Korea for denuclearization. Rather, cooperation is a powerful mechanism to change the internal and external behavior of North Korea.[24] Economic change has the potential to induce and reinforce a peaceful transition in North Korea, from a dysfunctional country to one that can better provide for its people's welfare and engage with other countries in a non-hostile manner.[25]

Concluding Remarks

Since 2001, North Korea has been showing signs of positive change in all economic activities through the adoption of the policy of "new thinking" and the market principle of "guarantee of material gain." These developments have occurred in concert with the gradual extension of North Korean reform and openness. In July 2002, North Korea undertook economic reform, which many feared would lead to a sharp increase of prices and wages, an incentive wage system, devaluation of the North Korean won (currency), and a self-supporting system.[26] In September 2002, the North Korean government designated Sinuiju as a special administrative region and stipulated Mt. Kumgang as a SEZ. Late that year, the North Korean Supreme People's Conference Standing Committee adopted the Kaesong Industrial District Law and designated Kaesong an SEZ.

The primary purpose of the new SEZs in North Korea has been to build the domestic economy through induction of foreign capital, improvements in foreign exchange, broader employment, and reinforcement of international economic linkages. Related goals include boosting production and supply to stabilize the success of economic reform and reinvigorating the Rajin-Sunbong SEZ, which was established in 1991. Today, North Korean SEZs include the Rajin-Sunbong SEZ, the Sinuiju SEZ, the Mt. Kumgang SEZ, and the Kaesong SEZ. Although the Rajin-Sunbong SEZ has been regarded as a failure and the Sinuiju SEZ is developing more slowly than expected, the Kaesong SEZ and the Mt. Kumgang SEZ have been making constructive progress. There are two main reasons for the disparity among the four SEZs: Rajin-Sunbong and Sinuiju could not attract serious potential investors, and there was no attractive local market potential to entice MNEs.

The deficiencies in North Korean investment and market potential are stark in contrast with the highly successful Chinese Shenzhen SEZ. To encourage serious investment, the North Korean government must focus on attracting South Korean companies with substantial investment incentives. In China, the government encouraged SEZ activities, with preferential policies for Chinese residents abroad, such as those in Hong Kong and Taiwan. In 1981, the Chinese government abolished tariffs on transactions with Taiwan, regarding business with the country as inter-province trade. In 1983, Beijing promulgated an SEZ Investment Special Treatment Management for Taiwan Compatriots policy and, in 1988, prescribed a Taiwan Compatriot Investment Encouragement Regulation policy to attract nationwide Taiwanese investment.

Preferential policy toward Taiwanese investment contains four principal points: First, the denationalization of Taiwanese investing companies; second, the liberalization of regulations to acquire Chinese company shares, bonds, and land use; third, taxation preferences; and fourth, the indefinite maintenance of invested companies. Such measures allowed Chinese SEZs to attract capital from Chinese residents in Hong Kong and Macao. This capital was a critical driving force for SEZ development. In the case of Shenzhen, a majority of the investment came from Chinese residents in Hong Kong, Macao, and Taiwan.[27]

By contrast, in North Korea, there is little provision in the existing investment laws for preferential treatment toward South Korean companies. For the first time, North Korea approved South Korean company investment in the Kaesong Industrial district through the Kaesong Industrial District Law in October 2002. There is, however, a marked difference from the Chinese approach, which attracts investment from expatriate Chinese in Taiwan, Hong Kong, and other countries by providing them with preferential services.

Clearly, the North Korean government should focus on transferring South Korean market competitiveness to North Korean SEZs. China and North Korea are different in their domestic market potential. MNEs have generally focused on utilizing abundant cheap labor in developing countries such as China, Vietnam, and others throughout Southeast Asia. Eventually, though, these MNEs become interested in selling their products in local markets. In the long term, the foreign capital introduced into Chinese SEZs will develop an interest in the Chinese market because of its population of 13 billion. In the case of North Korea, a smaller population, less developed economy, and weak domestic market potential would seem to limit purchasing power. Accordingly, North Korean SEZs should adopt a gradual strategy that fully utilizes South Korean market demand and competitiveness.

Clearly, success for North Korean SEZs lies in adopting a sequential approach, rather than adopting a simultaneous approach. Furthermore, each SEZ should have distinct strategies with regard to their function and targeting of industry: manufacturing industry in the Kaesong SEZ, service (tourism) and primary industry in the Mt. Kumgang SEZ, physical distribution and trade for the Rajin-Sunbong SEZ, and creating an international business complex for the Sinuiju SEZ.

South Korean competitive power will be crucial in linking the Kaesong SEZ and Pyongyang to the Sinuiju SEZ. The strategy for attracting foreign investment to the SEZs is to emphasize the economy of North Korean labor forces and attractive South Korean market demand. Competitiveness in labor forces will appeal to MNEs seeking production efficiency. The Seoul metropolitan area adjacent to the Kaesong SEZ will also be an attractive foreign direct investment climate for MNEs seeking potential markets.

The cooperative SEZs have direct and indirect effects on the prospect of Korean unification. The two cooperative SEZs, the Kaesong and Mt. Kumgang SEZs, are unique so far because they were established by two countries that are technically at war and because the two countries have vastly different economic systems. The cooperative SEZs are areas in which the two divergent economic systems (i.e., planned economy versus free market economy) can meet. If a business model were to succeed in these SEZs, it could be applied to the entire Korean peninsula after eventual unification. There is a substantial difference between the national income and development levels of the two Koreas. The successful development of North Korean SEZs and the cooperative SEZs should help enhance the national income and economic development of North Korea. Therefore, the success of the cooperative SEZs would help lower unification costs significantly.

The countries that would benefit most from the success of the cooperative SEZs are the two Koreas, but other countries in the region can benefit as well. The reason is because the SEZs not only promote détente on the Korean peninsula, but also bring peace to Northeast Asia. Thomas Friedman's book *The World Is Flat* notes that no two countries with McDonald's restaurants have ever gone to war.[28] Friedman has made a similar point about states with the Dell global sourcing system. The logic is that entrepreneurs worried about political instability hurting their business will try to convince politicians and government functionaries to reduce the risk of conflict. That is how economic cooperation between the two Koreas should operate in order for it to work as leverage aimed at unification.

Notes

1. "North Korea Gives Up on Sinuiju Project," *Korea Times*, November 7, 2002.
2. Harpal Sandhu, "A Doomed Reform: North Korea First with the Free Market," *Harvard International Review* 25, no. 1 (Spring 2003): 36–39.
3. "North Korea Ramps Up Threats Over Mt. Kumgang Tours," *Choson Ilbo*, March 19, 2010.
4. The Mt. Kumgang SEZ has been closed since the unfortunate death of a South Korean tourist who was shot by a North Korean soldier after she entered a prohibited area on July 11, 2008. The South Korean government immediately suspended the Mt. Kumgang SEZ, and the two Koreas are negotiating its reopening.
5. "Reopening of the Mt. Kumgang SEZ, Ties with the Cheonan Incident," *Choson Ilbo*, October 5, 2010.
6. Ministry of Unification, *Statistics Data (Kaesong Industrial Complex Project)*, http://www.unikorea.go.kr/CmsWeb/viewPage.req?idx=PG0000000240 (accessed November 28, 2010).
7. Ministry of Unification, *Overview of Exchange and Cooperation for January 2010* (Seoul: Ministry of Unification, 2010).

8. "Wages of the Kaesong Industrial Complex, 100 Times More Than the Ordinary Amount of Wage for North Korean Workers at the Most," *Yonhap News*, October 22, 2010.

9. Kwan Yiu Wong and David K. Y. Chu, "Export Processing Zones and Special Economic Zones as Locomotives of Export-led Economic Growth," in *Modernization in China*, eds. Kwan Yiu Wong and David K. Y. Chu (Oxford: Oxford University Press, 1985).

10. Xie Wei, "Acquisition of Technological Capability Through Special Economic Zones (SEZs): The Case of Shienzhen SEZ," *Industry and Innovation* 7, no. 2 (2000): 199–221.

11. *Dictionary of Economics* (Pyongyang: Social Science), 1985, p. 116.

12. Ibid., p. 176.

13. Sandhu, 2003.

14. Bin Xue Sang, "Pudong: Another Special Economic Zone in China? An Analysis of the Special Regulations and Policy for Shanghai's Pudong New Area," *Northwestern Journal of International Law and Business* 14, no. 1 (1993): 130–160.

15. Sung-Hoon Lim, *Locate in the DPRK, Buy in the DPRK* (Seoul: Hanol, 2008).

16. Sung-Hoon Lim, "Seven Business Models for North Korea's Special Economic Zones," *North Korean Review* 6, no. 2 (2010): 86–99.

17. Kaitlin Bonenberger, "Kaesong Industrial Complex Inter-Korea Test Bed Rests on Political, Not Economic," *SERI Quarterly* (July 2008): 102–107.

18. Annex 22-B of the proposed FTA, however, provides for a Committee on Outward Processing Zones to be formed. This committee is to meet annually to consider geographical areas that may be designated as outward processing zones and whose products can qualify as goods originating in South Korea. The committee also establishes criteria to be met to include, but not to be limited to, "progress toward denuclearization of the Korean Peninsula; the impact of the outward processing zones on intra–Korean relations; and the environmental standards, labor standards and practices, wage practices and business and management practices prevailing in the outward processing zone with due reference to the situation prevailing elsewhere in the local economy and the relevant international norms." Dick K. Nanto and Mark E. Manyin, *CSR Report for Congress, The Kaesong North-South Korean Industrial Complex*, Congressional Research Service, February 14, 2008.

19. "Obstacle to the Inter-Korean Economic Cooperation: The Korea-U.S. FTA," *PRESSian*, July 4, 2007, http://www.pressian.com/article/article.asp?article_num=6007 1004125843&Section= (accessed November 28, 2010).

20. Thomas F. Cargill and Elliott Parker, "Economic and Financial Reform: Alternatives for North Korea," *North Korean Review* 1, no. 1 (Fall 2005): 5–21.

21. Bank of Korea, *Estimations on North Korea's Economy Growth Rate 2006* (Seoul: Bank of Korea, 2007).

22. Peter M. Beck, "Contemplating Korean Reunification: The North Could Collapse More Quickly Than We Think," *The Wall Street Journal*, January 5, 2010.

23. Goohoon Kwon, "A United Korea? Reassessing North Korea Risks (Part 1)," *Global Economics Paper* 188, Goldman Sachs Global Economics, Commodities and Strategy Research, September 21, 2009.

24. *North Korea Inside Out: The Case for Economic Engagement*, Asia Society Center on U.S.-China Relations and the University of California Institute on Global Conflict and Cooperation, October 2009.

25. Ibid., p. 11.

26. Yukie Yoshikawa, "The Prospect of Economic Reform in North Korea," *The DPRK Briefing Book*, The Nautilus Institute, March 2004; Marcus Noland, "Life in North Korea," *Congressional Testimony*, Peterson Institute for International Economics, June 5, 2003.

27. *Shenzhen Statistics Yearbook* (Shenzhen, China Statistics, 2001).

28. Thomas L. Friedman, *The World Is Flat* (New York: Farrar, Straus and Giroux, 2005).

CHAPTER 10

Violence from Within: North Korea's Place in East Asian Community Debates

Mikyoung Kim

Abstract

Debates regarding the East Asian Community project the region as one integral unit amid rapid shifts in the socio-political and economic landscapes. The tension between the old order and emerging hierarchy defines the promises and challenges of the community debates where North Korea plays a crucial role despite being a largely ignored member of the community. This chapter analyzes North Korea's place in the East Asian community by examining the regional governments' reactions to the sinking of a South Korean warship, the *Cheonan*. These responses to the *Cheonan* incident demonstrate two dynamics: One is that domestic political needs supersede normative community rhetoric. Ruling elites prioritize domestic governance before the cultivation of communal spirit. Secondly the manageability of the North Korean regime will determine the next regional hegemon. North Korea exerts substantial influence on the competition among the big regional players.

Introduction

The South Korean corvette of the 2nd fleet, PCC-722 *Cheonan*, sank while conducting a mission in the vicinity of Northern Limit Line (NLL) in March 2010. The South Korean government, aided by experts from the United States, Australia, the United Kingdom, Canada, and Sweden, concluded that a North Korea midget submarine fired a 500-pound torpedo at the ship on March 26, 2010, killing forty-six seamen.

The Northeast Asian region has been rattled over the sinking of the

South Korean warship. The responses of the governments in the region have ranged widely from blatant accusations to cautious ambivalence. The wide spectrum of reactions to the alleged North Korean belligerence shed an interesting light on the on-going East Asian Community debates. "Community" being a different "association" often assumes shared cultural ethos among members who try to defend and protect the common interests and values. Then how can the East Asian Community sustain itself with the existence of North Korea, the pariah and perennial underdog of the region? It is not surprising that the debates over community in East Asia have been largely oblivious to the regime of Kim Jong-il.[1] The community discourse with the assumptions of shared values and binding goals is yet to address the existence of threat and danger within. This chapter argues that the North Korean regime simultaneously consolidates and divides the community, as seen in the aftermath of the *Cheonan* incident. I conclude by presenting the need for the inclusion of North Korea in the debates for the sake of regional cohesiveness and sustainability.

While Japan's stance vis-à-vis China dictates the shifting regional landscape, the two Koreas maintain their status quo as medium powers. The DPRK (Democratic People's Republic of Korea) continues to insist on bilateral dialogue with Washington over its nuclear programs, while simultaneously maintaining a close trading relationship with Beijing. Seoul is trying to tread precarious waters among the American unipolar hegemon, the traditional Japanese front runner in East Asia, the Chinese impressive reemergence, and the North Korean ideological adversary and potential partnership with primordial linkage.

Efforts to assess and situate North Korea in East Asian Community debates entail ideational variables formed through repeated interactions with reference groups.[2] Identity of a state, the manifestation of cognitive framework, influences national interests, preferences, and foreign policy behaviors. The "politics of labeling and framing" compounded with strategic calculations determine North Korea's place in the region.[3] As a state in the international system understands other states' perceptions, it reacts accordingly. North Korea is no exception to this.[4]

This chapter limits its scope to Japanese, North Korean, and South Korean governments' circumstances in regards to the *Cheonan* incident. This focus, however, does not imply that the three countries constitute the core members of the regional community. They are instead the biggest stakeholders when it comes to regional security. Japan under the Peace Constitution is very alert to potential threats. The probable motivations behind North Korea's provocation deserve a close examination. The reactions of South Korea, the victim, are also instructive in understanding its security dilemmas.

The *Cheonan* incident is an instructive empirical case testing the validity of norm-based community discourse. The violence within community, an inevitably disruptive influence, consolidates domestic interests over ideational construction of an international community. Violence deepens division of pre-existing rivalry by reopening the old wounds and reviving competitive modus operandi. It, as a consequence, grants bigger power to a party which can exert influence over the perpetrator shifting regional order. The *Cheonan* incident, therefore, has reversed the romanticized prospects of community discourse to the Cold War–like competitive modality. The incident has reminded the community that realpolitik supersedes normative rhetoric. Before moving on the incident's implications for the East Asian community, the existing debates on East Asia and community will be revisited respectively.

Definitions of East Asia and Community

What Is East Asia?

The unit of "East Asia" poses conceptual problems as there are many different definitions of the region. In geographical terms, the area would envelope China, Japan, the Korean peninsula, Mongolia, Taiwan, and parts of eastern Russia. Political currents, however, blur the line among geography, national boundary and identity. Although much of Russia resides in Northeast Asia, most Asians regard Russia as European. Mongolia shares substantial ethnic and racial similarities with Asia, but its relations with China are distant while its alliance with Russia is close, going back to the 1924 proclamation of the Mongolian People's Republic. And finally Taiwan's sovereign identity is in flux between indigenous roots and China.[5] Geography compounded with complicated political and historical trajectories makes the clear definition of East Asia a challenge.[6]

Scholars like Tsuneo Akaha see East Asia largely as a geographical entity. His definition of the region includes Mongolia and Russia along with the three core states (i.e., South Korea, Japan and China), the United States, Taiwan, and Hong Kong. North Korea is conspicuously absent in Akaha's typology despite geographical proximity. Akaha's typology is derived from what the region lacks (e.g., regional consciousness, regional institutions, deep economic integration, political community, effective leadership, and vibrant transnational actors). On the same token, he groups the unit by what it shares (e.g., national rivalries, unresolved historical animosities, negative mutual images, political and ideological conflicts, divided states, incompatible economic systems, crumbling economies, and cultural divide).[7] "Imagined community" as propositioned by Anderson has no relevance for Akaha because a geographically defined East Asia Community has more divisive elements than binding forces within it.[8]

South Korea, North Korea and Japan have been described as neighbors stuck with each other through interdependence, hierarchy, identification and rivalry. The three states are the main driving force of East Asian regionalism,[9] with Japan and, to a lesser extent, two Koreas, "at its financial, capital, techno-industrial centre and China at its market and low cost production centre."[10] The United States maintains its interests in the region as a crucial economic and military player.[11]

North Korea is a part of Northeast Asia, but its isolation makes a systemic study of the nation much more difficult than other societies. North Korea nevertheless is an East Asian nation sharing Confucian cultural tradition, geographical proximity, linguistic affinity, and racial similarity with other states. Along with entangled historical memories, the DPRK's dynastic socialist dictatorship makes regional cohesion challenging. The *Cheonan* incident's circumstances and post-hoc trajectory were the telling case in point. How do the similarities and differences shape the community discourse?

What Is Community?

Similarly to "East Asia," the concept of "community" is used with great fluidity. Toennies (1988), for instance, juxtaposed affection-based Gemeinschaft and contract-based Gesellschaft in his typological taxonomy. Gemeinschaft is closer to community, whereas Gesellschaft is more like society.[12] Making a clear distinction between the two is not simple given the complex dynamics within East Asia. The region entails both aspects of community and society where traditional security concerns such as nuclear threats intersect with rising attention to nontraditional security concerns such as human rights as an example.

Poplin (1979), on the other hand, emphasizes moral and psychological aspects for communitarian consciousness. In order for a group to constitute a community, he argues, the members should share a consensus that they belong to a meaningful group. They also should pursue common goals and identify with other members. Shared destiny and camaraderie are supposed to be internalized for a community to sustain itself. Poplin describes a community by the concepts of homogeneity, interdependence, shared responsibility, and common goals.[13] This position is contrary to Akaha's conceptualization based on contention, competition and division. These differences make Poplin's community a normative entity, whereas Akaha's an empirical unit.

We would need to discern different types of communities per its origin, goal, and qualifications. Various types of communities, political-security, economic-institutional, and cultural-ideational, can exist. "East Asian Community," therefore, should be approached as an encompassing and fluid concept gearing towards convivial co-existence and collective identification being devoid of security threats. Caveat in this normative statement comes from many cases of inter- and intra-community violence.[14] Then what are the functions of violence committed within the community?

Violence Within the "Community": The Cheonan Incident

The Natural Suspect

The dust on the sunken ROK Navy warship, *Cheonan*, has far from settled. The more we hear about the accident, the more confused we become. The ROK (Republic of Korea) government's May 20 report on the results of the joint investigation team failed to create a consensus on the circumstances of the accident. Instead it further widened ideological divides.[15] Since the Seoul government has filed a lawsuit against the Korean Broadcasting System for having shown a U.S. helicopter carrying a certain object near the "third" spot where Warrant Officer Joon-ho Han died, the major South Korean news media have projected the North Korean belligerence in a unanimous voice. The government has also filed more than a dozen lawsuits, accusing citizens who publicly raised suspicions of the report, of libel and National Security Law violations.[16]

The unquestioned acceptance of the report by the major media in this monotone chorus[17] is a reflection of widespread disappointment among ordinary citizens who believe that the North Korean leadership has not changed after a decade of engagement. The talks of hereditary succession add more to discredit the Kim Jong-il regime as a responsible member of the community. Other intermittent factors also contributed to the shifting perceptions from charged denouncement of the DPRK to confusion.[18] The factors include North Korea's adamant and persistent denial, China and Russia's skepticism, the ROK government's sequencing of evidence presentation, UN Security Council's ambivalent statement,[19] and alternative scenarios in circulation.

The current Japanese government is on a similar wavelength with the Lee Myung-bak administration in denouncing the DPRK, the natural suspect. North Korean threats are an effective means to sustain domestic power grip and instill fear among the domestic populace. Having an external danger is helpful for internal cohesion. The general sentiment can be described in words of suspicion, disillusion, and frustration towards the Pyongyang regime. The popular media both in Japan and South Korea reflect this widespread perception, while contributing to the creation and perpetuation of negative perceptions towards the de-stabilizer. Such popular perceptions are, in part, an outcome of decade-long elites' efforts to frame the country as the biggest source of regional instability. North Korea can be convenient for the Tokyo government. The reactions to this accident can be summarized as 'if not North Korea, who else?' North Korea is the natural suspect regardless of its persistent denials. One hundred thousand Pyongyang citizens, for example, protested against the accusations on May 30.

Rashomon-like

The reactions of "who else?" gets us nowhere in reconstructing what actually happened to the ship. When a hypothetical attack occurs, common sense makes us assume hostile intentions, and North Korea fits the usual criminal profile. It kidnapped Japanese citizens in the 1960s and 1970s, committed terrorist acts against the South Korean government delegation in Rangoon, Myanmar, in 1983, and tried to hijack the KAL 858 in 1987. Pyongyang's criminal record is long enough to raise suspicion. But when we start pondering without the presumption of intended hostility, the picture becomes fuzzy. An accident scenario has been presented by a Japanese freelance journalist, Mr. Sakai Tanaka, formerly of the Kyodo News, and has been in wide circulation.[20] Tanaka's reconstruction of the incident along with the statement by Mr. Don Gregg, the former U.S. Ambassador to ROK, adds more to the accident speculations. Amid increasing confusion, the *Cheonan* case has become more like Kurosawa Akira's film, *Rashomon*, where the eyes of the beholder narrate what s/he claims to have seen. South Korea, Japan and the U.S. joined by common interests point their fingers to Pyongyang. China and Russia remain skeptical about the ROK government's assessments. China's stance towards the *Cheonan* incident is an outcome of strategic calculations rather than a conviction from careful assessment of scientific evidence. Considering the close coordination among the United States and Japan after September 2010 Senkaku Islands (Diaoyu Islands in Chinese) disputes, Beijing is trying to strengthen Sino-DPRK ties in order to keep it a buffer from the rest of regional players.[21] Russia, a regional player with relatively minor influence, sent an investigative team which reported that a mine, not by a torpedo, was the cause of the explosion. The report contradicts the ROK government's evidence adding more confusion to the incident. North Korea's threats and denials are mostly dismissed by nearby listeners, except for China and Russia. A state believes what it wants to believe in the *Cheonan* incident.[22]

Seoul's Stance

The conservative government is back in power after 10 years of progressive rule. In South Korea the so-called "South-South divide" means that support of North Korea is automatically translated into anti–U.S. attitudes, and vice versa. Progressives believe in helping Pyongyang escape from international isolation in order to build peace on the Korean peninsula. That was one of the primary motivations behind the previous administrations' engagement policies. Conservatives, on the other hand, prioritize domestic welfare and relations with allies before improving inter–Korea relations. They believe that Pyongyang will never abandon its ambition for Communist unification, and aid from the South will keep the regime alive rather than reforming it.

The current ROK administration values its ties with Washington more than those with Pyongyang. The very existence of the DPRK makes the U.S.-ROK alliance more cohesive. The close coordination with the United States is important to protect the ROK from the DPRK's provocations, according to many in the Lee Myung-bak government. In due process, the progressive's romanticization of their brethren in the North has been replaced by national security pragmatism, a drastic departure from the previous administrations. Seoul's security dilemma originates from its dependence on the United States under the U.S.-ROK security treaty of 1953.

The George W. Bush administration's DPRK orientation and the current Obama administration's "nuclear free world" policy have made the Lee Myung-bak government's stance towards the Kim Jong-il regime more precarious. The G. W. Bush government shunned working directly with the Kim Jong-il regime out of moral contempt and its preoccupation with anti-terrorism. The resulting multilateral format of the Six Party Talks has failed to produce any tangible results. The Obama administration's NPT policy inevitably implicates North Korea's nuclear programs. The cacophonous leadership pairings (engaging Clinton and conservative Kim Young Sam, and conservative G.W. Bush and engaging Kim Dae Jung/Roh Mu Hyun administrations) for the past decade have been detrimental to regional security coordination. In the meantime, the DPRK's nuclear program grew, and the cacophony between Washington and Seoul contributed to a chasm in the bilateral alliance.

The *Cheonan* scenario argued by Tanaka, and any other alternative scenarios for that matter, could have been devastating for the current Seoul administration. Tanaka' friendly fire argument between the U.S. and ROK navy during a joint exercise, in particular, could have instigated widespread anti–American sentiment.[23] The massive explosion of anti–Americanism took place after the 2002 traffic accident where a U.S. armored vehicle flattened two middle schools girls to death during an exercise. The United States initially regarded it as a simple traffic "accident" which was not supposed to have any political ramifications. The incident became a major political issue for the ROK presidential elections helping Roh Mu-hyun win on his nationalist and anti–American platform. The current government would not have wished the same history to repeat itself with the rumor implicating the U.S. military. It could have been déjà-vu all over again. The Seoul administration can never go anti–American because it is the trading mark for the progressives vis-à-vis their accommodative posture towards North Korea.

Highlighting circumstantial dubiousness, the June 2, 2010, local government elections were fast-approaching when the ROK government was preparing a fact finding mission on the sinking. And the report of the joint investigation team was released on May 30, right before the election. South Korean elections have a long history of the so-called "Northern wind blowing to the South" just in time for elections. The fear and intimidation by North Korean threats proved to be helpful for the incumbent to garner votes. The close race between the ruling and opposition parties suggests suspicion-stirring timing of events on the part of Lee Myung-bak administration. This chronological sequencing of events is one of the important circumstantial variables in (re-)constructing the *Cheonan* incident.

Tokyo's Stance

The resigned Japanese Prime Minister, Yukio Hatoyama, reiterated his ardent support to South Korea after the *Cheonan* investigation during his Seoul visit on May 29. His successor, Mr. Naoto Kan, is not likely to change his position toward the Pyongyang regime. Prime Minister Kan has made it very clear that his administration will continue the previous regime's policy. The Democratic Party's top leaders have a very similar assessment of the DPRK to their rivals in the Liberal Democratic Party. While admitting the existence of U.S.-Japan secret agreements regarding the introduction of U.S. nuclear warheads into Japanese territory, the Democratic Party government utilized the *Cheonan* incident to create maneuvering room for the future revision of Japan's three non-nuclear principles (no introduction, no production and no usage of nuclear weapons). The Kan administration has made it clear that Japan favors the U.S. nuclear umbrella against the hypothetical possibility of North Korea's nuclear attack, and, therefore, puts the U.S. considerations before the Japanese peoples' anti-nuclear sentiments. Even though the truths about the U.S.-Japan nuclear secret pact was unearthed during the previous Hatoyama administration in November 2009, many believe that the DPJ's motivation was to inflict wounds on the previous LDP governments' moral principle on anti-nuclear pacifism rather than to seriously revisit the behind-the-curtain dealings made in the 1960s and 1970s.[24]

The Tokyo government did not express the keen interests in the *Cheonan* incident until their approach towards U.S. base relocation issues in Okinawa came to a dead-end. Prime Minister Hatoyama initially insisted that an alternative site to the Futenma base in the Okinawa prefecture should be found either abroad (e.g., Guam) or in other parts of Japan (e.g., Kyushu area). When he could only succumb to the high-handed approach by the U.S. government that the issue had been already settled without leaving much room for re-negotiations, Mr. Hatoyama turned the nation's attention to the *Cheonan* incident. It suddenly became a powerful symbol of Pyongyang's looming military threats to Japan. The incident took place at an opportune moment when the Tokyo government could conveniently justify the change in its policy towards the U.S. military bases in Okinawa Prefecture. At this moment, Seoul and Tokyo are hand-in-hand over Pyongyang's culpability for the sunken ship. And this is despite the existence of many other areas of bilateral disagreements including Dokdo/Takeshima disputes.[25] The *Cheonan* incident became timely material for Japan.

Pyongyang's Stance

The Kim Jong-il regime has utterly failed in its governance as manifested by the massive famine pushing the hungry out of their homeland. It is under mounting pressure to tread much in more precarious waters domestically as well as internationally. Just to name a few are Kim Jong-il's failing health, the succession move to his 27-year-old son, a failed economy and increasing isolation in the international community.

Under the George W. Bush administration, North Korea and its leader were the target of contempt, dismissal and verbal attacks. The politics of "naming, labeling and framing" set the two governments significantly back in any pre-existing bilateral progress. Needless to say North Korea's nuclear development program and evidence of its proliferation activities further aggravated U.S.-DPRK relations. The DPRK has a history of deception such as the IAEA's 1992–93 Yongbyon site investigation and its subsequent withdrawal from the NPT in 1993. The DPRK declared itself to be a nuclear state in 2005 and went on to conduct underground nuclear tests in 2006 and 2009. North Korea's recidivism in traditional and non-traditional security areas has made it a natural suspect of the *Cheonan* incident in the eyes of the Obama administration. The progressive Seoul governments of Kim Dae Jung and Roh Mu-hyun came to Pyongyang's rescue during the Washington-Pyongyang strain via engagement policy. At the end of the Bush administration's second term,

Pyongyang had high expectations for the incoming Obama administration. North Korea expected Obama to be different from George W. Bush. The Lee administration was pushed aside as a negotiation partner.

The Bush administration was a challenging partner for it tried to differentiate itself from the previous Clinton administration's engagement strategy. The post–9/11 atmosphere compounded with President Bush's dogmatic worldviews made the neo-conservative camp more vocal in the U.S. foreign policy behaviors. The camp led by Cheney, Rumsfeld and Bolton advocated distancing from the Kim Jong-il regime and avoided coming to the table with the evil regime. The formation of ineffectual Six Party Talks was an end result. The stalled multilateral negotiation has turned out to be a failure where each member brings its own issues to the community agenda. They appeared together at the venue, but were alone in pursuing separate agendas.[26] The representation at the community of Six Party talks revealed more chasm than consensus when it came to nuclear North Korea.

Pyongyang's anticipation for improved bilateral relations with the United States turned out to be false. The Kim Jong-il regime was anything but shy in expressing its bitter disappointment for the U.S.-ROK joint military exercise in March 2009. With President Obama's criticism of Pyongyang's missile (or satellite) launch in his Prague speech on April 5, 2009, North Korea responded with a second nuclear test the following month. The region has since reverted back to the old Cold War tension in the mood for tit-for-tat.

Under the flurry of speculation on North Korea's nuclear capability, Pyongyang keeps repeating the need for self-vigilance since President Truman's remarks on possibly using atomic bombs against the country in October 1950. Nobody knows for sure how real their fear is towards the possibility of a U.S. attack. The existing educational materials, for instance, repeatedly indoctrinate the people of fear, hatred and self-vigilance against the "imperial powers." The question of whether the indoctrination is to sustain the elite's power grip, or whether it is a reflection of felt reality is a topic for a different essay. Adding to the fire, the Pyongyang regime has recently claimed to have developed hydrogen bombs of cutting-edge technology. The DPRK's frustration with the United States could have been a probable motivation behind the attack. But it is only a speculation.

At the same time Pyongyang's distrust towards Japan has deepened. Japan's handling of the abduction issues, the thorniest topic between Japan and the DPRK, has made the Tokyo government more untrustworthy. The Tokyo government rebuked its deal with Kim Jong-il by not sending back the five Japanese abductees to North Korea after their Japan visit as originally promised. The DPRK is aware of Japan's utilization of the threats, imagined or real, to domestic advantage. And the *Cheonan* incident is just another case in point.

Under the strain and history of tit-for-tat over unfulfilled promises and empty words, neither Japan nor South Korea could provide a convincing motivation behind DPRK's attack on the *Cheonan*. The initial speculations were on the succession move that the heir needed to flex his muscles not only to the DPRK military, but also to neighboring countries. The September Communist Party meeting, however, suggested a rather mixed dynamics in power transition. Kim Jung-un debuted, but with his patrons, Sung-taek Jang (uncle) and Kyung-hee Kim (aunt). The overall assessment is that the heir could not have ordered an attack alone, and the power elites had very little incentive to induce another source of tension in the region.

The Implications

A self-serving interpretation of the confusing circumstances of the *Cheonan* incident is to respond with the equally irresponsible cliché "time will tell." There is no question that time will tell in this increasingly democratizing world where past wrongs and hidden truths get to be unearthed under the bright gaze of historical fact-finding. The U.S. Freedom of Information Act and the Japanese equivalent will be legally bound to shed light on this incident twenty five years from now. The South Korean eyewitnesses will survive to testify what they saw on March 26, 2010. The lingering question, however, is what to do meanwhile. What does the *Cheonan* mean for the East Asian Community?

If the accusation towards North Korea is wrong by any chance, we would need to be mindful of similar precedents. The rule of thumb should be universal in that every suspect is innocent until proven guilty. In 1992–3, for instance, the surrounding countries suspected North Korea for its clandestine nuclear development which led to military crisis on the peninsula, and it eventually paved the road for the new U.S.-Japan military guidelines. History repeated itself in 2002 when North Korea was accused of developing a uranium enrichment program that helped the Liberal Democratic Party of Japan to enact a series of wartime legislations in 2003. The U.S.-Japan 2+2 consultations mechanism was established which transformed the bilateral alliance into one with sharper teeth. Japanese political elites and President Lee Myung-bak frequently cite the current threat to justify their respective domestic policies. This brand of history will continue to repeat itself unless we are ready to think outside the usual politics of blaming and framing. No matter how natural the natural suspect appears, the case still requires a judicious consideration.

The confrontation in the community continued on June 14, 2010, when both North and South Korean representatives made contrasting accusations towards each other at the United Nations Security Council. The South blamed Pyongyang for sinking the ship, whereas the North accused the Seoul government of fiction writing. The unsettling *Cheonan* incident shows that the needs to serve domestic political needs in the cases of Japan and South Korea prevail over the spirit of community in the region. The behaviors of China are to serve its regional prerogatives as an emerging hegemon. Had the communal spirit been counted in, the procedures and reactions could have been more judicious. The rush to finger-pointing has added more plausibility to the alternative scenarios. Careful collection, examination, and presentation of evidence, a fundamental principle in building a case, was notably absent in South Korea. It could have taken much longer time, but could have won more hearts and minds about this tragedy. Also if Japan had been more mindful of the collective regional security, it could have acted less self-absorbent in utilizing the *Cheonan*. The ship's tragic drama demonstrated the fragility of the community discourse with the occurrence of violence from within.

Conclusion: Where to from Here?

The community debates project the region as one integral unit amid the rapid shifts in its socio-political and economic landscapes. While many things are undergoing changes, many other things remain the same. North Korea's place in East Asia Community debates plays a crucial role, as indicated by the *Cheonan* incident.

Amid the flurry of predictions, one thing that does not cause much disagreement is Japan's relative position vis-à-vis China over the next few decades—military strength, economic competitiveness and political influence. The changes cause anxiety in Tokyo, whereas China reacts with ambivalence towards the speculation. Japan is trying to balance between the United States, its traditional ally, and China, the emerging partner and rival. Current skirmishes over the military bases in the Okinawa Prefecture are just one of the examples showing Japan's confusion between the dependence on the United States and its self-reliance midst the security architecture created in the Cold War era. China's rise and Japan's relative decline are at the epicenter of the changing regional dynamics.[27] Considering the current Naoto Kan administration's declared policy continuity with the previous Hatoyama government, East Asian Community debates in rhetoric, not necessarily the tangible substance, are highly likely to expand and prosper in Japan for years to come.[28]

The caveat lies with discerning normative rhetoric on the community from empirical reality of divisive positions.

In an effort to shed light on the implications of inter-community violence, European experiences suggest that violence (or war) was not excluded from its vision for regional integration. As there was Sino-centric world order before the encroachment of Western powers in the nineteenth century later to be replaced by Japan's Greater East Asian Co-prosperity Sphere theorem, a few powerful European nations attempted to unify the countries into one integrated region. Napoleon's France in the early nineteenth century, and Hitler's Germany and Mussolini's Italy in the early twentieth century used unbridled violence to rule and unify Europe. There was countervailing reactions to the bloodshed and war-making as well. The Austrian Duke, Graf Richard Coundenhove-Kalergi, initiated a pan–European movement in 1923 followed by the French Foreign Minister Briand's call for the creation of a European Union in 1929, for example. All these efforts failed because of resistance from the international community and the emergence of nation-states on the continent.[29] North Korean threats are, of course, discernable from the European cases: it exercises power of the powerlessness.[30] The defiant regional underdog persists and intimidates the strong. The danger posed by the DPRK is, of course, by no means parallel to the previous violence committed in Europe. Unlike Japan, Italy and Germany, the DPRK does not have enough military strength to launch a total war. The difference in scale, however, does not necessary mean that violence can be easily brushed off in our community debates. It is a disruptive and divisive variable dampening the communal spirit. Even though North Korea is a medium power, its threats and violent propensities exert substantial influence on the region. The *Cheonan* incident shows that only the perception of violence can be detrimental enough to push each member state to engage in strategic calculation for self-vigilance.

Community observers are busy speculating on the next hegemon of the regional hierarchy. What the *Cheonan* Incident suggests is that Pyongyang manageability will be one of the determining factors for the next regional hegemon. Considering the age-old rivalry and competition among the member states, the party which can control, manipulate and mobilize the source of danger can become the leader of the collective. Japan as an economic superpower obviously looms large in East Asia's regional international politics. However, the difficulty of Japan's role as a regional hegemon is vastly compounded by the long shadows of the Greater East Asian Co-Prosperity Sphere, an ever poignant reminder of pernicious regionalism during the heyday of Japanese imperialism. The possibility seems rather distant given Japan's past record compounded with Tokyo's inability and unwillingness to extend heartfelt apologies for imperial atrocities.[31]

The "Great China" prospect is potentially more promising, but it depends on a host of unpredictable variables including, most importantly, the sustainability of China's relentless economic growth and its international conduct as a responsible great power in the uncertain years ahead. Applying the thesis of the clash of civilizations, as a form of structural realism, to the debate on the rise of China, Huntington, for instance, argues that Asian countries will be more likely to bandwagon with China than to balance against it, and that Asia's Sino-centric past, not Europe's multi-polar past, will be Asia's future, even as China is resuming its place as regional hegemon.[32] China's cautious ambivalence regarding the *Cheonan* incident makes this scenario more persuasive than others. As of now, it is only China which stays engaged with the DPRK, and that grants substantial power to Beijing when it comes to managing regional security.

South Korea, a medium power, has been advocating the European Union as a model for East Asian community. Except for the cultural differences of Judeo-Christian world views of Europe and Confucian ethics of Asia, both the European Union and East Asian Community have overlapping goals such as war prevention, peace building, economic cooperation and cultural exchanges. The South Korean government's reactions to the violent incident reveal the need for more trust, less suspicion and judicious preponderance in the spirit of community.

The *Cheonan* incident and regional reactions to North Korea's alleged provocation demonstrate dramatic diversions among the member states. Other than geographical proximity, the binding elements such as shared worldviews, ethos, mutual identification and common ideational values are notably missing. Amid rising concerns and anticipations, the future trajectory of East Asian Community remains to be seen. The (re-)constructed narratives surrounding the violence within the community suggest more room for pessimism for its future. The sunken *Cheonan* reminds us of two unspoken mishaps: dismissal of North Korea as a legitimate party of the discourse and potent implications of inter-community violence. The multilayered readings of the *Cheonan* incident alert us to what we have refused to see, and why. The unfolding saga of past several months was a self-reflexive momentum. This chapter has described the circumstantial stories of each stakeholder—Japan, South Korea and North Korea. The irony is that confusing state of affairs makes us reveal the hidden intentions: the sunken *Cheonan* is instructive for its unsolved mysteries.

Notes

1. For the latest calls for the inclusion of North Korea for the East Asian Community debates, see Young-seo Baek, "'Higashi Ajia Kyoudotai'to Chousenhantou, SositeNikanrentai ['East Asian Community,' the Korean Peninsula and Japan-Korea Coalition]," *Sekai*, May 2010, pp. 53–62; Sakamoto Yoshikazu, "Higashi Ajiawokoeta 'Higashi Ajia Kyoudotai'nokoujyouwo: Hyumanitito Dabunkasekai [Towards the Conceptualization of East Asian Community That Transcends East Asia: Humanity and Multi-culturalism]," *Sekai*, January 2010, pp. 169–180.

2. Barry Buzan, Ole Waever, and Jaap De Wilde, *Security: A New Framework for Analysis* (Boulder, CO: Lynne Rienner, 1997).

3. Mikyoung Kim, "North Korea: Beyond the Name Game," *The Oregonian*, July 25, 2005.

4. The psycho-cultural tenets of identity construction theories (e.g., constructivism) suffer from two shortcomings. The variation in state behavior is assumed to be absent. If a state reacts and reconstructs its own identity according to salient others' perceptions, the interaction leaves little room for change. The overall picture remains static rather than interactive. See Yangmo Ku, "Reckoning with Forced Labor/Sexual Slavery Issues in Germany and Japan: The Nature of Ruling Coalition and the Mobilization of Societal Groups," a paper presented at the Hiroshima Peace Institute Memory Workshop, February 10, 2010, Athens, GA.

5. Taipei's main adversary has been mainland China, as it has been maintaining security coordination with the United States since the 1954 U.S.-R.O.C. mutual defense treaty. Unlike China, Korea and the United States, the Taiwanese bear little resentment toward Japan in spite of colonial occupation. Taiwan's security obsession lies with China, and vice versa. See L. T. S. Ching, *Becoming "Japanese": Colonial Taiwan and the Politics of Identity Formation* (Berkeley: University of California Press, 2001); R. Eskildsen, "Taiwan: A Periphery in Search of a Narrative," *The Journal of Asian Studies* no. 2 (May 2005): 281–94; cf. P. R. Katz, "Governmentality and Its Consequences in Colonial Taiwan: A Case Study of the Ta-pa-ni Incident of 1915," *The Journal of Asian Studies* no.2 (May 2005): 281–94.

6. Entangled among these factors is also a dense cultural memory. See John Bohman, "The Globalization of the Public Sphere: Cosmopolitan Publicity and the Problem of Cultural Pluralism," *Philosophy and Social Criticism* 24(2/3) (1998): 199–216; J. Habermas, *The Structural Transformation of the Public Sphere: An Inquiry into a Category of Bourgeois Society* (Cambridge, MA: MIT Press, 1989); Marc Lynch, *State Interests and Public Spheres: The International Politics of Jordan's Identity* (New York: Columbia University Press, 1999).

7. Akaha, Tsuneo, ed., *Politics and Economics in Northeast Asia: Nationalism and Regionalism in Contention* (New York: St. Martin's, 1999).

8. Anderson's *Imagined Communities* argues that it is modernity that gives rise to nations and nationalism. Nationalism, he argues, arises through the creation of an imagined community, where one member is able to conceive of another being part of the same nation, without necessarily knowing or encountering them. In Benedict Anderson, *Imagined Communities: Reflections on the Origin and Spread of Nationalism* (New York: Verso, 2006).

9. Regionalism and regionalization are often used interchangeably, but are discernable in the concepts. According to Kim (2004: 12–13), regionalism is a normative concept that refer to shared values, norms, identity, and aspiration. Regionalization, on the other hand, implies a series of complex, interrelated processes of interregional interconnectedness in political, economic, and social relations.

10. C. M. Dent and D. W. F. Huang, eds., *Northeast Asian Regionalism: Lessons from the European Experience* (London and New York: Routledge Curzon, 2002).

11. As for the latest development on the U.S. membership in the East Asian Community, the former Japanese Prime Minister Hatoyama stated that he wanted the United States "to join us in the security area" in reference to his "East Asian Community" proposal. *Asahi Shimbun*, November 14, 2009.

12. Ferdinand Toennies, *Community and Society: Gemeinschaft and Gesellschaft* (New York: Transaction, 1998).

13. Similar position to Poplin, see Patricia Hill Collins, "The New Politics of Community," *American Sociological Review*, 75(1) (2010): 7–30.

14. See, for example, E. E. Evans-Pritchard, *The Nuer: A Description of the Modes of Livelihood and Political Institutions of a Nilotic People* (Oxford, UK: Oxford University Press, 1969); Benjamin Talton, *Politics of Social Change in Ghana: The Konkomba Struggle for Political Equality* (London and New York: Palgrave Macmillan, 2010).

15. For different reactions from the conservative and the progressives in South Korea, see http://news.khan.co.kr/kh_news/khan_art_view.html?artid=201009132005355&code=910302 (accessed October 22, 2010), and http://news.chosun.com/site/data/html_dir/2010/10/24/2010102400026.html?Dep1=news&Dep2=headline1&Dep3=h3_06 (accessed October 22, 2010).

16. Sakai Tanaka (trans. Kyoko Selden), "Who Sank the South Korean Warship *Cheonan*? A New Stage in the US-Korean War and US-China Relations," *Japan Focus*, http://www.japanfocus.org/-Tanaka-Sakai/3361, accessed May 15, 2010.

17. As for the exceptions to the media monotone, see, for example, http://www.pressian.com/article/article.asp?article_num=10100622152932&Section=05 (accessed October 22, 2010) and http://news.khan.co.kr/kh_news/khan_art_view.html?artid=201009132005175&code=910302 (accessed October 22, 2010).

18. For instance, according to a July 2010 opinion survey conducted by the Institute of Peace and Unification Studies (IPUS) at Seoul National University, those who responded positively to a questionnaire item, "I trust the government's report on the sunken *Cheonan*," was at 32.5 percent, while 35.7 percent expressed doubts (*The Daily Chosun*, September 8, 2010, p. 4). These survey results reveal perceptual change from June 2010 survey taken by the Ministry of Public Administration and Security, where 75.4 percent of the adults and 75.1 of the teenagers responded positively to the DPRK's accountability of the incident.

19. The July 9 UN Security Council statement did not specify the responsible party for the ship sinking (see http://www.un.org/News/Press/docs/2010/sc9975.doc.htm, accessed October 21, 2010) drawing mixed reactions. Some of the South Korean news media called it a "half success" (*The Daily Joongang*, July 9, 2010), while others were more critical calling it a "failure" (*The Kyunghyang Shinmun*, July 9, 2010).

20. Tanaka, ibid.; the former U.S. Ambassador to the ROK Don Gregg also has expressed reservations towards the May 20 report of the civilian-military multinational joint investigation team led by the ROK (http://www.koreaherald.com/national/Detail.jsp?newsMLId=20100916000866, accessed October 21, 2010).

21. Bao Daozu, October 26, 2010, "China, North Korea enhances ties," *China Daily*, http://www.asianewsnet.net/home/news.php?id=15113 (accessed October 26, 2010).

22. John McGlynn, "Politics in Command: The 'International' Investigation into the Sinking of the *Cheonan* and the Risk of a New Korean War," *Japan Focus* (http://www.japanfocus.org/-John-McGlynn/3372, accessed June 15, 2010).

23. This alternative scenario has drawn audience for its relatively persuasive reconstruction of the incident. The ROK Ministry of Defense responded by clarifying the Foal Eagle exercise date earlier than March 26, 2010. The response was to clear the United States of any involvement.

24. The U.S.-Japan secret pact includes the following four agendas: (1) January in 1960, introduction of nuclear weapons into the Japanese territory was agreed upon during revision of the U.S.-Japan Security Treaty; (2) in January 1960, a joint military operation was agreed upon in the case of contingency on the Korean peninsula; (3) in 1972, introduction of nuclear weapons into the Japanese territory was agreed upon during bilateral negotiations of the Okinawa base return; and (4) in 1972, Japan agreed to bear the financial cost of reverting the Okinawa base to the previous non-military use during the bilateral negotiations of Okinawa base return.

25. Dokdo/Takeshima disputes regard territorial contention between Korea and Japan. The two main islets and 35 small rocks (aka Liancourt Rocks) are currently administered by South Korea, while Japan classifies the area as Okinoshima, Oki District of Shimane Prefecture. With Japan's annexation of Korea in 1910, Dokdo/Takeshima belonged to Imperial Japan. Korea's liberation in 1945 and subsequent San Francisco Peace Treaty in 1953 did not make the islets' ownership clear because of Korea's exclusion from the Treaty's signatory and Japan's rising strategic importance to the United States amid unfolding Cold War rivalry with the former USSR. The territorial disputes have been continuing for the past several hundred years with each side presenting disputable evidence. As of now, two South Korean fishermen and 37 South Korean police personnel (in rotation) are residing on the islets (http://media.joinsmsn.com/article/035/456 4035.html?ctg=1200&cloc=portalxhomexnews_media).

26. Jefferey Lewis, October 15, 2010. "The Cooling Tower," http://38north.org/ 2010/10/the-cooling-tower/print/ (accessed October 26, 2010).

27. Eric Talmadge, October 26, 2010, "Japan, Worried by China, May Boost Submarine Fleet," Associated Press, http://news.yahoo.com/s/ap/20101026/ap_on_re_as/as_japan_military_2;_ylt=AslB2jw0y7TqHBMP7XnYrI4AS5Z4, (accessed October 26, 2010).

28. Former Prime Minster Hatoyama wrote in his opinion piece published in the *New York Times*: "Current developments show clearly that China will become one of the world's leading economic nations while also continuing to expand its military power. The size of China's economy will surpass that of Japan in the not-too-distant future.... How should Japan maintain its political and economic independence and protect its national interest when caught between the United States, which is fighting to retain its position as the world's dominant power, and China, which is seeking ways to become dominant? This is a question of concern not only to Japan but also to the small and medium-sized nations in Asia. They want the military power of the U.S. to function effectively for the stability of the region but want to restrain U.S. political and economic excesses. They also want to reduce the military threat posed by our neighbor China while ensuring that China's expanding economy develops in an orderly fashion. These are major factors accelerating regional integration." http://www. nytimes.com/2009/08/ 27/opinion/ 27iht-edhatoyama.html?_r=1&pagewanted=2, (accessed August 27, 2009). Chinese Vice President Xi Jinping also stated that he hoped to see the "realization of both the Korea-China free trade agreement and an East Asian community in the not distant future." *The Korea Times*, editorial, December 16, 2009, p. 8.

29. Another wave of regionalism in Western Europe in the 1950s surfaced in the Paris Agreement of April 1951, and Rome Agreement of March 1957. It faded in the 1960s and early 1970s, especially in the wake of the 1965 European Community crisis and the challenge to super-nationalism posed by de Gaulle's high politics. The second wave of regionalism came about as a result of a series of momentous developments in the late 1980s and early 1990s, all of which are said to have greatly increased the significance of the intrinsic dynamics of regional and sub-regional forces.

30. Kyung-Ae Park, "North Korean Strategies in the Asymmetric Nuclear Conflict with the U.S.," a paper presented at the annual meeting of the American Political Science Association, Toronto, Canada, September 3–6, 2009.

31. Richard J. Samuels, "Wing Walking: The US-Japan Alliance," *Global Asia* 1, no. 1 (Spring 2009): 14–19.

32. Samuel P. Huntington, *The Clash of Civilizations and the Remaking of World Order* (New York: Simon and Schuster, 1966). Wyne, on the other hand, asserts that the Chinese authoritarian capitalism can be as influential as the American model of democratic capitalism. He argues that East Asia will be a part of highly polarized twenty-first century world order, but not necessarily as a more influential bloc of the international community. See Ali Wyne, "A Skeptical View of Asia's Rise," *Global Asia* 4, no. 3 (Fall 2009): 50–52.

CHAPTER 11

The Northern Limit Line and North Korean Provocations

*Terence Roehrig**

Abstract

The South Korean warship *Cheonan* sank off the southwest coast of *Baengnyeong* island on the evening of March 26, 2010. The island is one of five South Korean islands that lie along the Northern Limit Line (NLL), the maritime boundary between North and South Korea in the West Sea (Yellow Sea). The South Korean government, aided by experts from the United States, Australia, the United Kingdom, Canada, and Sweden, concluded that a North Korean submarine fired a 500-pound torpedo at the ship killing forty-six seamen. The *Cheonan* incident is part of a broader context that includes the dispute over the NLL. This chapter examines the sinking of the *Cheonan*, the dispute along the NLL, and role these issues play in North Korea's overall survival strategy. Though difficult to ascertain with any certainty, it is likely that the explanation for Pyongyang attacking the *Cheonan* are a combination of several explanations that include: demonstrating its unhappiness with the NLL maritime boundary, revenge for the November 2009 clash when a North Korean ship crossed the NLL, and the efforts to secure the transition of Kim Jong-il's third son, Kim Jong-un to leadership of North Korea.

Introduction

On the evening of March 26, 2010, the South Korean corvette, *Cheonan* was on patrol off the southwest coast of *Baengnyeong* island. The island is one of five South Korean islands that lies along the Northern Limit Line, the maritime boundary between North and South Korea in the West Sea (Yellow Sea).

*The views expressed in this chapter are the author's alone and do not represent the official position of the Department of the Navy, the Department of Defense, or the U.S. government.

A sudden explosion split the ship in two causing it to sink within minutes. Forty six of the ship's crew of 104 lost their lives in the tragedy. The origin of the explosion was uncertain that night, but eventually suspicions turned to North Korea. However, the Lee Myung-bak administration was quick to downplay any speculation of the causes or culprit until authorities conducted a thorough investigation. Seoul assembled a multinational team composed of members from South Korea, the United States, the United Kingdom, Canada, Australia, and Sweden to conduct a thorough investigation. On May 20, after taking almost two months, the team released a report that concluded the explosion was caused by a torpedo launched from a North Korean submarine that had snuck into South Korean waters. North Korea denied these actions strenuously and indicated that any attempt to punish it through military force or economic sanctions would be considered an act of war. There remains some disagreement over the formal investigation,[1] but a recent ROK (Republic of Korea, or South Korea) survey indicated that close to 68 percent of respondents believed North Korea was responsible for sinking the Cheonan.[2]

North Korean motivation for the strike on the Cheonan remains a mystery, as is often the case when attempting to examine Pyongyang's actions. Yet, the Cheonan incident is part of a broader context that includes the dispute over the Northern Limit Line (NLL). There have been several confrontations along the NLL with the most serious in 1999, 2002, and 2009 that have resulted in the deaths of a number of South and North Korean sailors. These confrontations may be part of the Democratic People's Republic of Korea's (DPRK) efforts to force a change to the NLL that are part of Pyongyang's larger national strategy of regime survival. This chapter examines the sinking of the Cheonan, the dispute along the NLL, and role these issues play in North Korea's overall survival strategy. Though difficult to ascertain with any certainty, it is likely that the explanation for Pyongyang attacking the Cheonan are a combination of several explanations that include: demonstrating its unhappiness with the NLL maritime boundary, revenge for the November 2009 clash when a North Korean ship crossed the NLL, and the efforts to secure the transition of Kim Jong-il's third son, Kim Jong-un to leadership of the DPRK. All of these issues share a common thread of being elements of North Korea's survival strategy.

History of the Northern Limit Line

The sinking of the Cheonan along with other naval clashes in 1999, 2002, and 2009 occurred along the North-South maritime boundary known as the

Northern Limit Line. The Northern Limit Line was drawn at the end of the Korean War as a maritime boundary between the two Koreas in the West Sea. During armistice talks, negotiators settled on a land border, the military demarcation line (MDL) and granted the United Nations Command (UNC) the rights to five small islands (Woo-do, Yeonpyeong-do, Socheong-do, Daecheong-do, and Baengnyeong-do) on the west coast of Korea. Despite lying off the North Korean coast, the islands were under UNC control at the time of the armistice and Pyongyang did not dispute the islands remaining in South Korean hands. However, negotiators could not agree on a maritime boundary due to disagreements over the extent of North Korea's territorial sea.[3] Moreover, South Korean President Syngman Rhee had made known his displeasure with the armistice and pledged to continue the fight if given the opportunity.[4] To ensure that naval forces and fishing boats did not spark a renewal of the conflict, on August 30, 1953, the UNC promulgated the NLL. The line was drawn approximately mid-channel between the Ongjin Peninsula and the five islands under UNC/ROK control. For the next 20 years, little was said between the two Koreas regarding the NLL, and North Korea did not lodge any formal protests regarding the line.

In 1973, North Korea appears to have made its first formal protest of the NLL at the 346th Military Armistice Commission meeting where the DPRK representative proclaimed that the five islands under UNC/ROK control as specified in the armistice were in DPRK territorial waters. In addition, transit to and from these islands would require North Korean permission.[5] However, Pyongyang did not challenge ROK control of the five islands. In 1977, North Korea proclaimed two additional maritime zones: its 200 nautical mile (nm) economic exclusion zone (EEZ) and a 50 nm military boundary zone. According to the United Nations Convention on the Law of the Sea, within the 200 mile EEZ, states have "sovereign rights for the purpose of exploring and exploiting, conserving and managing the natural resources, whether living or non-living, of the waters superjacent to the seabed and of the seabed and its subsoil, and with regard to other activities for the economic exploitation and exploration of the zone, such as the production of energy from the water, currents and winds."[6] The designation of a military boundary zone was unusual and not in keeping with international law. According to DPRK authorities, the purpose of the military zone was "to reliably safeguard the economic sea zone" and defend "militarily the national interests and sovereignty of the country."[7] The DPRK announcement also stated that within this zone and the sky above, foreign military vessels and planes were prohibited, and any civilian ships, excluding fishing boats, must obtain approval before entering the zone. Enforcement of these measures would have been in conflict with accepted norms of maritime transit and international law. In addition, the five ROK islands were also fully within the military boundary zone making travel to and from the islands problematic. Despite the declaration of these zones, South Korea continued its regular ferry service between the islands and the mainland, and North Korea refrained from enforcing its claims. For the next 20 years, the NLL remained fairly quiet.

The peace was shattered on June 15, 1999, when ROK and DPRK ships clashed along the NLL. The culmination of nine days of tense activity at sea, on June 15, over a dozen North Korean fishing vessels crossed the NLL followed by several North Korean patrol boats. As the ROK naval ships attempted to turn back the DPRK vessels, a North Korean torpedo boat fired on the ROK ships with its 25 mm guns, possibly in a fit of panic. The ROK ships returned fire and after a brief exchange, the DPRK ships sped back across the NLL. Soon after, two of the North Korean ships sank.[8] Later reports indicated that close to 30 DPRK sailors died and four other vessels were badly damaged. ROK naval forces suffered only minor casualties and its ships sustained little damage.[9]

After the clash, on September 3, 1999, the North Korean Army General Staff issued a special communiqué that repeated its condemnation of the current NLL and declared the line void. In addition, the statement proposed a new line that was approximately equidistant from the North and South Korean coasts, and was essentially an extension of the provincial boundary line between Hwanghae-do and Kyonggi-do. Pyongyang's NLL proposal provided for two corridors, each 2 nm wide leading to the ROK's five islands for all commercial transit. Travel outside these lines would violate North Korean sovereignty, and Pyongyang maintained it would be justified to use force to defend its waters. Despite the proclamation, South Korea continued to conduct its business as before, and North Korea chose not to enforce its proposed line.

On June 29, 2002, North and South Korean ships clashed again along the NLL. Two DPRK patrol boats traversed the line at different points and several minutes apart in a move that appeared to be a coordinated effort intended to separate ROK forces. Contrary to previous crossings of the NLL, this time, the North Korean naval vessels were not escorting fishing boats or chasing illegal foreign fishermen. The ROK Navy sent patrol boats to intercept the incursions and after closing to approximately 500 yards, one of the North Korean ships opened fire killing five South Korean sailors and Marines while wounding 19 on one of the ROK patrol craft. The ship was badly damaged and sunk while being towed back to port. The skirmish lasted only 20 minutes and when DPRK vessels withdrew, the South chose not to pursue. Though formal numbers have never been released by Pyongyang, most estimates cite DPRK losses at approximately 30 sailors. South Koreans now refer to these the 1999 and 2002 clashes as the First and Second Battles of Yeonpyeong. For the next seven years, the NLL remained relatively quiet though both sides continue to accuse the other of violating the line.[10]

While tension remained, on several occasions, the North and South attempted to address the issue in formal talks. On a regular basis, Pyongyang tried to raise the issue but the positions held by both sides was so distant that progress was next to impossible. In early October 2007, South Korean President Roh Moo-hyun traveled to Pyongyang for the second ever summit meeting between the two countries. Prior to the meetings, stories began to surface in the ROK press that President Roh might be willing to raise the NLL issue and be amenable to addressing some of the North's concerns. Unification Minister Lee Jae-joung who was well known as an enthusiast of engaging North Korea noted "I don't think that the NLL is basically a territorial concept, but a security concept to prevent military clashes. Now we need a concrete measure to prevent clashes in the West Sea."[11] Many in South Korea were very upset with the possibility of negotiations to change the NLL. One vocal critic was ROK Defense Minister Kim Jang-soo, who maintained he would not support a change to the NLL if it came up during the summit meeting because the issue was too complex to be on the summit agenda.[12] In the face of such strong opposition, the Roh administration backed down and did not raise the NLL issue during the meetings. However, the summit communiqué did address a few issues that involved the NLL including the development of a joint fishing area in the West Sea, along with a maritime peace zone, greater joint usage of Haeju harbor, and joint use of the Han River estuary.[13] The details for implementing these provisions were not included in the communiqué and were left for future meetings.

When President Roh returned home from the summit, he faced a barrage of criticism for these proposals, especially from conservatives. In testimony to the National Assembly following the summit, Defense Minister Kim argued that "to make any concessions or to open up the Northern Limit Line is out of the question."[14] Yet, Roh continued to question the NLL maintaining the line was not a border but rather "a limit line for our naval operations. Some people are calling it a 'border' these days. This is a concept that misleads people."[15] Furthermore, Roh also maintained that "We need to admit that the NLL was drawn unilaterally by [the United States and South Korea] with no bilateral agreement reached."[16] North and South Korean officials held a series of meetings to try to implement the agreement but made little progress and by November 2007, the issue was dropped. Soon after, South Koreans went to the polls and elected a new president, Lee Myung-bak from the conservative Grand National Party and ROK policy toward North Korea shifted in a more hardline direction. President Lee decided that South Korea would no longer provide aid to North Korea without a greater degree of reciprocity and inter–Korean relations soon began to deteriorate.

Another bloody clash occurred along the line on November 10, 2009. The confrontation was part of an increase in tension that had begun months earlier with a second nuclear weapon test and another round of ballistic missile tests. At around 11:30 A.M. on November 10, a North Korean patrol ship crossed the NLL close to Daechong-do. Four South Korean ships intercepted the vessel and fired warning shots. The North Korean ship returned fire shooting 50 rounds at the ROK ships which sustained only minor damage. The ROK ships then returned fire at the North Korean ship which sustained heavy damage with one DPRK sailor killed and three injured. The North Korean ship could be seen ablaze as it limped back across the NLL. North Korea was outraged over the incident and demanded an apology along with the punishment of those involved in the incident. The DPRK also indicated afterward that it would "take merciless military measures to defend" the maritime border that it established in 1999.[17] South Korea did not respond to Pyongyang's demands.

Importance of the Northern Limit Line

The dispute over the NLL is a contentious issue where the stakes are high for both sides. Both Seoul and Pyongyang have significant security and economic interests at stake in the region. There are four primary issues involved with the NLL: fishing; commerce and access to the West Sea; sovereignty; and security.

Fishing

The area around the NLL is a prized fishing ground for many types of species. Every spring the region attracts fishing boats to catch the highly valued blue crabs that migrate through these waters. Thus, it is not a coincidence that the 1999 and 2002 NLL clashes occurred in June during crab season. As the crabs move through the area, fishing boats must follow the crabs, which sometimes cross the maritime border making it difficult to maintain the integrity of the maritime line. In fact, sometimes ships, including illegal Chinese fishing vessels, dart across the border for a quick harvest and move back across the line before the ROK navy can reach the area. Fishing is an important industry in the region for both North and South, and access to as much of these waters as possible is important for the economies of both sides.

Policing the NLL has been more difficult because of illegal Chinese fishing in the region. DPRK efforts to prevent incursions often result in pursuing these vessels across the NLL. South Korean patrol boats warn the DPRK ships to return to their side of the line but sometimes the pursuit continues into ROK waters. On occasion, North Korean ships have been seen towing Chinese fishing boats back across the NLL. Some of these Chinese boats have paid the North Korean government for permission to fish on the DPRK side of the line but cross the NLL nonetheless. Given the profits to be made in fishing here, it is a difficult region to manage.

Commerce and Access to the West Sea

The NLL has another important economic impact that complicates inter-Korean trade and the North's access to the West Sea. Prior to restrictions imposed as a result of the *Cheonan* attack, over 90 percent of North-South trade passed through these waters between the DPRK port of Nampo and Incheon.[18] Commercial transit across the NLL is prohibited for both countries which requires DPRK ships to travel north beyond the northernmost island of Baengnyeong to enter the West and destinations beyond. This indirect route adds many extra miles and the related fuel costs onto trips. The line also blocks shipping lanes between Haeju, one of the North's major ports and the Gaeseong Industrial Complex from Incheon and Seoul in the South. The NLL complicates the possibilities of cheaper, ocean-born commerce for both Koreas.

Sovereignty

In addition to economic factors, the NLL is also an issue of sovereignty for both Seoul and Pyongyang based on important economic, political, and security factors. Other than during the Roh Moo-hyun administration, South Korea has been determined to maintain the NLL as it is and to retain its sovereignty over the region. This is particularly so when concerns for security run high and the *Cheonan* attack only reinforces the need to maintain the NLL. North Korea believes that the line is illegal, was imposed unilaterally, and restricts them from access to what it believes are its sovereign, territorial waters. However, sovereignty here may be a complicated issue. Both North and South maintain that the division of the peninsula is temporary. In the 1992 North-South Agreement on Reconciliation, Nonaggression, and Exchanges and Cooperation, both parties acknowledge "that their relationship, not being a relationship as between states, is a special one constituted temporarily in the process of unification."[19] Article 3 of the ROK Constitution states that "the territory of the Republic of Korea shall consist of the Korean peninsula and its adjacent islands" (Republic of Korea Constitution 1948). Consequently, it is not entirely clear if this is a boundary dispute between sovereign states or a temporary division drawn predominately as a military requirement.

Security

The final and perhaps most important issue concerning the NLL is security. Several important DPRK naval installations are located on the nearby Ongjin Peninsula along with the North Korean city of Haeju. If the NLL were moved farther south, North Korean warships could patrol closer to Incheon and the Han River estuary that in turn, leads to Seoul. This would reduce ROK warning time for a North Korean attack and move the DPRK's special forces, one of its chief military strengths, closer to South Korea. North Korean incursions into the South over the years such as the commando raids in 1968, the submarine incursions of 1996 and 1998, and the sinking of the *Cheonan* have been particular dangers for the South. North Korean leaders have their own security concerns and would be delighted to see ROK naval vessels patrolling farther from their shores. Moving the NLL farther south would provide the DPRK a larger ocean buffer in this area from South Korean patrols and intelligence gathering.

The Positions in Pyongyang and Seoul on the Northern Limit Line

Though fairly quiet on the NLL for the first 20 years of its promulgation, since 1973, North Korea's position has been clear: the NLL line should be null and void. After the June 2002 confrontation, the *Korean Central News Agency* proclaimed "it is well known to the world that the 'northern boundary line' ... is a bogus line unilaterally and illegally drawn by it [the UNC] in the 1950s and our side, therefore, has never recognized it."[20] North Korea has not challenged the South's possession of the five islands included in the armistice but makes clear that it believes these islands fall completely in the territorial waters of the DPRK.

North Korea's relative silence on the NLL until 1973 raises an interesting question under international law. During the first 20 years of the line's existence, North Korea did little to challenge the legitimacy of the line. This is an important consideration due to the concepts of customary law and "acquiescence" where states choose to not exercise a certain right or to protest an action they oppose. As a result of a state's inaction or failure to protest, the measure may become binding. Customary law can be defined as "international custom, as evidenced by a practice generally accepted as law."[21] To become customary international law, a practice must be largely accepted, though not universally adopted by states. This concept is often applied to large, multinational treaties and obligations that are certainly binding on those who sign and ratify the agreements. However, customary law also maintains that "if there is a sufficiently general acceptance of treaty rules by non–Parties ... those rules may become binding as a matter of customary law."[22]

While states are generally bound by customary law, they have the right to demonstrate they are not acquiescing to the law and will not follow it. Thus, according to Churchill and Lowe,

> if a state persistently objects to an emerging rule of customary law, as a matter of strict law it will not be bound by that rule. The objection must be persistent: States will not be permitted to acquiesce in rules of law and later claim exemption from them at will.... Thus, even if a general practice has generated a rule of customary law, which is in principle binding upon all States, particular States may be able to claim the status of persistent objectors, with the result that they will not be bound by the rule [p. 8].

As a result, if a state regularly expresses its objections to a rule of customary law, it is not bound by that law. Failure to register dissent gives tacit consent to the matter in question and implies that one is relinquishing any right to challenge an issue or a decision. Thus, even though a state may be unable to alter a perceived injustice, it might choose to transmit an annual letter of protest to demonstrate that it has not acquiesced to the situation.

It is not clear whether North Korea's actions, or lack thereof, from 1953 to 1973 constitute acquiescence to the UNC-designated NLL or not, and if after 20 years, the DPRK was still able to challenge the NLL. In fact, North Korea's continued violations of the NLL, the 1999, 2002, and 2009 naval clashes along with the attack on the *Cheonan* may have been an effort to challenge the line and refrain from any recognition of the line that would support an accusation of acquiescence.

For South Korea, the NLL is the de facto maritime boundary and a legitimate line drawn at the end of the Korean War. The line is crucial for ROK security and in March 2008, General Kim Tae-young, chairman of the ROK Joint Chiefs of Staff stated the NLL "should be defended under any circumstance. It is a quasi-border, part of the nation's territorial sovereignty."[23] Until the security situation changes in the region, South Korea is unlikely to show much flexibility. In the past, President Lee has indicated a willingness to pursue a West Sea peace zone that includes a joint fishing zone, development of the Haeju economic zone, and cooperation on the Han River Estuary project. However, given the incidents of the past, ROK leaders believe it is too dangerous to move the NLL further south at this point in time.[24]

ROK officials also maintain that in the past, Pyongyang has given several indications that it has accepted the NLL as the border. First, as indicated earlier, from 1953 to 1973, North Korea lodged no formal protest of the NLL, implying its acquiescence of the line. Second, in 1991, North Korea signed the "Agreement on Reconciliation, Nonaggression, and Exchanges and Cooperation between South and North Korea." In Article 11 of the agreement it notes "the South-North demarcation line and the areas for nonaggression shall be identical with the Military Demarcation Line provided in the Military Armistice Agreement of July 27, 1953, and the areas that each side has exercised jurisdiction over until the present time" (Agreement on Reconciliation). For South Korea, the North's assent to this wording demonstrates that Pyongyang again accepted the NLL as the maritime border of the Koreas.

Events of the Cheonan

On the evening of March 26, the ROKS *Cheonan* (PCC-772) was rocked by an explosion that split the ship in two killing 46 of the crew of 104. In the early hours after the event, speculation for the cause of the explosion included several possibilities such as accidental contact with a sea mine, an internal explosion on board the *Cheonan*, or a torpedo fired by a North Korean submarine. Speculation quickly settled on North Korea and the submarine explanation but South Korean President Lee was quick to call for caution in assigning blame. He maintained that hasty judgments were counterproductive and that an investigation must be objective and based on facts so that no one can deny blame for perpetrating the tragedy.[25] To ensure transparency and objectivity, Seoul conducted the investigation jointly with representatives from the United States, the United Kingdom, Australia, Canada, and Sweden. China may have also been invited but declined, and Pyongyang offered to send a delegation to participate in the query but were turned down. Russia sent a team of investigators to conduct their own independent assessment after the report was released but have indicated they will not make their results public. Prior to the release of the Russian report, Russia's ambassador to South Korea, Konstantin V. Vnukov, told a South Korean audience, that "journalists mention 'even China and Russia, as closest allies of North Korea,' but we are not an ally of North Korea." Referring to the 1995 Moscow-Pyongyang agreement that changed the relationship to a "friendship" treaty and removed its formal security guarantee, "we don't have such obligations, so our relationship with North Korea is very practical."[26] However, reports indicated that Russian authorities confirmed that the *Cheonan* was sunk by a torpedo but would not confirm that it was fired from a North Korean submarine.[27]

After close to two months of investigation, the final report was released on May 20, 2010, and confirmed many of the details that had been present in the press. The ship was sunk by a CHT-02D acoustic/wake homing torpedo that exploded approximately 6 to 9 meters below the *Cheonan*. The explosion produced a "bubble-jet" effect that caused the ship to split in two and sink. Investigators discovered a section of the torpedo that survived the blast that included the propellers, propulsion motor, and steering section. According to the report, the torpedo pieces "perfectly match the schematics of the CHT-02D torpedo included in introduction brochures provided to foreign countries by North Korea for export purposes."[28] In addition, one of the sections had written "No. 1" in Korean script that was consistent with the markings on North Korean torpedoes that the South had acquired previously. The torpedo was likely fired by a small 130 ton Yeono class mini-submarine. North Korea is believed to have ten of these boats in its navy. The report notes that "a few small submarines and a mother ship supporting them left a North Korean naval base in the West Sea 2–3 days prior to the attack and returned to port 2–3 days after the attack. Furthermore, we confirmed that all submarines from neighboring countries were either in or near their respective home bases at the time of the incident." To end the report, the investigators state that the *Cheonan* "was sunk as a result of an external underwater explosion caused by a torpedo made in North Korea. The evidence points overwhelmingly to the conclusion that the torpedo was fired by a North Korean submarine. There can be no other plausible explanation."

North Korea Motives for the Cheonan

Determining the motivations of the North Korean regime is a difficult task; it is one of the most opaque regimes in the international system. There is some debate concerning whether North Korea purposely crossed the NLL and provoked the clashes of 1999, 2002, and 2009. However, there can be little room to argue that the attack on the *Cheonan* was accidental. The reasons why North Korea took this provocative act remain a matter of speculation but several possibilities exist.

First, the attack may have been an act of revenge for the November 2009

NLL incident that left a North Korean ship ablaze. Some argue that soon after the North was embarrassed by this skirmish with the South, Kim Jong-il ordered preparations to begin for retaliation.

Second, the attack may have also been an effort to embarrass the Lee Myung-bak administration. Lee had campaigned on taking a tougher line with North Korea arguing that he would continue efforts to engage Pyongyang as had his successors but would expect greater reciprocity from the North. Thus, financial and political engagement from the South would require compromise from the North and progress toward denuclearization. Pyongyang viewed this policy shift harshly and soon began to spew invective at Lee calling him a "traitor," "political charlatan," "reckless," "anti-reunification," and a "sycophant toward the US."[29] Inter-Korean relations have been decidedly worse since President Lee came into office, and Pyongyang may have been intent on sending a message of its unhappiness with Lee's North Korea policy.

Third, the attack may also be part of an ongoing test of wills over the NLL. For over 40 years, Pyongyang has asserted that the line is illegal. On numerous occasions, North Korean ships tested the line and crossed either intentionally or accidentally. In 1999, Pyongyang proposed an alternate line but there has been little interest in the South to negotiate a maritime border or give the issue over to an international tribunal for a solution. Another incident along the NLL may be an effort to raise international pressure on the South and address what Pyongyang sees as the inequities of the line. It may be far easier and less risky for the North to push a provocation along the NLL than it is to do so along the DMZ.

Fourth, increasing tension along the NLL may be an attempt to generate greater bargaining leverage for North Korea and remind all the key players in the region that increased tension is still possible. In the past year or so, North Korea has pressed its demands for the conclusion of a formal peace treaty to replace the 1953 armistice in a bid to formally end the Korean War. Moreover, the position of Seoul, Washington, and Tokyo regarding Six Party Talks has been that North Korea has already agreed to relinquish its nuclear weapons. The goal of further talks is to seek ways to make this happen. It is possible that North Korean leaders believed that a serious NLL incident might remind all of the gravity of peace in Korea, soften President Lee's current policy, and motivate South Korea, the United States, and Japan to return to the Six Party Talks with a more flexible negotiating posture.

Finally, there is a good possibility that the main explanations are rooted in domestic politics. North Korea is undergoing a leadership transition with Kim Jong-il attempting to transfer power to his third son, Kim Jong-un. The transition has been relatively late in coming in comparison to similar events when Kim Il-sung began the process of transferring power to his son, Kim Jong-il. By most accounts, that transfer started in 1974 when Kim Jong-il was 33 years old. For the next 20 years, he was slowly given positions of authority to help establish his leadership credentials since he was sorely lacking in the "revolutionary experience" of his father. When Kim Il-sung died on July 8, 1994, his son had spent close to 20 years in preparation for the job and still there were worries that the transition would be smooth and that the younger Kim would be accepted by the older elites, especially those in the military.

For reasons unknown, Kim Jong-il delayed preparation for a transition until after an apparent stroke in August 2008. As speculation over the exact nature of his illness grew, the contours of a possible urgent succession also began to take shape. For a variety of reasons, Kim Jong-il's first two sons, Kim Jong-nam and Kim Jong-chul, were eliminated as possible candidates and most of the attention focused on the third son, Kim Jong-un. Little is known about the 28-year-old Kim except that he was educated in part at a Swiss boarding school. The past 18 months have witnessed a sporadic effort to elevate Kim Jong-un's position in the government and party hierarchy to prepare him to lead the DPRK. However, prior to the October 2010 Party Congress, he received a position of four-star general, was named a vice chairman of the Central Military Commission of the Korean Worker's Party, and appointed to the Party's Central Committee. In addition, Kim Jong-il has elevated some of his most loyal followers to higher positions of authority, most notably his brother-in-law, Jang Song-taek, to the number two position, Vice Chairman, in the National Defense Commission which effectively places him in the number two power position in all of North Korea. Jang is known to be a loyal supporter of Kim Jong-il and the succession of Kim Jong-un. Kim Jong-il's sister and wife of Jang Song-taek, Kim Kyong-hui, also received a position of four-star general

It is possible that the attack on the *Cheonan*, after the embarrassing clash in November 2009, was an effort by Kim Jong-il to shore up support for his rule and the transition among conservatives, especially those in the military. In addition, within inner circles, Kim Jong-un is likely being given credit for "masterminding" the operation in order to build his credentials. For the sake of this domestic agenda, North Korean leaders may have believed that they could "push the envelope" while being able to absorb any costs from a South Korean or international response. Moreover, criticism from the South and the rest of the world can be turned to support the regime in domestic circles and helps to maintain North Korea's fortress mentality. After the disastrous currency revaluation in November 2009, public discontent with Kim Jong-il and the regime was considerable.[30] An international crisis that "falsely" accuses North Korea can be used to mobilize "rally 'round the flag" support for government.

What to make of the possible reasons for the North Korean attack on the *Cheonan*? It is likely that all of these may have been part of the explanation for why North Korea took the action it did and are linked to a broader North Korean survival strategy. However, the succession issues appear to be the foremost explanations along with the continuing dispute over the Northern Limit Line. Giving South Korea a bloody nose is always good politics in North Korea and helps to secure the regime internally. North Korean leaders made a calculated decision that the costs of pursuing the attack on the *Cheonan* were tolerable in comparison to the domestic political benefits they would be able to gain. Yet, the sinking of the *Cheonan* has not been cost free as the loss of trade with South Korea will have a considerable impact on the DPRK economy. However, the political survival of the North Korean State and the Kim Jong-il regime was more important than further jolts to the country's economy. Thus, the regime believed it could absorb further costs to its economy for the sake of gains in securing the succession and the survival of the regime.

Conclusion

The sinking of the *Cheonan* with the loss of 46 South Korean sailors has plunged inter–Korean relations to their lowest point in many years. South Korea's response has been calculated and careful, focusing largely on economic and political measures while refraining from a military response. It is absolutely important that a firm response be given to Pyongyang but one that does not escalate the crisis, particularly with a military response. South Korean President Lee Myung-bak was cautious and wise in his handling of this affair. While this sort of behavior by Pyongyang cannot be tolerated, the South Korean and international response must be measured and cognizant of the DPRK's domestic politics at work here. North Korea's chief goal internally and internationally is regime survival and Pyongyang's actions need to be understood in that context. The costs the North Korean regime is willing to bear to secure its regime internally as well as externally are high and will make it difficult for others to drastically alter the calculations of the North Korean leadership. But South Korea, the United States, and other concerned states must do their best to deter North Korea from taking similar actions while refraining from escalating tensions further. It is a delicate balance but so far, South Korea has done well in walking this tightrope.

Notes

1. J. McGlynn, "Politics in Command: The 'International' Investigation into the Sinking of the Cheonan and the Risk of a New Korean War," *Japan Focus*, http://japanfocus.org/-John-McGlynn/3372 (accessed October 22, 2010); and S. Lee and J. Suh, "Rush to Judgment: Inconsistencies in South Korea's Cheonan Report," *Japan Focus*, http://japanfocus.org/-JJ-Suh/3382 (accessed October 22, 2010).

2. "S. Koreans Solidly Blame N. Korea for Cheonan Sinking," *Chosun Ilbo*, October 20, 2010, http://english.chosun.com/site/data/html_dir/2010/10/20/2010102000428.html (accessed October 22, 2010).

3. T. Roehrig, "North Korea and the Northern Limit Line," *North Korean Review* 5, no. 1 (Spring 2009), and B. Howe, "Insecurity Dilemma" *North Korean Review* 6, no. 2 (Fall 2010).

4. M. Kang, *A History of Contemporary Korea* (Kent, UK: Global Oriental, 2005), p. 191; and A. Nahm, *Korea: Tradition and Transformation* (Elizabeth, NJ: Hollynym, 1988), pp. 431–32.

5. J. Prescott, *Maritime Jurisdiction in East Asian Seas* (Honolulu: East-West Environment and Policy Institute, 1987), pp. 48–49, and J. Kim, "Reflections on the Attitude of North Korea Toward the Law of the Sea Treaty (UNCLOS II)," in C. Park and J. Park, *The Law of the Sea: Problems from the East Asian Perspective* (Honolulu: Law of the Sea Institute, University of Hawaii, 1987), pp. 219–223.

6. United Nations Convention on the Law of the Sea (UNCLOS), Part V, Article 56, 1982, http://www.unorg/Depts/los/convention_agreements/texts/unclos/part5.htm (accessed October 22, 2010).

7. Korean Central News Agency, August 1, 1977, as quoted in C. Park, "The 50-Mile Military Boundary Zone of North Korea," *American Journal of International Law* 72, no. 4 (October 1978): 866

8. J. Bermudez, Jr. *The Armed Forces of North Korea* (New York: I.B. Tauris, 2001), p. 93.

9. B. Glosserman. "Crab Wars: Calming the Waters in the Yellow Sea," *Asia Times Online*, June 14, 2003, http://www.atimes.com/atimes/Korea/EF14Dg03.html (accessed September 29, 2008).

10. Bruce E. Bechtol, Jr., *Red Rogue: The Persistent Challenge of North Korea* (Washington, DC: Potomac, 2007); D. Kirk, "Legality of UN-Drawn Line Is at Issue: Two Koreas Defiant in Yellow Sea Dispute," *International Herald Tribune*, July 11, 2002, http://www.iht.com/articles/2002/07/11/korea_ed3_2.php (accessed May 14, 2008); and D. Macintyre, "Guns and Crustaceans," *Time*, July 15, 2002, http://www.time.com/time/magazine/article/0,9171,320797,00.html (accessed September 29, 2008).

11. S. Jung, "Will Leaders Agree on Tension-Reduction Plan?" *Korea Times*, August 13, 2007, http://www.koreatimes.co.kr/www/news/special/2008/05/180_8269.html (accessed June 22, 2010).

12. "Defense Minister Stands Up for Northern Limit Line," *Chosun Ilbo*, August 22, 2007, http://english.chosun.com/site/data/html_dir/2007/08/22/2007082261025.html (accessed June 22, 2010).

13. Joint Communiqué, "Declaration on the Advancement of South-North Korean Relations, Peace and Prosperity," October 2–4, 2007, http://www.usip.org/files/file/resources/collections/peace_agreements/n_skorea10042007.pdf (accessed October 22, 2010).

14. Brian Lee, "Minister Vows No Concessions Over Northern Limit Line," *JoongAng Daily*, October 18, 2007, http://joongangdaily.joins.com/article/view.asp?aid=2881655 (accessed June 22, 2010).

15. "Northern Limit Line Not a Border: Roh," *Chosun Ilbo*, October 12, 2007, http://english.chosun.com/site/data/html_dir/2007/10/12/2007101261012.html (accessed June 8, 2010).

16. Ibid.

17. Korean Central News Agency, "DPRK Takes Merciless Action to Defend MDL," November 13, 2009, http://www.kcna.co.jp (accessed June 8, 2010).

18. J. Olsen, M. Vannoni, and J. Koelm, "Maritime Cooperation for the Koreas," Cooperative Monitoring Center, Sandia National Laboratories, SAND 2003-1834P, 2003, http://www.cmc.sandia.gov/cmc-papers/sand2003-1843p.pdf (accessed July 3, 2008).

19. "Agreement on Reconciliation, Nonaggression, and Exchanges and Cooperation Between South and North Korea," February 19, 1992, http://www.international.ucla.edu/eas/documents/korea-agreement.htm (accessed June 10, 2010).

20. Korean Central News Agency, "S. Korean Military to Blame for Armed Clash in West Sea," June 30, 2002, www.kcna.co.jp (accessed May 3, 2008).

21. R. Churchill and A. Lowe, *The Law of the Sea*, 3d ed. (Manchester, UK: Manchester University Press, 1999), p. 7.

22. Churchill and Lowe, p. 8; and M. Mendelson, "The International Court of Justice and the Sources of International Law," V. Lowe and M. Fitzmaurice, eds., *Fifty Years of the International Court of Justice* (Cambridge, UK: Cambridge University Press, 1996), pp. 63–89.

23. "Designated Military Chief Backs Northern Limit Line," *Chosun Ilbo*, March 27, 2008, http://english.chosun.com/w21data/html/news/200803/200803270010.html (accessed April 14, 2008).

24. S. Song, "Timely Summit Enables Two Koreas to Play a Key Role in Peace Efforts," *Korea Policy Review* 3, no. 11 (November 2007): 15.

25. "A Time That Tries Our Patience," *JoongAng Daily*, April 10, 2010, http://joongangdaily.joins.com/article/view.asp?aid=2919018 (accessed June 22, 2010).

26. "Russia 'Not an Ally' of Pyongyang," *JoongAng Daily*, June 17, 2010, http://joongangdaily.joins.com/article/view.asp?aid=2921957 (accessed June 23, 2010).

27. "Russian Experts 'Unconvinced by Cheonan Evidence,'" *Chosun Ilbo*, June 10, 2010, http://english.chosun.com/site/data/html_dir/2010/06/10/2010061001164.html (accessed June 23, 2010).

28. "Investigation Result on the Sinking of ROKS 'Cheonan,'" 2010, http://news.bbc.co.uk/nol/shared/bsp/hi/pdfs/20_05_10jigreport.pdf (accessed June 10, 2010).

29. "Lee Myung Bak Regime's Sycophancy Towards U.S. and Anti-DPRK Confrontation Hysteria Blasted," Korean Central News Agency, April 1, 2008, http://www.kcna.co.jp (accessed July 2, 2010).

30. S. LaFraniere, "Views Show How North Korea Policy Spread Misery," *New York Times*, June 9, 2010, available at http://www.nytimes.com/2010/06/10/world/asia/10Koreans.html (accessed June 10, 2010).

CHAPTER 12

Lessons Learned from the North Korean Nuclear Crises*

Siegfried S. Hecker

Abstract

In October 2006, some 50 years after North Korea began its nuclear journey, it detonated a nuclear device and declared itself a nuclear power. A second explosion, in May 2009, erased lingering doubts about its ability to build the bomb. It is instructive to learn how, but even more important to understand why, it built the bomb. Pyongyang has proclaimed its reason for going nuclear: "The DPRK made nuclear weapons and has strengthened its self-defensive war deterrent to maintain the sovereignty and the right to existence of the nation in the face of the increased aggressive threat by the U.S."[1] But is the alleged threat to Pyongyang's security the only reason it built the bomb? This chapter briefly reviews what North Korea's nuclear capabilities are and shows how technical capabilities and political intent were inextricably intertwined in shaping the program. The chapter then turns to Scott Sagan's theoretical framework of three models for the bomb[2] to show how Pyongyang's deep security fears, augmented by domestic and diplomatic drivers, have dominated its decision to build and keep the bomb. The chapter concludes with lessons learned from North Korea for the nonproliferation regime.

How Did North Korea Develop the Bomb?

The promise and peril of nuclear energy share a common technological foundation. Pursuit of a civilian fuel cycle—making fuel, building reactors to burn the fuel, and maintaining the back-end to deal with nuclear waste, includ-

---

*This essay originally appeared as "Lessons Learned from the North Korean Nuclear Crises," *Daedalus* (Winter 2010): 45–56. © 2010 by the American Academy of Arts and Sciences.

ing the option of extracting some of the valuable by-products from burning reactor fuel—enables nations to develop the capability to make bomb fuel, either highly enriched uranium (HEU) or plutonium. North Korea mastered the plutonium fuel cycle ostensibly for nuclear power and then used it to build the bomb.

This brief review of North Korea's acquisition of nuclear capabilities will only touch on the important political milestones that helped to shape it; a more complete discussion will be presented in the next section. Kim Il-sung, the country's founding father, laid the foundation for nuclear technology development in the early 1950s. The Soviet "Atoms for Peace" initiative, modeled after President Eisenhower's initiative of the same name, enabled several hundred North Korean students and researchers to be educated and trained in Soviet universities and nuclear research centers. The Soviets built a research re-actor, the ITR-2000, and associated nuclear facilities at Yongbyon in the 1960s. North Korean specialists trained at these facilities and by the 1970s were prepared to launch a nuclear program without external assistance.

North Korea's decision to build gas-cooled, graphite-moderated reactors was a logical choice at the time for an indigenous North Korean energy program because gas-graphite reactors can operate with natural uranium fuel and, hence, do not require enrichment of uranium.[3] Although North Korea may have experimented with enrichment technologies, commercial enrichment capabilities were beyond its reach and difficult to acquire.[4] North Korea's ambitious program began with an experimental 5 megawatt-electric (MWe) reactor, which became operational in 1986. Construction of that reactor was followed by a scaled-up 50 MWe reactor and a 200 MWe power reactor, although neither was ever completed.

North Korea quickly mastered all aspects of the gas-graphite reactor fuel cycle. It built fuel fabrication facilities and a large-scale reprocessing facility, which enabled extraction of plutonium from spent fuel.[5] Unlike the Soviet built research facilities, the new facilities were built and operated without being declared to or inspected by the International Atomic Energy Agency (IAEA). Pyongyang had no legal obligation to declare these facilities because it was not a member of the Nuclear Non-Proliferation Treaty (NPT). American reconnaissance satellites picked up signs of the reactor construction in the early 1980s and the reprocessing facility in the late 1980s. It was not until 1989, when South Korea leaked American satellite data of the reprocessing facility that the international community first became aware of and concerned about North Korea's indigenous nuclear program. The concern stems from the fact that gas-graphite reactors are capable of producing weapons-grade plutonium while generating electrical power and heat. So, whereas Pyongyang's choice of gas-graphite reactors for its energy program was logical, it was also the best choice to develop a nuclear weapons option.

In parallel, North Korea asked the Soviets to build light water reactors (LWRs) to help meet North Korea's energy demands. North Korea joined the NPT in 1985 because the Soviets made consideration of LWRs contingent upon joining the Treaty. These reactors, though, never materialized because of the demise of the Soviet Union. Pyongyang kept inspectors out of its new facilities until 1992, by which time it had all of the pieces in place for the plutonium fuel cycle. This move coincided with several diplomatic initiatives and President George H.W. Bush's decision to withdraw all American nuclear weapons from South Korea. By this time, the 5 MWe experimental reactor produced electricity and heat for the local town, as well as approximately 6 kilograms (roughly one bomb's worth) of weapons-grade plutonium per year. The fuel fabrication and reprocessing facilities were operational, and the two bigger gas-graphite reactors were under construction.

In 1992, Pyongyang opened the window on its nuclear program for diplomatic reasons explained below, but closed it quickly when IAEA inspectors uncovered discrepancies between their own nuclear measurements at Yongbyon and Pyongyang's declaration. Pyongyang responded to IAEA accusations by announcing its intent to withdraw from the NPT. Pyongyang was apparently surprised by the sophistication of the IAEA's nuclear forensics and by the strictures of the NPT. Negotiations started in June 1993 but stalemated. In 1994, when North Korea unloaded the reactor's fuel containing an estimated 20 to 30 kilograms of plutonium, Washington and Pyongyang came close to war before former President Jimmy Carter intervened and brokered a freeze.

Intense negotiations in Geneva led to the Agreed Framework,[6] which changed North Korea's nuclear technical trajectory dramatically. Pyongyang agreed to give up its indigenous gas-graphite reactor program for the promise of two LWRs to be supplied by the United States, South Korea, and Japan. The spent fuel rods unloaded from the 5 MWe reactors were repackaged by an American technical team and stored in the cooling pool for eventual removal from North Korea. Operation of the 5 MWe reactors, the fuel fabrication plant, and the reprocessing facility was halted and monitored by IAEA inspectors per special arrangement under the Agreed Framework. Construction of the two larger reactors was stopped.

Although Pyongyang halted its plutonium program during the Agreed Framework, it continued to expand its missile program, including by conducting a long-range rocket launch over Japan in 1998. It also explored uranium enrichment.[7] During its first formal encounter with Pyongyang in October 2002, the Bush administration, which was adamantly opposed to the

Agreed Framework, accused Pyongyang of covertly pursuing the alternative HEU path to the bomb. This altercation effectively ended the Agreed Framework and changed Pyongyang's technical and political trajectory again.

In 2003, North Korea became the first nation to withdraw from the NPT. It expelled international inspectors and announced that it would strengthen its nuclear deterrent. By the end of 2003, which also marked the invasion of Iraq and the fall of Saddam Hussein, Pyongyang was eager to have Washington believe it had the bomb. It used my first trip to North Korea, an unofficial, Track II trip led by my Stanford University colleague John W. Lewis, to send that message back to Washington. In a carefully choreographed tour of the Yongbyon nuclear complex in January 2004, Pyongyang gave me remarkable access to nuclear facilities and nuclear scientists and allowed me to hold nearly half a pound of plutonium bomb fuel (in a sealed glass jar), all to convince me it had a "deterrent."

Over the next five years, Pyongyang built and demonstrated its nuclear weapons capabilities while it was engaged off and on in the six-party talks, which it joined only because of Chinese pressure.[8] We do not know exactly when Pyongyang got the first bomb, but we know it made significant strides during the past five years. In the early 1990s, the CIA reported that North Korea may have had enough plutonium for one or two bombs. Albright and O'Neill[9] reported the uncertainty in that estimate, noting that it varied from 10 kilograms plutonium to perhaps less than 2 kilograms. They also reported that non-nuclear explosive experiments, which are prerequisites for a plutonium bomb, were conducted at Yongbyon in the 1980s, leaving little doubt that Pyongyang was pursuing the bomb.

Since its restart in 2003, the 5 MWe reactor has operated for approximately three years, but is currently not operational. The reprocessing facility is operational, but extensive corrosion of fuel fabrication equipment that occurred during the Agreed Framework left that facility only partially operational.[10] North Korea has conducted three reprocessing campaigns since 2003. The reprocessed plutonium, combined with the roughly 2 to 10 kilograms North Korea may have produced before 1994, yields an estimated plutonium production of 40 to 60 kilograms, of which 24 to 42 kilograms are available for weapons today.[11]

North Korea also conducted two nuclear tests of plutonium devices, the first in October 2006 and the second in May 2009. The first was only partially successful; its explosion yield was estimated as slightly below 1 kiloton (compared to roughly 21 kilotons for the bomb at Nagasaki). The second was more successful, with an estimated yield of 2 to 4 kilotons. We know nothing about North Korea's nuclear design capabilities. I believe the test results indicate that North Korea can build a Nagasaki-like simple plutonium bomb with a yield of 20 or so kilotons, and most likely possesses a nuclear arsenal of four to eight such primitive weapons today. Based on the experience of other nuclear countries, North Korea appears a long way from developing both a missile and a warhead to launch a nuclear weapon to great distances. Fielding a nuclear weapon on its shorter-range No-Dong missiles would take less time, but it may require another nuclear test.

Following the initial 2002 altercation with the Bush administration over North Korea's alleged uranium enrichment program, Pyongyang denied ever having pursued such a program in spite of overwhelming evidence to the contrary. As part of its response to UN sanctions following the April 2009 missile launch, Pyongyang announced that it would now pursue enriching uranium for a domestic LWR program. On September 3, it informed the UN Security Council that it was in the final stages of enriching uranium, something that it could only have accomplished if it already had an active program long before April 2009. It appears that Pyongyang used the current crisis as an opportunity to admit to having a uranium program; however, that admission changes the North Korean threat very little. I still believe that Pyongyang has experimented with uranium enrichment for decades, but never developed it on an industrial scale.[12]

Pyongyang has pursued an extensive missile program for decades. It built its initial capability, obtained from the Soviets, into a formidable short-range missile force and developed an ambitious export business for re-engineered Soviet missiles. Its principal customers have been Pakistan, Iran, Syria, Libya, Egypt, and Burma. Pyongyang's long-range missile development has been slow and not a great technical success. After the 1998 launch, it delayed its second launch until July 2006, primarily because of the missile moratorium it declared in 1999. However, the second launch failed instantly when the rocket apparently hit the gantry. Its third test, in April 2009, successfully lifted the first two stages over the Pacific, but the third stage failed.

Many observers now look at the last two decades as a dismal diplomatic failure because Pyongyang's nuclear program was not eliminated. Let's take a closer look at what Pyongyang actually achieved technically—or, perhaps more importantly, what it did not achieve. It failed to get commercial nuclear power. Although Pyongyang now has nuclear weapons, its weapons program is much smaller than it would have been if left unchecked. With the capabilities it already had or was soon to complete by the early 1990s, Pyongyang today could have an arsenal of a hundred or more nuclear weapons. Instead, it has enough plutonium for four to eight weapons and currently is not producing more. It has the capacity to put the 5 MWe reactor back into operation and produce one bomb's worth of plutonium annually for the foreseeable future, but it has not taken steps to do so, perhaps indicating that it believes its small nuclear arsenal provides a sufficient nuclear deterrent.

Did North Korea Export Its Nuclear Technologies?

However, Pyongyang's export of missiles and nuclear technologies appears not to have been constrained. It has widely exported short-range missiles and manufacturing technologies. We have much less information about its nuclear exports. However, evidence is overwhelming that Pyongyang built a plutonium-producing reactor for Syria that was destroyed by an Israeli air raid in September 2007. It appears quite likely that it exported to Libya uranium hexafluoride, the precursor to HEU. There are also grounds to suspect nuclear cooperation with Pakistan and Burma.[13] Cooperation with Iran is the greatest concern because Iran is putting in place all of the pieces for a nuclear weapons option, and its nuclear capabilities complement those of North Korea.[14] The nature of the nuclear exports also suggests that North Korea may have undeclared uranium facilities.

No one outside Kim Jong-il's inner circle understands the decision-making process and motivations of North Korea's regime. I will use Sagan's framework to analyze Pyongyang's nuclear decisions and try to answer why it built the bomb. Sagan postulates three models for the bomb: the security model, the domestic politics model, and the norms model. The security model calls for states to build nuclear weapons to increase their security against foreign threats, especially nuclear threats. States that face nuclear-armed or vastly superior conventionally armed adversaries will eventually attempt to develop their own nuclear arsenals unless credible alliance guarantees with a major nuclear power exist.

Security concerns have been the central driver of the North Korean ruling regime since the birth of the nation after World War II. Much of Pyongyang's nuclear decision-making can be understood by examining how Pyongyang saw its security environment evolve over the years. The devastating Korean War, resolved only by an armistice, and the U.S. threat to use nuclear weapons likely moved Kim Il-sung to pursue nuclear weapons early on. He likely strengthened his resolve to pursue his own bomb when China, shortly after its own first nuclear test in 1964, turned down his request to share its atomic secrets.

The late 1960s were turbulent times in Pyongyang's relations with the West. South Korea's military was bolstered by U.S. troops and U.S. nuclear weapons on its soil. Pyongyang watched the Cuban missile crisis unfold in a manner that shed doubt on Soviet commitments to its allies. It witnessed the Sino-Soviet split and the Chinese Cultural Revolution. Each of these developments reinforced the notion that Pyongyang could only rely on itself for the North's security. Although Pyongyang fielded an immense conventional army and its deadly artillery along the Demilitarized Zone (DMZ) was poised to destroy Seoul, nuclear weapons would help to balance the U.S. nuclear presence in the South. Therefore, the political drivers existed to match Pyongang's sustained technological drive to develop or import the necessary reactor and reprocessing facilities to eventually build nuclear weapons, a technological base that it completed by 1990.

By the early 1990s, Pyongyang's security environment deteriorated dramatically. As the Cold War drew to a close, Pyongyang lost financial assistance from the former Soviet bloc. Its archrival, South Korea, had pulled ahead economically as well as strengthened its military. China focused on its economic rise and reached out to South Korea, and Russia recognized the South as well. Pyongyang was devastated by these changes and began seriously to explore accommodation with the West, especially with the United States. Carlin and Lewis[15] believe that Kim Il-sung made the strategic decision to engage the United States and even accept U.S. military presence in the South as a hedge against potentially hostile Chinese or Russian influence.

Kim Il-sung took bold steps toward reconciliation with the South. He signed a North-South reconciliation agreement and North-South denuclearization agreement, which altered the security landscape and offered a potential resolution to the nuclear issue.[16] Following a difficult start with the Clinton administration, Pyongyang agreed to trade its gas-graphite reactors and associated fuel-cycle facilities for two LWRs and interim energy assistance in the form of heavy fuel oil. Carlin and Lewis point out that Pyongyang viewed the political provisions of the Agreed Framework, which called for both sides to move toward full normalization of political and economic relations, to be the heart of the pact.

However, reconciliation between and Pyongyang proved difficult, as Washington saw the Agreed Framework primarily as a nonproliferation agreement. Struck by the Clinton administration as the best alternative to avoid war and put the North on a path to denuclearization, the Agreed Framework was opposed immediately by many in Congress who believed that it rewarded bad behavior. Congress failed to appropriate funds for key provisions of the pact, causing the United States to fall behind in its commitments almost from the beginning. The LWR project also fell behind schedule because the legal arrangements were much more complex than anticipated. The Agreed Framework, which began as a process of interaction and cooperation, quickly turned into accusations of non-compliance by both parties.

The 1990s were also particularly difficult times domestically for North Korea. In addition to geopolitical changes, North Korea lost Kim Il-sung and had to cope with a series of natural disasters that added to its economic devastation and decimated its industrial capacity. Its once mighty conventional military was decaying. Its hope for receiving the benefits of nuclear electricity to help bolster its sagging economy appeared a distant hope because of delays in implementation of the Agreed Framework. However, the diplomatic crisis resulting from its 1998 rocket launch over Japan was resolved by the Perry Process, which brought Pyongyang's second-ranking official, Vice-Marshal Jo Myong-rok, to the White House in October 2000.[17] The two sides issued a joint communiqué that pledged "neither would have hostile intent toward the other and confirmed the commitment of both governments to make every effort in the future to build a new relationship free from past enmity." This communiqué signaled to Pyongyang for the first time that the United States recognized the right of North Korea to exist. The follow-up meeting between Secretary of State Madeleine Albright and Kim Jong-il that was held in Pyongyang a couple of weeks later appeared to put the nuclear crisis on a path to final resolution.

With the change in administrations in Washington, hope for a settlement was quickly dashed. Whereas Pyongyang was waiting for a U.S. response to the Perry Process, it ran into the Bush administration's adamant opposition to the terms of the Agreed Framework and to political accommodation. Pyongyang practiced restraint with the incoming Bush administration until North Korea was accused of a covert uranium enrichment program and saw the Agreed Framework come to an end. During the confrontation over enrichment in October 2002, First Vice Minister of Foreign Affairs Kang Sok-ju told his American counterpart, "We are a part of the axis of evil.... If we disarm ourselves because of U.S. pressure, then we will become like Yugoslavia or Afghanistan's Taliban, to be beaten to death."[18] Pyongyang withdrew from the NPT and restarted its dormant Yongbyon facilities to produce fuel for a plutonium bomb.

Pyongyang's security fears were further heightened by the invasion of Iraq. Pyongyang now believed the bomb would assure its survival, so it no longer hid its nuclear weapons aspirations. At the six-party negotiations, Pyongyang again declared its willingness to denuclearize in return for political accommodation and economic and energy assistance. Although Pyongyang signed the Joint Denuclearization Statement on September 19, 2005, the talks were mired in distrust and accusations. They led to alternate cycles of dialogue and confrontation.

Pyongyang viewed U.S. financial sanctions imposed at the same time as a breach of the denuclearization pact. It withdrew from the talks and launched a second long-range rocket in July 2006 and conducted its first nuclear test in October 2006. The test drew UN Security Council sanctions, but Pyongyang appeared to offset the negative effects of sanctions with increased diplomatic leverage. Later that year, the Bush administration radically changed its negotiating strategy with Pyongyang for the remainder of its term. It conducted bilateral negotiations under the umbrella of the six-party talks, something that Pyongyang had desired but that the Bush administration had refused to do for six years. Pyongyang viewed this change as a direct result of its new nuclear status, whereas domestic U.S. politics and the results of the 2006 congressional elections may have played a greater role.

During the remainder of the Bush administration, Pyongyang agreed again to halt its nuclear program, but not to eliminate it. During my visit three weeks after the nuclear test in 2006, North Korean officials made it clear that their negotiation strategy had changed. They considered North Korea to be a nuclear power and wanted to talk arms control with Washington, not denuclearization focused on the North.[19]

In early 2009, Pyongyang decided not to wait for engagement by the Obama administration, but instead took aggressive steps to enhance its missile program. These steps prompted more UN sanctions, which Pyongyang used as an excuse to walk away from all its international nuclear obligations and to restart its nuclear program, including testing a second nuclear device in May. Although security concerns continue to dominate its decision-making, Pyongyang's actions were most likely driven by domestic and diplomatic factors rather than an increased sense of insecurity.

Scott D. Sagan's Domestic Politics Model

Sagan's domestic politics model posits that nuclear weapons may serve the bureaucratic or political interests of individual actors, such as the military, the nuclear establishment, politicians, or the public. Such actors or coalitions of actors may influence the state's decision-making. Sagan cites the Indian nuclear program as a particularly convincing case of the importance of domestic politics and the influence of domestic advocacy groups. He further demonstrates that domestic political factors played strong roles in nuclear decision-making in South Africa, Ukraine, Argentina, and Brazil.

Domestic politics are clearly different in North Korea. The Kim dynasty, father and son, has ruled the country with an iron fist and based its legitimacy, in large part, on a cult of personality of its leaders. To stay in power, the regime tightly controls all information, limits contact of its people with the outside world, and warns its people that external forces constantly threaten the very existence of their nation. External threats are used to justify keeping the country on a constant war-footing that requires continued sacrifices by and harsh treatment of its people. Natalia Bazhanova[20] points out that in communist countries the pursuit of nuclear weapons to meet external threats helps to increase tensions at home and distract people's attention from their daily grievances and the failures of the regime. The need for nuclear weapons drives home the severity of the external threat.

The need for nuclear weapons was not directly invoked with the public until 2003, when Pyongyang openly declared its pursuit of nuclear weapons. Propaganda was greatest after the long-range missile and nuclear tests in 2006 and 2009. Although Pyongyang's leaders have not had to contend with political opposition or public uprisings, the nuclear card, along with the missile program, has helped to emphasize the power and prestige of the regime. There was much speculation that a succession crisis was driving Pyongyang's decision making in 2008, after Kim Jong-il was reported to have suffered a stroke and appeared frail. Kim Jong-il reemerged and appeared to have rearranged the domestic power structure and solidified his control. Still, any future succession crisis in the DPRK may make cooperation with the United States less likely, as potential leaders would want to avoid being branded as "weak" or as "appeasing" Washington in negotiations about the nuclear program.

Sagan's norms model views nuclear decisions as also serving important symbolic functions externally—both shaping and reflecting a state's identity. Norms and shared beliefs about what is legitimate and appropriate in international relations can drive nuclear decision-making. Symbolism becomes important. Nuclear weapons become part of what defines a legitimate, modern state. Sagan contends that the French decision to build nuclear weapons was more the result of French leaders' perceptions of the bomb's symbolic significance than its security calculus. Sagan also shows how international norms, such as the NPT, helped to restrain nations' nuclear ambitions and, in cases such as Ukraine, to relinquish a nuclear arsenal inherited from the Soviet Union.

Pyongyang does not appear to have allowed international norms to influence its nuclear decision-making. The record shows that its own needs always trumped international norms and obligations. Pyongyang signed the NPT because of the promise of Soviet LWRs, but did not sign the required safeguards agreement with the IAEA for years because it wanted to keep its nuclear construction hidden from the world.

Pyongyang withdrew from the NPT in 2003 and defied international norms and UN sanctions with its two nuclear tests and long-range missile launches. Pyongyang decided to hedge its bets during the Agreed Framework, violating the agreement and its NPT commitments by acquiring export-controlled materials and equipment from abroad in order to explore the uranium enrichment route to the bomb.

However, international symbolism and prestige derived from nuclear technologies and weapons played an important role. North Korea views itself as a small and weak nation in spite of its domestic propaganda to the contrary. Once Pyongyang acquired and demonstrated the bomb, it used the power and prestige derived from the bomb as a diplomatic lever to strengthen its negotiating position. Its decision to confront the Obama administration with a missile launch and a nuclear test was more likely an attempt to gain diplomatic leverage and possibly to support domestic changes, rather than an effort toward deterring an increased security threat.

Pyongyang may also simply have decided to take advantage of the transition to accomplish two objectives while the Obama administration was still formulating its Northeast Asia security policies and assembling its executive team. North Korea's long-range missile program needed additional flight tests, and Pyongyang needed to demonstrate to itself and the world that its nuclear weapons could do better than the 2006 test. The missile and nuclear tests must have been on the shelf ready to go for some time, looking for a convenient window.

Will North Korea Give Up the Bomb?

What can we learn from how and why North Korea built the bomb? North Korea is unlikely to give up its nuclear arsenal anytime soon because it has become crucial to how the regime assures its security. Nuclear weapons also play a supportive role domestically and provide diplomatic leverage. Pyongyang views its security concerns as existential. They are deeply rooted in history and, hence, are unlikely to be resolved by alliances with its neighbors, each of which North Korea believes to have ulterior motives. Pyongyang turned to the United States, but it found Washington unreliable and inconsistent. In spite of having received numerous security guarantees that promised to respect its sovereignty along with assurances not to invade the country, Pyongyang still feels threatened today. It will require much more than another security guarantee to make Pyongyang feel secure.

Even if North Korea's security fears are assuaged, domestic factors favor keeping the bomb. The external threat is used to justify the need for the bomb and the sacrifices North Korea's people are asked to make. That threat also helps keep its people submissive and isolated from the international community. It also helps the regime continue to control all information and to blind its people to progress in the rest of the world, especially south of the DMZ. Paradoxically, compared to a more democratic country, an autocracy like North Korea may find it easier to give up its weapons if doing so is seen to help the regime survive, because it does not have to deal with domestic opposition.

Military might is the only source of Pyongyang's diplomatic power today. Nuclear weapons have become central to the projection of its military might, in spite of the fact that its nuclear arsenal has little war-fighting utility. Pyongyang views nuclear weapons as diplomatic equalizers with its much more prosperous and powerful, but non-nuclear rivals, South Korea and Japan. Without nuclear weapons, North Korea would get scant attention from the international community.

Many believe that the bomb is only a bargaining chip and that North Korea is willing to sell it for the right price. However, for reasons stated above, there is no price high enough for Pyongyang to sell. It is also not about to give up its nuclear weapons first as a condition of normalization. Pyongyang may agree to denuclearize in principle, but it will drag out implementation as it did during the six-party process.

It is also unlikely that North Korea can be forced to give up the bomb. Realistically, military options are off the table unless North Korea initiates a conflict. Additionally, sanctions are ineffective without China's support, but China will not support sanctions that bring Pyongyang to its knees. Beijing fears U.S. intervention in North Korea more than it does nuclear weapons in its neighbor's hands. It wants peace and stability on the Korean peninsula.

As undesirable as it may sound, the best hope is a long-term strategy to contain the nuclear threat while tackling the North Korean problem comprehensively, but in discrete steps.[21] Both Beijing and Seoul favor taking the long view. Time is not on Pyongyang's side. The greatest threat to the regime is not from the outside, but from within. It can't hold back its people forever from the tide of change surrounding its borders. In the meantime, it is important to avoid a clash between Pyongyang and Seoul or Tokyo. And it is essential to stop Pyongyang from doing additional damage around the world through nuclear cooperation and exports. Beijing is likely willing to restrain North Korea from expanding its nuclear program and, most importantly, to stop it from exporting its nuclear materials or technologies. That is how our joint efforts should be directed to reduce this dangerous threat.

The lessons of North Korea will not be lost on other potential proliferators, particularly Iran. Pyongyang broke new ground in defying international norms and took advantage of the international community's inability to respond effectively. Restricting supply of nuclear technologies through international treaties, norms, and arrangements slows down, but does not stop determined proliferators. We must understand the demand side of nuclear proliferation. Motivation may change over time; it becomes more difficult to reverse proliferation the longer a nuclear program has been pursued and the more successful it has become. In North Korea's case, the security motivation was augmented by domestic and diplomatic considerations and also by time and increased programmatic success. Many have called Pyongyang's actions unpredictable and bizarre, but I find that they are most likely based on a deliberate calculus of its needs, its negotiating strategy, and the necessarily inexact science of negotiations and implementation.

Conclusion

North Korea demonstrated how a sustained technical effort can develop the nuclear weapons option under civilian nuclear energy cover and, by exercising its NPT Article X rights to withdraw from the Treaty, how that option can be exercised quickly once proper political conditions emerge. The choice of fuel cycle for the civilian cover is important. Pyongyang selected the gas-graphite reactor technology, which was the best dual-use option. A lack of transparency and cooperation with the IAEA should serve as a red flag of a state's nuclear weapons aspiration. Pyongyang also confirmed that producing the fissile material—plutonium in this case—is the critical step. It was able to build the bomb rapidly once it had plutonium because it had tested the non-fissile components of the weapon beforehand. North Korea taught us that we should not underestimate the indigenous capabilities of nations willing to commit resources to build the bomb. Both Russia and China underestimated this capability and, consequently, misjudged the severity of the threat. In Washington, the threat was often exaggerated for political purposes. Hence, it is important to get accurate, publicly available technical assessments of nuclear capabilities.

Pyongyang showed that a nuclear arsenal does not have to be large or sophisticated to be politically effective. Nuclear tests strengthened the country's hands and tied the hands of the international community. Thus, it is crucial to stop aspiring programs short of demonstrating their capabilities. All nuclear threats are not equal; prioritization is critical. The Bush administration killed the Agreed Framework for domestic political reasons and because it suspected

Pyongyang of cheating by covertly pursuing uranium enrichment. Doing so traded a potential threat that would have taken years to turn into bombs for one that took months, dramatically changing the diplomatic landscape in Pyongyang's favor. On the other hand, the Bush administration did not deal effectively with North Korea's egregious, secret construction of a plutonium production reactor in Syria, which constituted a serious proliferation threat. Moreover, Pyongyang may also be engaged in similar, and perhaps even more dangerous, liaisons with the likes of Iran and Burma.

The United States plays an indispensable role in proliferation prevention, but it can't go it alone. It cannot afford to sit at the sidelines as it has done with Iran. We found that Pyongyang was willing to slow its drive for nuclear weapons only when it believed the fundamental relationship with the United States was improving, but not when the regime was threatened. Pyongyang was willing to tolerate the six-party negotiations, but progress was made only when Washington agreed to bilateral dialogue. Washington holds the key to incentives, but by itself cannot impose sufficient disincentives to eventually convince North Korea to give up its weapons. It must have support from Beijing and Seoul, both of which have very different strategic objectives.

The more divided we are at home, the more we yield advantage to the adversary. Political divisions in Washington in recent years resulted in our inability to negotiate the nuclear crisis effectively. American diplomats lament that it has been more difficult to negotiate in Washington than at the six-party table. Not only have we not been able to negotiate effectively, but also we have allowed Pyongyang to cross with impunity every red line we have drawn. The U.S. negotiating position has also been hampered by our inability to sustain consistent policies through transitions in administrations. Pyongyang has taken advantage of our political divisions to play a weak hand with success. Unless we learn from the lessons of North Korea, others may be able do the same.[22]

Notes

1. See the article by So Ki-sok, senior researcher from the DPRK (Democratic People's Republic of Korea; or, North Korea) Institute for Disarmament and Peace, in "Three Perspectives on Korean Developments," presented at a July 2009 meeting of the Council for Security Cooperation in the Asia-Pacific (CSCAP) Study Group on Countering the Proliferation of Weapons of Mass Destruction, http://csis.org/publication/pacnet-55-three-perspectives-korean-developments.

2. Scott D. Sagan, "Why Do States Build Nuclear Weapons? Three Models in Search of a Bomb," *International Security* 21 (3) (Winter 1996/1997): 54–86; also updated in Scott D. Sagan, "Rethinking the Causes of Nuclear Proliferation: Three Models in Search of

a Bomb," in *The Coming Crisis: Nuclear Proliferation, U.S. Interests, and World Order*, ed. Victor A. Utgoff (Cambridge, MA: MIT Press, 2000), 17–50.

3. The gas-graphite reactors were patterned after the British Calder Hall Magnox reactor, whose technical specifications were readily available because they were widely disseminated in the United Kingdom.

4. The alternative path for natural uranium-fueled reactors is a heavy water reactor, such as the Canadian CANDU reactor. This was India's choice for its first reactor, which was constructed by Canada with U.S.-supplied heavy water. However, after India used the plutonium produced by that reactor for its first nuclear test in 1974, it would have been difficult for North Korea to get external assistance. North Korea required external assistance because it did not have the capacity to produce heavy water.

5. The reprocessing facility resembles an extension of the design of the Eurochem reprocessing plant in Belgium.

6. The Agreed Framework signed between the United States and North Korea on October 21, 1994, in Geneva agreed to have North Korea freeze its existing nuclear program. In addition to U.S. supply of LWRs and delivery of heavy fuel oil, the two sides agreed to move toward full normalization of political and economic relations and work together for peace and security on a nuclear-free Korean peninsula. See Joel S. Wit, Daniel B. Poneman, and Robert L. Gallucci, *Going Critical: The First North Korean Nuclear Crisis* (Washington, DC: Brookings Institution, 2004) for informative discussions of the Agreed Framework and North Korean crisis in the 1990s.

7. In the late 1990s, Pyongyang is reported to have acquired centrifuge technology from Pakistan's A.Q. Khan, as reported by Pervez Musharraf in his book *In the Line of Fire: A Memoir* (New York: Free, 2006). Additional evidence, including the purchase of aluminum tubes suitable for centrifuge rotors from Russia and attempted purchase from Germany, is discussed in Hui Zhang, "Assessing North Korea's Uranium Enrichment Capabilities," *Bulletin of the Atomic Scientists* (June 18, 2009), http://www.thebulletin.org/web-edition/features/assessing-north-koreas-uranium-enrichment-capabilities.

8. The six-party talks, which were initiated in 2003, involved the United States, North Korea, and its four neighbors: South Korea, China, Japan, and Russia.

9. David Albright and Kevin O'Neill, eds., *Solving the North Korean Nuclear Puzzle* (Washington, DC: Institute of Science and International Security, 2002).

10. For a detailed assessment of the state of the Yongbyon nuclear complex, see Siegfried S. Hecker, "Denuclearizing North Korea," *Bulletin of the Atomic Scientists* 64 (2) (2008): 44–49, 61–62.

11. All of the plutonium estimates have high uncertainties. If we estimate a 10 percent loss during reprocessing (which includes waste and material held up in plant equipment), that reduces the amount to 36 to 54 kilograms before testing, leaving an estimated 24 to 42 kilograms after testing, assuming that North Korea expended 6 kilograms per test (roughly the amount in the Nagasaki plutonium bomb). In 2008, North Korea declared that it had 26 kilograms reprocessed and weaponized. (By that time, it had conducted one nuclear test and it still had roughly 8 kilograms in the fuel rods that were reprocessed in 2009.) Although that number is low, it is possibly correct.

12. This point has been made in Siegfried S. Hecker, "The Risks of North Korea's Nuclear Restart," *Bulletin of the Atomic Scientists* (May 12, 2009).

13. The evidence for North Korean assistance to Syria is strong; see David Albright and Paul Brannan, "The Al Kibar Reactor: Extraordinary Camouflage, Troubling Implications," Institute for Science and International Security (ISIS) Report, May 12, 2008, http://isisonline.org/publications/syria/index.html. Evidence of cooperation with Libya is less conclusive, yet likely; see David E. Sanger and William J. Broad, "Tests Said to Tie Deal on Uranium to North Korea," *The New York Times*, February 2, 2005. Evidence of nuclear cooperation with Burma is weak, but possible; see Julian Borger, "Burma Sus-

pected of Forming Nuclear Link with North Korea," Guardian.co.uk, July 21, 2009, http://www.guardian.co.uk/world/2009/jul/21/burma-north-korea-nuclear-clinton.

14. Siegfried S. Hecker and William Liou, "Dangerous Dealings: North Korea's Nuclear Capabilities and the Threat of Export to Iran," *Arms Control Today* 37 (2) (2007), http://www.armscontrol.org/act/2007_03/heckerliou; and Siegfried S. Hecker, "From Pyongyang to Tehran, with Nukes," op-ed, *Foreign Policy* (May 26, 2009).

15. Robert Carlin and John Lewis, *Negotiating with North Korea: 1992–2007* (Center for International Security and Cooperation, Freeman Spogli Institute for International Studies, Stanford University, January 2008), http://iis-db.stanford.edu/pubs/22128/Negotiating_with_North_Korea_1992-2007.pdf.

16. The North-South Denuclearization Agreement signed on December 31, 1991, vowed that neither would test, manufacture, produce, receive, possess, store, deploy, or use nuclear weapons. The Agreement on Reconciliation, Nonaggression, and Exchanges and Cooperation between South and North Korea (also known as the Basic Agreement), signed on February 19, 1992, reaffirmed a 1972 Joint Communiqué that the North and South are determined to end the state of political and military confrontation and achieve national reconciliation; to avoid armed aggression and hostilities; and to ensure the lessening of tension and the establishment of peace and the desire to realize multifaceted exchanges and cooperation to promote interests and prosperity common to the Korean people. At the time, this agreement was the more significant of the two. The denuclearization agreement never received serious consideration for implementation.

17. Former Secretary of Defense William J. Perry led a North Korea policy review for President Clinton. The full report can be found at http://www.state.gov/www/regions/eap/991012_northkorea_rpt.html.

18. Charles L. Pritchard, *Failed Diplomacy: The Tragic Story of How North Korea Got the Bomb* (Washington, DC: Brookings Institution, 2007), 25.

19. For a detailed description of the political developments in North Korea during the past decade, see Mike Chinoy, *Meltdown: The Inside Story of the North Korean Nuclear Crisis* (New York: St. Martin's, 2008).

20. Natalia Bazhanova, "Economic Factors and the Stability of the North Korean Regime," in *The North Korean Nuclear Programs*, ed. Clay Moltz and Alexandre Mansourov (London: Routledge, 2000), 60.

21. In his 1995 analysis of the North Korean nuclear crisis, Michael Mazarr argued that complete denuclearization may be too high a standard for hard-core proliferators; progress will come instead in fits and starts. Michael J. Mazarr, *North Korea and the Bomb: A Case Study in Nonproliferation* (New York: St. Martin's, 1995).

22. The author is indebted for close readings and suggestions on an earlier draft made by Chaim Braun, Robert Carlin, Thomas Fingar, John Lewis, Michael May, Niko Milonopoulos, Scott Sagan, David Straub, Kevin Veal, and Philip Yun.

CHAPTER 13

Channels of Engagement with North Korea: Academic Exchanges
Bernhard J. Seliger and *Suk Hi Kim*

ABSTRACT

If North Korea collapses sometime in the future, it will be because of its economic problems. Observers describe the North Korean economy in a number of distinct ways, such as state ownership of the means of production, centralized economic planning, and an economic system designed to be self-reliant and closed; all of which has made the country's economy highly inefficient. To overcome problems arising from these types of economic management, North Korea began to reform its economy almost ten years ago. There have been numerous attempts by North Korea to liberalize its ailing economy; however, to date, these measures have been peripheral and completely inadequate to pull the economy out of the nosedive. If North Korea wants to survive as an independent state in the long run, it will have to liberalize its economy as much as China or Vietnam. But there is a catch. Any economic reform by North Korea will not succeed unless it has enough managers and administrators who understand the principles of the market economy and practice them. Apparently, North Korea appears to be aware of this problem, because the country has begun to allow foreign organizations and individuals to train North Korean professionals and to send its promising young people to study abroad and attend international conferences. By the end of the 1990s, for example, North Korea had begun to allow an unprecedented number of its officials and civilians to travel abroad for training purposes in a variety of areas.[1] There is reason to believe that North Korea may be ready to integrate its economy with the world economy. Thus, the United States and its allies should consider their engagement with North Korea as a long-term strategy to complement the short-term focus on North Korea's nuclear capabilities.

Although there are several channels of engagement with North Korea, this chapter will focus on academic exchanges, because they would generate a vested interest in continued reform without strengthening the coercive power of North Korea, as is the case with foreign aid.[2]

Introduction

In the early years following the Korean War (1950–1953), the centrally directed economy of North Korea had been larger in per capita income and had grown more rapidly than the more loosely controlled economy of South Korea. However, in the absence of rational and strategic economic planning, these advantages soon reached their limits. By the mid–1970s, South Korea's two successful five-year economic plans put it ahead of North Korea. Loss of allies in the early 1990s, consecutive floods in 1995 and 1996, and a severe drought in 1997 caused the North Korean economy to shrink in the 1990s. Thus, while North Korea had gradually reformed its troubled economic system since the early 1990s, these measures were different from market-oriented reform. However, in July 2002, North Korea began to introduce the most significant liberalization measures since the start of communist rule in 1948.

A series of crises since 1990 have forced North Korea to think seriously about the future of its autarkic system, resulting in a host of new laws on foreign investment, relations with capitalist firms, currency reforms, new zones of free trade, and other reforms. North Korea has promulgated many banking, labor, and investment laws over the last 20 years. It could reap numerous benefits from its expanded economic cooperation with South Korea and other countries. The direct benefits include the creation of infrastructure and facilities, employee wages paid by South Korea or foreign companies, the sale of raw materials, and the development of related industries and neighboring areas. The indirect benefits include the attraction of foreign capital, improved country risk ratings, and the easing of the economic sanctions imposed by the United States and its allies. However, these measures have not gone well, thereby making the North Korean economy even worse than before.

We consider recent reforms in North Korea as a signal that its authorities recognize that its long-term survival may depend on returning to sustained economic growth.[3] Any economic reform by North Korea will not succeed unless it has enough managers and administrators who understand the principles of the market economy and practice them. Apparently, North Korea appears to be aware of this problem, because the country has begun to allow foreign organizations and individuals to train North Korean professionals and to send its promising young people to study abroad and attend international conferences. Thus, it is about time for the United States and its allies to consider economic engagement with North Korea as a central part of their long-term strategy in dealing with Pyongyang. Such an economic engagement could induce and reinforce North Korea's peaceful transition into a country that can better engage with other countries in a nonhostile manner.[4]

This chapter introduces six organizations that engage in the training of North Korean professionals: the Hanns Seidel Foundation Korea, the Nautilus Institute for Security and Sustainability, Pyongyang International Business School, Syracuse University, Pyongyang University of Science & Technology, and Chosun Exchange.

The Hanns Seidel Foundation Korea

The Hanns Seidel Foundation (HSF), a German nonprofit organization funded mainly by the German Ministry for Economic Co-operation, is active in more than 55 countries worldwide to promote economic and political development. In South Korea, where the HSF has had an office since 1987, the focus of the work is the preparation for reconciliation and eventual peaceful unification on the Korean Peninsula. Among other cooperation projects with NGOs, universities, and research institutes, the HSF has cooperated with Gangwon province on sustainable development in the border area between the two Korean states.

In North Korea, the HSF has been active since 2003 with capacity-building measures. In the series "International Finance," seminars on "International Financial Institutions, Financial Integration and Transformation" and on "Monetary and Exchange Rate Policy" were carried out with the Economic Institute of the Cabinet, a governmental research institute. Among the participants of the training units were employees of the Ministry of Finance and the Economy, the central bank, specialized banking and financial institutions of North Korea, and academic institutions such as Kim Il-Sung University.

A new series, the "EU–North Korea Trade Capacity Project," began in 2006, with funding from the European Union. In three 2006 seminars, basic aspects of international trade from the perspective of economics and management were discussed, and the functioning of chambers of commerce as business intermediaries was explained. In two basic training units, professors of economics and business administration made the case for participation in international trade and showed the advantages of international trade integration, in particular for small economies.

The aim of the first two seminars was to open the eyes of participants to the many prerequisites and preparations for international trade and integration into the international division of labor. The following topics were addressed: the theoretical foundations of international business; multinational companies as actors in international trade; entry modes of international business; human resource management in international business; European integration as an example for successful trade integration; the trade policy of the small country Estonia, as an example of successful transformation and opening; and world trade policy and institutions.

Did the programs succeed? It is generally more difficult to measure the direct impact of seminars on the mindset of the participants than it is to measure more technically defined skills. However, the Q&A sessions in particular gave some insights into business methods and business thinking in North Korea. For example, the more sophisticated foreign packaging and marketing activities were often discussed as a form of deception. For example, in the local markets, Chinese foods that were well packed and that carried expiration dates, but that had allegedly inferior quality, were denounced as a way of cheating customers. In other words, the companies are particularly aware of the lack of these elements (marketing, attractive packaging, etc.) in their own products. Another set of questions regarded real or alleged trade barriers from the European Union and worldwide, foremost among them being the restrictions on financial transactions through the U.S. threats to freeze financial assets. However, the lack of experience with the competition, and the perceived lack of competitiveness of their own products, also were topics.

Business intermediaries are an important way to help companies establish international trade links. In particular, the North Korean companies with few existing outside links need the support of business intermediaries. In cooperation with the "European Business Organizations," the network of European Chambers of Commerce abroad, the participants in the last training unit were introduced to the tasks, structure, financing, and activities of European Chambers of Commerce abroad. The participants in all of the training units came from exporting companies, governmental agencies such as the Ministry of Foreign Trade, and academic institutions such as Kim Il-Sung University.

Both programs will be extended into the future, if political circumstances allow. Additionally, in 2005 two North Korean students went to Germany with a scholarship from the HSF to study business administration for one year at Deggendorf University of Applied Sciences. Other exchange programs are currently being discussed with the North Korean authorities. Also, in 2007 the HSF donated economic textbooks to North Korean universities. There is no doubt that the twin missile and (alleged) nuclear tests did not improve the situation for exchange and cooperation.

Overall, the experience of the first year of the EU–North Korea Trade

Capacity Project is mixed. On an operational level, the goal of the project to carry out three capacity-building measures was achieved. Grave problems existed in the communication with the Korean partners concerning the selection of approved North Korean participants. This selection has been a unilateral choice by North Korea, often not completely according to the ideas of the Hanns Seidel Foundation. This is due to the fact that the Korean European Cooperation Coordinating Agency (KECCA), a front organization of the Ministry of Foreign Affairs of North Korea, has been set up to centralize relations of European organizations with North Korean partners, effectively barring them from independent communication. The month of December 2005, when these changes were introduced and when many European aid workers had to leave North Korea, was the real watershed for European activities in North Korea, and this also affects the EU–North Korea Trade Capacity Project. Nevertheless, the success of the three capacity-building measures remains evident.

How these measures can be expected to contribute to real-world changes in North Korea—given that trade and opening up in general become less and less of a realistic alternative, in the face of tensions and the bunker mentality of the North Korean leadership—is another question altogether. One important aspect here is the creation of new ideas in a mid-level field of bureaucrats and managers, based on the already visible divergence of interests of many participants. North Korea is far from being a homogenous mass, though its politics always stress this aspect of its policy-making. It remains important to encourage discussions about openness, and this event gains in importance with the increased tensions created by the leadership. Another important aspect is the trust-building effect of such measures, which are aimed at helping to improve of the North Korean economy. Given that, at least in part, the North Korean stance toward the international community is one of a lack of trust, such trust-building efforts, though not immediately measurable, might be an important investment in the possibility of future reconciliation.

Naturally, there are strict limits to such an idea of capacity building. Ultimately, a clear decision in favour of opening up at the very highest level has to precede any effective reform measures, and there are good reasons, related to the internal stability of the regime, that make such a decision unlikely for the time being. Also, a united and clear response to the nuclear tests, as the latest breach of international treaties and rules, is important to bring North Korea back to the negotiating table. Capacity-building projects cannot be insulated from such policies, as the distinction between "purely political" and "purely capacity-building" actions does not exist; ultimately, capacity-building efforts are part of the package "European Policies towards North Korea." Each time relations worsen between the EU and North Korea, the possibilities for capacity-building projects are reduced. It is to be hoped that future multilateral negotiations will lead to an improved environment, making such projects more and more feasible and effective. Those who would like to know more about the activities of the HSF are encouraged to visit http://www.hss.or.kr.

The Nautilus Institute for Security and Sustainability

Since its foundation in 1992, the Nautilus Institute has evolved into a thriving public policy think-tank and community resource. Along the way, it has addressed critical security and sustainability issues such as the U.S. nuclear policy in Korea and the effect of the U.S.-China relationship on environmental insecurity. The Institute has built a reputation not only for innovative research and analysis of critical global problems; it also translates ideas into practical solutions, often with high impact. Now with a branch office in Melbourne, Australia, at the Royal Melbourne Institute of Technology, Nautilus pursues its mission through a highly networked organization. Two of the Institute's 14 projects are designed to help North Korea improve the use of its scarce energy resources.

DPRK Building Energy Efficiency Training (BEET)

Nautilus of America, working with partners in China and the Global Cities Institute in Australia, has performed an energy efficiency upgrade of a building in Pyongyang. This project built trust and reinforced communication between North Korea and the outside world. It also exemplified the best way to build energy security in North Korea for negotiations with the North over nuclear weapons, and made an important intervention in the lives of North Korean people.

Humanitarian energy cooperation with North Korea has a direct and significant impact on the lives of many North Koreans, builds in-country human capacity, and helps to open the door to further engagement. Moreover, demonstration of the benefits of energy efficiency will help to focus policy-makers' attention on those energy aid options that offer the best long-term prospects to sustainably improve the North Korean energy sector and economy.

The project also provided an opportunity to engage North Korean energy-sector exports on what energy aid is needed in the North and it allowed the Nautilus staff to assess North Korea's energy infrastructure. This will help improve the Institute's unique database and set of quantitative and qualitative analytic tools to evaluate and track North Korea's energy economy. These tools then can be used to prepare energy analyses of the DPRK's energy sector, and energy aid and engagement options to support efforts to denuclearize the DPRK.

North Korea Energy Experts Working Group

Energy insecurity is a critical dimension of the North Korean nuclear challenge, both in its making and in its reversal. The Nautilus Institute maintains a unique database and set of quantitative and qualitative analytic tools to evaluate and track the North Korean energy economy, and has maintained working relations with North Korean scientists and technical personnel from the energy sector for more than a decade. With this capacity, Nautilus has provided a stream of policy analyses and briefings at their request to the United States, South Korea, and other officials on the North Korean energy needs, its likely negotiating postures and demands, and possible negotiable options. The need for such expertise in support of the Six-Party Talks is increasing.

This project ensures that the underlying data and technical analysis available at Nautilus is as up to date as possible, and that analysis and policy advice are available when needed by U.S. and other officials.

The North Korean Energy Expert Working Group updates the Nautilus Institute's North Korean energy database and related analysis by compiling the latest data from a wide array of sources, including North Korean announcements and analyses, input from experts who work in or visit North Korea on energy issues, and elsewhere, in a consistent physical framework for accounting for supply and demand over time, and forecasting future supply and demand levels based on different underlying drivers of the North Korean energy economy. This database underlies all Nautilus' research and policy analysis on the North Korean energy economy, and due to the nature of the underlying algorithms and coefficients that enable us to partly dissolve the granite curtain of opacity in North Korea, it is essential that the database be updated regularly. Those who would like to know more about the Nautilus Institute are encouraged to visit its website at http://www.nautilus.org/projects.

Pyongyang International Business School

The Pyongyang Business School was launched in 2004, under Swiss sponsorship, and enjoys the advisory support of the European Business Association. Its director, Felix Abt, oversees a program that includes 12 three-day seminars per year, sanctioned by examinations. The program covers a broad range of themes relevant to business management and administration. A number of

North Korean companies, ministries, and institutions register their senior professionals with the school. The lecturers are top managers from leading European corporations or prominent academics from European and Asian universities. The prominent Hong Kong Management Association regularly mandates lecturers. The school also publishes its lectures and associated texts, in Korean and English, for dissemination to North Korean firms, universities, ministries, and institutions; they are also posted on the North Korean intranet.

Context and Background

A need for further education and training in business management and administration tools was noted by the North Korean government, which resulted in discussions about parameters for a business program with the North Korean authorities and the Swiss Development Cooperation.

In the context of severely restricted financial resources, one very cost-effective means of ensuring capacity building in the import-export domain is to provide extensive training and appropriate exposure to its activities. Indeed, there is a need for Korean management staff to be trained in international state-of-the-art practices to meet the requirements of foreign investors and contribute to more foreign investment as another important hard-currency earner for the national economy. Dealing with foreign investors also requires the ability for policy-makers and officials to develop a legal framework to promote an attractive investment terrain in North Korea.

Partners

The school works with the North Korean authorities, companies, and universities and with the Swiss Development Cooperation. The director represents several international industrial groups in North Korea and ensures that the school reaches out to the wider community according to the school's objectives. His extensive experience in the North Korean business environment allows him to discern shortcomings associated with training requirements. Partnerships with the University of Applied Sciences in Northwest Switzerland and the Hong Kong Management Association provide scope for thematic approaches.

At present, the Swiss Development Cooperation (SDC) finances this venture. It is hoped that the EU, the UN, foundations and companies will take a financial interest in the school and contribute to its operational budget. Indeed, the European Business Association in Pyongyang actively promotes the school at the EU in Brussels and among European as well as Asian chambers of commerce in major cities.

As sponsorship becomes more diverse, the SDC's contribution will decrease. In the medium term, the school is intended to be self-reliant, operating by means of school fees and corporate sponsors rather than donations.

Business schools are often part of a university. This ensures a combined practical approach and professional experience with an academic approach. The Pyongyang Business School and its host university would both benefit from such exchanges. At the same time, university integration would ensure the program's sustainability.

Objectives

The Business School seeks to equip North Korean enterprises with the necessary tools to flourish and successfully compete in domestic and foreign markets. The medium- to long-term goal of the school is to provide an academic program commensurate with internationally recognized Master of Business Administration (MBA) programs.

The Business School also serves as a meeting platform for North Korean companies to exchange with foreign companies who could become customers, suppliers, or investors; for example, one lecturer has started to give contracts to North Korean software companies. The Asia Division Human Resources Director of a world-renowned chemical corporation has lectured at the school and subsequently generated an interest in investment opportunities for the North Korean environment.

A public management seminar is being considered. It would capitalize on experiences with market reforms in other countries where capacity building at different levels has helped to create favorable framework conditions for domestic and foreign investment, triggering a significant boost to national economies. Finally, the Pyongyang Business School collaborates with the DPRK government to promote exports.

Program Lectures Grouped According to Themes

- New Markets and Marketing, Marketing and New Enterprise Development Strategic Management Marketing Concepts and Strategy (Marketing Plan), International Marketing, Marketing Research, New Product Development and Corresponding Marketing Strategies, Advertising and Promotions Management, Buyer Behavior.
- Major Export Markets for North Korean Companies, Asian Markets of Choice, The New Europe and its Markets: Structure and Trends, International Trade Finance, Cross-Cultural Management.
- Organizational Behavior and Human Resource Management: Corporate Social Responsibility.
- Legal Issues in International Business.

- Management Issues: Management Decision-Making, Operations Management, Accounting and Financial Management Manufacturing Systems Management Supply Chain Management, E-commerce, Management of Information Systems, Strategic Quality Management.

Outcome Challenges

- To ensure a consistency of teaching and an up-to-date selection of seminars that remains relevant to both North Korea and the global environment.
- To maintain the quality of teaching and the subsequent sustainability of the school.
- To maintain the combination of academic and applied learning.

Monitoring and Evaluation

Seminar participants engage in discussions, and ask and answer questions. At the end of each seminar, they are required to take an examination and subsequent results establish that the teaching is relevant, clear, and interesting to the senior professionals who attend the seminars.

The North Korean partners, the director of the School, and the SDC meet regularly to discuss issues relevant to the School's operations, new programming, and potential links with universities, with domestic companies, and with companies or universities abroad. Those who would like to know more about Pyongyang International Business School are encouraged to visit its website at http://www.business-school-pyongyang.org/.

Collaboration: Syracuse University and Kim Chaek University[5]

Since 2001, Syracuse University (USA) and Kim Chaek University of Technology (Pyongyang, North Korea) have, with involvement of The Korea Society, been engaged in the only sustained U.S./North Korea academic science collaboration to date. Seven times in the first five years, North Korean scientists visited Syracuse for research collaboration on information technology (IT). Six times, the Syracuse team met with its North Korean counterparts in North Korea or China. The exchange enhanced IT capability in North Korea and provided an area of cooperation between the United States and North Korea, a necessary step toward reconciliation. To get the project started, the University consulted, in 2001, with The Korea Society—an organization based in New York City that promotes understanding and cooperation between the United States and Korea—and approached North Korea's United Nations mission to discuss possible joint academic engagement. The American government has been consulted throughout the program.

Concrete outcomes of the collaboration include the first digital library in North Korea, a multilateral Regional Scholars and Leaders Seminar program, the first ever participation by North Korea's undergraduates in the Association for Computing Machinery's International Collegiate Programming Contest, the development of a Junior Faculty Leadership and Development program to bring young North Korean scholars to the United States for semester long study, and a national academic conference on scientific cooperation with North Korea.

In May 2007, the U.S.–North Korea Scientific Engagement Consortium was established to explore collaborative academic science activities between the United States and North Korea. This consortium consists of four organizations: the U.S. Civilian Research & Development Foundation, the American Association for the Advancement of Science, Syracuse University, and The Korea Society. Between 2007 and 2009, this consortium engaged in a number of activities, such as workshops, public panels, and others to work toward collaboration with North Korean academics in a variety of areas such as agriculture, information technology, and health. Participants in these activities, funded by the Richard Lounsbery Foundation, included representatives from nine universities, and high-level officials from the U.S. government, Congress, and NGOs.

Pyongyang University of Science and Technology

In these times of global and economic uncertainty, North Korea watchers have to wonder how these crises will affect North Korea. Does the country have in place the kind of infrastructure that will enable it to deal with these global challenges and economic uncertainties as they arise, both now and into the future? One way for any country to face its future successfully is to educate its people. Chin Kyung Kim, the founder of the Pyongyang University of Science and Technology (PUST), stressed the need to develop relations with North Korea by any means possible, believing that "the future will be brighter if we put our hands together." When China opened its doors in 1979, he realized that what was needed was a university to satisfy a populace hungry for education. A few years later, he founded Yanbian University in the heart of China's ethnic Korean region of Yanbian, near the Tumen River frontier, to fulfill this purpose. The university has become a successful model for cooperation. Now, he is trying the same model with North Korea, with PUST, expected to be opened with a few hundred students in the next few years. Eventually, the university plans to increase its student body to 2,500 students and hire 250 professors.

PUST is North Korea's first institution of higher education founded, operated, and funded by associations and people outside the country. Since 2001, Chin Kyung Kim, Chan Mo Park (the former president of Phohang University of Science and Technology), and Malcolm Gillis (the former president of Rice University) have spearheaded the establishment with these privately raised funds to construct the 16 buildings necessary for the opening of the university. The dormitories, and the academic and utility buildings, were almost completed as of the end of 2008. PUST plans to train talented young North Korean people in the fields of information and communication technology, industrial management, agriculture, food and life science, architecture, joinery and construction, and public health. The major challenge that faces the university is related to maintaining its financial resources. The founders and their supporters will need to provide PUST with its entire operating and capital expenditures almost permanently, because North Korea will continue to suffer economic difficulties for many years.

It is hard to believe that Mr. Chin Kyung Kim is the same man who was detained for six weeks in North Korea in 1998 and threatened with a death sentence by his interrogators. The establishment of PUST represents a shift in the outlook of North Korea's ruling elite, which counted on the former Soviet Union and its eastern allies for most of its technical aid and advice until the breakup of the Soviet empire in 1990. PUST, along with the Kaesong Industrial Complex, appears to be the best kept secret for the long-term survival of North Korea. Kim served as a panel member of a session "The Strategic Role of North Korea" at the 9th World Knowledge Forum, held in Seoul, South Korea, on October 14–16, 2008. During this session, he argued that Asia needed a union, similar to the European model, and that this union would not be possible without the inclusion of North Korea to bridge the gap between North and South East Asia. Kim hopes that this new university will be a first step toward bridging that gap. Those who would like to know more about PUST are encouraged to visit its website at http://pust.kr.

Chosun Exchange

Yale University fellow Geoffrey See founded Chosun Exchange to train young North Koreans, to host academic visits, and to carry out other educational activities in North Korea. The following information about Chosun Exchange has been extracted from its website.

Who We Are

We are a nonprofit organization pioneering knowledge cooperation between economic and academic institutions in North Korea and their foreign counterparts. We encourage interaction through sharing educational resources, arranging university visits, and providing training in the business, legal, and economic fields to promising young North Koreans (under the age of 40). We also support projects in other academic fields.

Through our projects, we build trust and encourage mutual learning. Our team takes a long-term view (10–15 years) toward creating social impact. The Choson Exchange team is based primarily in Singapore and Boston, but its Organizing Committee is present in and coordinates activities in the Greater China region, Southeast Asia, and Europe.

What We Do

We take an integrated approach to our programs. We train young North Koreans through on-site lectures and e-learning. Through these programs, we identify North Koreans who are best suited for overseas learning opportunities and seek out opportunities for them to study abroad. While our programs focus on economics, business, and law, we also support on an occasional basis projects in other fields. We also welcome and support new ideas from universities and student groups, and help organize visits to academic institutions for interested groups or individuals.

Training programs: Our innovative training platform integrates Open Courseware with on-site programs to train North Koreans less than 40 years of age. We focus on business, economics, and law, and run occasional programs in public health, architecture, and other fields.

Field notes: Posts from our globally dispersed team from inside and outside North Korea on our work, lives, and random thoughts. We brainstorm new ideas in our Field Notes, broadcast changes to our organization here, and encourage you to get to know our team through your visit to our website.

Academic visits: Interested in visiting North Korean academic institutions? Our Visiting Fellows program caters to students and academics who wish to do so, with proceeds going to our training programs. Check out Academic Visits for updates and feel free to email us with questions.

Evaluations and analysis: Program evaluations, North Korean survey results, and original analysis relevant to our training programs written by team members and guest writers. All views represent the opinions of their respective authors, and do not represent the position of Choson Exchange. Those who would like to know more about Chosun Exchange are encouraged to visit its website at http://chosonexchange.org/.

Conclusion

The North Korean economy has been prominently characterized by two unusual features: an aid-seeking strategy and a military-first economic policy. Historically, North Korea relied on aid from its communist allies, particularly the Soviet Union and China, to augment its imports. Since the early 1990s when the Soviet Union collapsed, however, North Korea's survival strategy—its foreign aid seeking strategy—has not changed, but its approach has changed: it has become a combination of humanitarian aid and economic aid extracted through military threats; some call the latter "international military extortion." In some years before 2002, the amount of foreign aid for North Korea was more than the amount of its exports. In addition, North Korea has obtained a substantial amount of money through illegal or questionable methods, such as counterfeiting of hard currently, illegal sales of military equipment or technology, sales of illegal drugs, and/or the shipment of illegal cargoes between third-party countries. At the end of the day, we will never know what would have happened if the United States, South Korea, and their allies in Asia and Europe had refrained from underwriting the survival of North Korea since the 1990s. No matter what happens in North Korea and no matter what North Korea does, the country will never receive more aid than is just sufficient to avoid mass starvation. However, North Korea will never give up the hyper-militarization of the economy and the so-called "military extortion" until the United States adopts a long-term strategy of economic engagement with North Korea, because this isolated country has an insecurity dilemma.

"Sanctions have a role in defending the U.S. against risks of proliferation, but they have not and can not provide a long-run solution to the North Korean problem."[6] "Combining targeted sanctions with robust engagement ... offers the best hope of changing the motivations and the actions of states that presently take a hostile stance toward the U.S. and the international community." There are several channels of engagement with North Korea whose aid cannot be diverted into its military forces: official contacts, unofficial country-to-country dialogues, academic exchanges, nongovernmental organizations, and international financial institutions. The engagement of activities by the academic exchanges described in this chapter, development training, and assistance is perhaps the easiest to initiate in the short run and should be expanded now, with no conditions attached.

Notes

1. Kyung-Ae Park, "Regime Change in North Korea: Reform and Political Opportunity Structure," *North Korean Review* 5, no. 1 (Spring 2009): 23–45.
2. Charles Kartman, Susan Shirk, and John Delury, "North Korea Inside Out: The Case for Economic Engagement," Asia Society and the University of California, October 29, 2009.
3. Thomas F. Cargill and Elliott Parker, "Economic and Financial Reform: Alternatives for North Korea," *North Korean Review* 1 (Fall 2005): 5–21.
4. Kartman, Shirk, and Delury, pp. 5–7; and Bernhard Seliger, "The July 2002 Reforms in North Korea: Liberman-Style Reforms or Road to Transformation," *North Korean Review* 1 (Fall 2005): 22–37.
5. For detailed information on this academic collaboration, see Hyunjin Seo and Stuart Thorson, "Academic Science Engagement with North Korea," Academic Paper Series, Korea Economic Institute, April 2009, pp. 1–10; George S. Bain, "One Korea," http://www.maxwell.syr.edu/news.aspx?id=36507226699, September 7, 2010; and Stuart Thorson, Thomas Harbin, and Frederick F. Carriere, "U.S.-North Korean Trust Building through Academic Science Cooperation," http://frederickfcarriere.cgpublisher.com/index.html?manage_tabs_message=Product+added+to+order+click+%27Your+Cart%27+in+the+top+right+corner+to+view+your+shopping+cart+and+proceed+with+your+order%21.
6. Kartman, Shirk, and Delury, p. 5.

CHAPTER 14

U.S. Policy Options on a Nuclear North Korea

Suk Hi Kim and *Bernhard J. Seliger*

Abstract

According to U.S. think tanks and policy analysts, the United States has four options in dealing with a nuclear North Korea:[1]

1. Give economic aid and a security assurance if North Korea dismantles its nuclear program.
2. Use a military strike against North Korean nuclear facilities.
3. Let North Korea develop nuclear weapons.
4. Starve the North Korean regime of money.

Oddly enough, the United States, North Korea, and many North Korean experts believe that the United States should hand out economic aid and a security assurance if North Korea dismantles its nuclear program to settle the nuclear deadlock. If so, why has this option not worked thus far, and how can we make it work? This chapter will try to answer these questions.

Consequences of Failure for U.N. Sanctions Against North Korea

The United States and its allies have suspended six-party talks and assistance to North Korea in recent years. On June 12, 2009, the United Nations Security Council unanimously voted to expand and tighten sanctions against North Korea after the nation's second nuclear test. In fact, the United Nations, the United States, South Korea, and their allies have taken a series of new hard-line actions—tougher sanctions, a stronger proliferation security initiative (PSI), and so on—to punish North Korea for its defiant May 25, 2009, atomic test and a barrage of missile tests. In March 2010, a North Korean submarine sank a South Korean corvette, the *Cheonan*, killing 46 sailors on board. South Korean leaders sought a tough UN Security Council resolution and increased sanctions. However, the Council could agree to give only a President Statement that condemned the attack but refrained from linking responsibility directly to North Korea.[2]

In November 2010, tension rose to unexpected levels with two serious events. First, Stanford University scientist and former director of the Los Alamos National Laboratory Siegfried Hecker announced that during a trip he had taken to North Korea in mid-November, he had been shown a new nuclear facility consisting of countless centrifuges used for uranium enrichment. North Korean officials told Hecker there were 2,000 of these aluminum tubes up and running but the functional state of the facility was uncertain. It was clear the facility had been recently constructed, likely after April 2009 and probably done with outside help and in violation of UN sanctions. North Korea claimed the facility was for producing fuel to generate power but few believe Pyongyang is not pursuing another route to nuclear weapons.[3]

According to a *New York Times* report, "The Obama administration has concluded that North Korea's new plant to enrich nuclear fuel uses technology that is 'significantly more advanced' than what Iran has struggled over two decades to assemble." In carefully worded public comments on December 14, 2010, "both senior American and South Korean officials have also argued that this plant could not have been constructed so quickly unless there was a sophisticated network of other secret sites—and perhaps a fully running uranium enrichment plant—elsewhere in the country. These conclusions strongly suggest that North Korea has evaded the many layers of economic sanctions imposed by the United Nations Security Council and America's allies in Asia."[4]

The shock of these revelations was soon overtaken by the North Korean shelling of the South Korean island of Yeonpyeongdo. On November 23, South Korea conducted military exercises that included live fire drills close to the disputed Northern Limit Line. North Korea warned Seoul to stop the exercise and when the South did not comply, North Korean shore batteries launched 170 to 200 rounds on the island of Yeonpyeong killing two Marines and two civilians. South Korean artillery on the island responded with approximately 80 shells but the effect was minimal. The South Korean military, along with the Lee Myung-bak administration, is undergoing intense scrutiny over its preparation and response to the North Korean action. Pyongyang's motives for the attack are unclear but speculation includes arguments tied to the ongoing succession of Kim Jong-un, the North-South dispute over the NLL, and efforts to push Washington and Seoul back to the negotiating table. President

Lee has promised that North Korea will "pay a dear price without fail" should it take another provocative action but the final outcome of these events remain uncertain.

Has this new round of tougher actions against a nuclear North Korea worked, or will it work? These tougher actions have not worked so far. If history repeats itself, they will again undoubtedly fail. U.S. economic sanctions against North Korea began on June 28, 1950, three days after the outbreak of the Korean War. Since then, the United Nations, the United States, and its allies have increasingly imposed economic sanctions on North Korea in an attempt to destabilize and contain the North Korean regime.

However, these sanctions and other hard-line measures have been largely ineffective in stopping North Korea from developing weapons of mass destruction (WMD) and from outrageous provocations including the sinking of the South Korean warship *Cheonan* and the shelling of Yeonpyeong island. A series of hard-line moves taken by North Korea and the United States over the last few years appear to have caused their relationship to deteriorate to the point where there are few options except for a war. However, once again, both sides began to take steps to alleviate tensions in their relationship since early 2011. These sorts of cycles have occurred quite a few times since the Korean War (1950–1953). According to one study, to balance the disincentives with the incentives, "the United States should review its diplomatic record with North Korea. Instead of remaining fixated on its inability to denuclearize North Korea, Washington should realize that, in spite of its own inconsistent and often contradictory policies during the past twenty years, diplomacy has left Pyongyang with only a handful of bombs, instead of the hundred or more it might have had by now, and essentially no significant nuclear-generated electricity."[5]

The current U.S. policy with respect to North Korea includes: (1) no diplomatic engagement through the six-party talks and related bilateral meetings since 2009; (2) non-proliferation efforts, including the proliferation security initiative; (3) international efforts to counter trafficking by North Korea in illegal drugs, counterfeit currency, or other contraband; (4) maintenance of military forces in South Korea, Japan, and other East Asian countries as a credible deterrent against North Korean aggression; (5) economic sanctions and diplomatic isolation; and (6) keeping North Korea from joining international institutions.[6]

In other words, President Barack Obama reinforced the hardliner's foreign policy agenda of his predecessor, George W. Bush, by expanding coercive options against Iran and North Korea at the top of his to-do list. However, many people believe that he should take a different approach in dealing with countries that are developing weapons of mass destruction. Ashton Carter, a former Defense Department official who helped set the Clinton administration policy on North Korea, warned that:

1. North Korea might sell or trade plutonium and nuclear technologies.
2. "Loose nukes" could fall into the hands of "warlords of factions" if the North Korean regime suddenly collapsed.
3. The prospect of war on the peninsula could rise if North Korea had a moderate-size nuclear arsenal, rather than just the one or two bombs it is believed to possess now.
4. Other developing nations would follow North Korea's example.[7]

Carter's 2003 warnings have become increasingly prophetic as time passes. Since 2003, North Korea has developed more sophisticated WMDs, such as nuclear weapons, missiles, and others. Now the country not only has sufficient bombs to deter a war, but enough to sell to other countries or even to terrorist groups. Pyongyang has widely exported missiles and nuclear technologies to Syria, Libya, Pakistan, Burma, and Iran.[8] Tougher economic sanctions, the proliferation security initiative, and other hard-line measures against North Korea have neither deterred the country from developing WMDs, nor stopped it from exporting missiles and nuclear technologies.

U.S. Policy Options on a Nuclear North Korea

The Korean nuclear standoff has become a high-stakes game, which poses greater threats than those posed by Iraq and Iran. North Korea sits in the heart of northeast Asia, amid some of the world's largest and fastest growing economies, which are alarmed by the prospect of war or the collapse of an impoverished regime. There are no easy solutions to the North Korean nuclear problem. The United States and its allies have used sanctions against North Korea for the last sixty years; at times they have been useful in moving North Korea back to negotiations and slowing down its development of nuclear weapons. However, in the long run, they have hardened North Korea's resistance to international cooperation and reinforced its isolation from the international community.[9]

According to U.S. think tanks and policy analysts, the United States has four options in dealing with a nuclear North Korea.

1. Provide economic aid and a security assurance if North Korea dismantles its nuclear program.

2. Use a military strike against the North Korean nuclear facilities.
3. Let North Korea develop nuclear weapons.
4. Starve the North Korean regime of money.

We will describe some of the details of these four options below. First, the United States could hand out economic aid and a security assurance if North Korea dismantles its nuclear program. Former President Bill Clinton tried this approach in 1994. That pact collapsed after the North violated the deal and pocketed the handouts, blaming Washington for not fulfilling its obligations. Second, the United States could use a military strike against North Korean nuclear facilities. This could trigger a full-scale war, with missile attacks, radioactive fallout, economic turmoil, and massive refugee flows. U.S. troops in Japan and South Korea could become nuclear hostages. Third, the United States could let North Korea develop nuclear weapons. If we allow North Korea to have nuclear weapons, we should also accept the fact that North Korea may export nuclear weapons. Also, this could spark an arms race where South Korea, Japan, and Taiwan become nuclear powers to defend themselves. Fourth, the United States could attempt to starve the North Korean regime of money, slapping sanctions and embargoes on the grounds that the North is breaching the nonproliferation treaty. In addition, the United States could block the country's hard cash from illicit trade and cut off food aid. This would likely worsen a massive humanitarian crisis in an economically isolated nation.

If the United States hopes that North Korea will either collapse or give up its nuclear weapons because of a U.S. policy of strangulation, the odds of success seem remote. North Korea has already survived for twenty years in a state of ongoing decline. Moreover, the U.S. strangulation policy may in effect increase the odds that it will sell nuclear weapons to the highest bidder to rescue its ailing economy. That would be the worst of all policy options for the United States. The U.S. strategy to force North Korea to dismantle its nuclear programs may not work either.

How the United States and North Korea Can Build Mutual Confidence

In the middle of a precarious and tough neighborhood, divided Korea stands as a strategic pivot. History and geography have consigned Korea to the position of a highly contested strategic crossroads, the site for over a century of recurrent collisions between great-power interests. However, four neighboring countries—Russia, China, Japan, and the United States—will eventually have to work together, because they will need each other's help on Korean issues for their national security, energy security, and economic security. In this book, we argued that North Korea's longevity and its role in Northeast Asia justify a strong case for a new way of thinking about the survival strategy of North Korea.

In an interview with the news media in 2009, U.S. Secretary of State Hillary Clinton stated "we should try to step back and see North Korean issues as the forest instead of the trees." Some observers suggest that we have to think about the North Korean nuclear standoff on the premise that the United States and the Northeast Asian countries will have to learn to work together. First, the United States and Northeast Asian countries have no choice but to resolve the North Korean nuclear standoff through peaceful negotiations, because a nuclear North Korea poses a greater threat than that posed by the Middle East. Second, the Northeast Asian countries are likely to cooperate for their national energy security, because this region is home for major energy consumers, such as China and Japan, as well as major energy producers, such as Russia. The United States is likely to support such regional cooperation because it does not want these countries to depend excessively on Middle Eastern oil. Third, scholars argue that Northeast Asia is a region that has every possibility of becoming the best trading bloc in the future, because of Japanese capital and technology, Chinese labor and money, Russian natural resources, and the Korean work ethic. In addition, the Northeast Asian countries and the United States have already had close economic ties for many years and have been increasingly economically interdependent. Eventually, these factors are likely to compel the United States, China, Japan, Russia, and South Korea to collaborate on their security, energy, and economic issues, even if they have some differences.

An important implication of U.S. relations with North Korea is the impact of those relations on other nations in the region, such as China, Japan, and South Korea. If North Korea were to face political and economic problems beyond its control due to the U.S. containment policy, there is a distinct possibility that North Korea could invade South Korea out of desperation. In fact, North Korea has repeatedly stated that it would not capitulate without bringing South Korea into a conflict. Seoul's location, just twenty-five miles south of the demilitarized zone, makes it virtually impossible to protect the city from unprovoked artillery attacks. Even without a direct invasion of the South, an induced collapse of North Korea through policies of containment would certainly lead to insurmountable problems for South Korea. In summary, North Korea is one of the few countries that could suddenly involve the four major powers—the United States, Japan, China, and Russia—in major military operations. Given this gravity and urgency, it is important for those studying North Korea to take a long-term view about North Korean problems and to start confidence building.

If the land bridge that passes through North Korea were to be restored, not only the Northeast Asian countries but also other parts of Asia, the Middle East, and Europe could be connected through a land transportation network, such as railroads, highways, and undersea tunnels. Such a land transportation network would open up the possibility of direct travel between Tokyo and London by train, car, and truck. Before the dream of such a transportation network comes true, however, transportation officials and government officials say that years of confidence-building talks and billions of dollars in investments in North Korea's decrepit rail and highway systems will be needed. Observers acknowledge that such a dream will not be made real until after North Korea gives up its nuclear weapons and improves its human rights. Those moves would help build public support in South Korea and other countries for large investments across the border, and would open the way for international development aid.

Targeted Sanctions and Robust Engagement[10]

How can we induce and reinforce North Korea's peaceful transition into a country that can better provide for its own people and engage with other countries in a non-hostile manner? The process of engagement with North Korea should focus on means that do not jeopardize U.S. and South Korean security concerns. The types of measures, such as a standing committee for Northeast Asian issues and The North Korean Bank for Reconstruction and Development, recommended in this book can neither be diverted to the North Korea military nor strengthen the coercive power of the North Korean regime. They will start a process that may bring significant benefits to the North Korean people in the long run without enhancing North Korean military capability or making the United States and its allies more vulnerable. Because these types of engagement would encourage North Korea to adopt a more open and market-friendly economic growth strategy as whole, they are likely to generate vested interest in continued reform and a less confrontational foreign policy. Sanctions have a role in defending the United States and its allies against risks of proliferation, but they cannot provide a permanent solution to the North Korea problem. Combining targeted sanctions with robust engagement appears to be the best option of alleviating the tensions on the Korean peninsula in the long run.

This argument sidesteps sanctions against North Korea because they have been tried for decades. Instead, it presents new, innovative ideas in building mutual trust between the United States and North Korea. In fact, a variety of ideas for robust engagement with North Korea have appeared in recent publications.[11] They include: (1) turn Korea's Demilitarized Zone into a UNESCO World Heritage Site; (2) perform an energy efficiency upgrade of buildings in Pyongyang; (3) undertake economic engagement through official contacts, unofficial country-to-country contacts, academic exchanges, NGO cooperation, and others; (4) replace the armistice with a conditional peace treaty; (5) establish a cultural office in Pyongyang as a first step of normalizing relations with North Korea; and (6) increase engagement to include positive incentives for reform over the long term (loosen sanctions, encourage reforms, facilitate foreign investment, allow North Korea to join international financial institutions). The remainder of this section discusses two such new ideas in some detail.

No stable and authoritative institution exists for the deliberation and development of multilateral security, energy, and economic cooperation in Northeast Asia. One potential candidate for the role of driving Northeast Asia's energy and economic cooperation is the six-party talks, informally put together to solve the North Korean nuclear dispute. Given the vital role of energy supply and economic growth in stabilizing the peninsula, it is conceivable that this grouping could develop into a more formal economic institution even before solutions to the challenge emerge. The European Union provides a precedent, as its origin also lies in political and security concerns.[12]

Although Asia does not have a strong trading bloc, such as the North American Free Trade Agreement or the European Union, it does have two loose affiliations: ASEAN plus Three and the Asia Pacific Economic Cooperation (APEC) forum. Created in 1967, ASEAN consists of Southeast Asian countries such as Indonesia, the Philippines, Vietnam, and Singapore. The ASEAN plus Three was institutionalized in 1999, when the ASEAN leaders and their counterparts in China, Japan, and South Korea issued a Joint Statement on East Asia Cooperation at their Third ASEAN plus Three Summit in Manila. Formed in 1989, APEC includes the United States, Japan, China, and South Korea. However, APEC and ASEAN plus Three do not focus on contemporary security issues of Northeast Asia. Economic patterns are, in fact, complementary, and can be transformed into a force that drives regional cooperation. North Korea can also become a potential market, because it is one of only a few countries that are still untapped by multinational companies.

Both sides should sit back and think about some type of permanent mechanism that will tackle North Korea as one of the broad issues for the United States and the Northeast Asian countries. For example, these six countries may establish some sort of standing committee under the auspices of the U.N. for negotiations over North Korea's nuclear standoff, along with other issues for these six countries. Six-party talks and bilateral talks have produced quite a few agreements, but not all of them have materialized, mainly because these agreements have been reached in a hurry, without confidence building.

The establishment of a development bank, The North Korean Bank for Reconstruction and Development, may be another good idea to resolve the half-century-old North Korean nuclear problem. This bank may be funded by the United States, China, South Korea, and other countries; but, for credibility, it may be better run by three countries—the United States, China, and a neutral third country, such as Switzerland. This bank can encourage development and construction in North Korea through loans, guarantees, and equity investments in private and public companies. The establishment of such a bank may convince North Korea that five other countries are indeed ready to provide the country with a security guarantee and economic aid in exchange for the abandonment of its nuclear program.

What Is the Best Option?

Oddly enough, the United States, North Korea, and many North Korean experts believe that the United States should hand out economic aid and security assurance if North Korea dismantles its nuclear program to settle the nuclear deadlock. The problem is that the United States and North Korea have been key enemies since the Korean War (1950–1953), and thus do not trust each other. Washington demands that North Korea destroy all its nuclear weapons in a complete, verifiable, and irreversible way before substantial rewards are delivered. Pyongyang, however, insists that only if the United States first provides economic assistance and a guarantee of security will it dismantle its nuclear weapons gradually.[13]

Of course, there is no guarantee that any negotiated strategy with the unpredictable regime will work, but only a serious proposal from the United States will put the other parties (South Korea, Japan, China, and Russia) in a position to increase pressure on North Korea in case a reasonable deal is rejected: "There will be no agreement on coercive measures unless the U.S. lays out a detailed plan of what North Korea can expect by way of economic assistance and security guarantees."[14] North Korea is only likely to accept a combination of economic and security inducements backed by the threat of coercive measures, such as sanctions. China and Russia are reluctant to impose further sanctions on North Korea.

A military strike on the nuclear plant might eliminate the North Korean nuclear program. The U.S. stealth aircraft in South Korea and heavy bombers in Guam sustain the specter of this option. Such a strike would risk a North Korean counterattack that could devastate South Korea, subject Japan to missile attacks, and even trigger a broader regional war involving China. Thus, "dialogue" is the only viable way to resolve the North Korean nuclear issue peacefully. Greater China (China, Taiwan, and Hong Kong), Japan, and South Korea are countries that the United States cannot afford to ignore, because they possess more than half of the world's total foreign reserves and comprise three of the world's ten largest economies. A U.S. policy of engagement and reconciliation with North Korea would make it possible to alleviate tensions on the Korean Peninsula as well as accelerate North Korean internal reform. Just as the United States won the Cold War against the Soviet Union without armed conflict, the solution to the crisis on the Korean Peninsula should also be engagement and reconciliation, not further disruption. In other words, combining targeted sanctions with robust engagement appears to be the best option to resolve a twenty-year-old North Korean nuclear problem.

Notes

1. M. Bray, "North Korea: What Are the Options?" www.cnn.com, December 10, 2003.

2. UN Security Council Presidential Statement, July 9, 2010, http://www.un.org/News/Press/docs/2010/sc9975.doc.htm.

3. David E. Sanger, "North Koreans Unveil New Plant for Nuclear Use," *New York Times*, November 20, 2010, http://www.nytimes.com/2010/11/21/world/asia/21intel.html (accessed December 2, 2010).

4. David E. Sanger and William J. Broad, "U.S. Experts Surprised by North Korea's Nuclear Skill," *New York Times*, December 14, 2010, http://www.nytimes.com/2010/12/15/world/asia/15nukes.html?_r=1&hp.

5. Siegfried S. Hecker, Sean C. Lee, and Chaim Brau, "North Korea's Choice: Bomb Over Electricity," *The Bridge* (Summer 2010): 5–15.

6. Dick K. Nanto and Emma Chanlett-Avery, "The North Korean Economy: Leverage and Policy Analysis," CRS Report: Order Code RL 32493, March 4, 2008.

7. B. Slavin, "US Fears Spread of North Korea Nukes," www.usatoday.com, February 4, 2003.

8. Siegfried S. Hecker, "Lessons Learned from the North Koran Nuclear Crises," *Daedalus* (Winter 2010): 5.

9. Charles Kartman, Susan Shirk, and John Delury, "North Korea Inside Out: The Case for Engagement," Asia Society and the University of California, October 2009, p. 39.

10. Some portions of this section depend heavily on, Kartman, Shirk, and Delury.

11. Seung-ho Lee, "A New Paradigm for Trust-Building on the Korean Peninsula: Turning Korea's DMZ into a UNESCO World Heritage Site," Nautilus Policy Forum 10-045, August 19, 2010; Kartman, Shirk, and Delury; Suk Hi Kim, "Editor's Comments:

The Third Wave of North Korean Collapse," *North Korean Review* 6, no. 1 (Spring 2010): 3–11; Anthony DiFilippo, "North Korea's Denuclearization and a Peace Treaty," *North Korean Review* (Spring 2011); Nautilus Institute for Security and Sustainability, "DPRK Building Energy Efficiency Training (BEET)," http://www.nautilus.org/projects/dprk-buildings, October 19, 2010; Yonhap News Agency, "France Seeks to Establish Cultural Office in Pyongyang," *Vantage Point: Development in North Korea*, May 20, 2010, pp. 24–25; Nanto and Chanlett-Avery.

12. P. Andrews-Speed, X. Liao, and P. Stevens, "Multilateral Energy Co-operation in Northeast Asia: Promise or Mirage?" *Oxford Energy Forum* (2005): 13–17.

13. K. Oh and R.C. Hassig, "North Korea's Nuclear Politics," *Current History* (September 2004): 273–279.

14. International Crisis Group, "North Korea: Where Next for the Nuclear Talks?" www.icg.org, November 15, 2004, p. 3.

About the Contributors

Thomas F. Cargill has taught and conducted research on financial and monetary economics at the University of California, Davis; California State University, Sacramento; Purdue University; and the University of Nevada, Reno. He has written extensively on U.S. financial and central banking issues and has also conducted similar research on Korea, Japan, and China. He is a member of the Advisory Council to the Korea Economic Institute and an associate editor of the *North Korean Review*.

Semoon Chang is a professor of economics and director of the Center for Business and Economic Research at the University of South Alabama and an associate editor of *North Korean Review*. His recent writings on Korean issues have appeared in the *Quarterly Journal of Labor Policy*, the *Journal of East Asian Studies*, the *International Journal of Korean History* and the *International Economics and Finance Journal*.

Bruce Cumings is the Gustavus F. and Ann M. Swift Distinguished Service Professor in History at the University of Chicago and the chairperson of the History Department. He specializes in modern Korean history and contemporary international relations in East Asia. He is the author of several books, including *The Origins of the Korean War* (2 volumes); *War and Television*; *Korea's Place in the Sun: A Modern History*; and *Dominion from Sea to Sea: Pacific Ascendancy and American Power*.

Peter Hayes is executive director of the Nautilus Institute for Security and Sustainable Development, a nongovernmental policy-oriented research and advocacy group. Professionally active as an environment and energy consultant in developing countries, he also writes widely about security affairs in the Asia-Pacific region. He is coauthor of *American Lake: Nuclear Peril in the Pacific* and *The Global Greenhouse Regime*.

Siegfried S. Hecker is co-director of the Stanford University Center for International Security and Cooperation, a senior fellow of the Freeman Spogli Institute for International Studies, and professor (research) in the Department of Management Science and Engineering at Stanford University. Joining the Los Alamos National Laboratory in 1973, he served as chairman of the Center for Materials Science and Division Leader of the Materials Science and Technology Division before becoming director of the Laboratory.

David von Hippel is a Nautilus Institute senior associate and independent consultant based in Eugene, Oregon. His work with Nautilus has centered on energy and environmental issues in Asia, and particularly in Northeast Asia.

Hwa-Kyung Kim is an associate professor at the Semyung University in Korea and an advisor to the Korea Ministry of Culture and Tourism and has been a frequent contributor to such Korean newspapers as *Dong-A Ilbo* and *Maeil Business* on matters of Korea's tourism.

Mikyoung Kim is an associate professor at the Hiroshima City University–Hiroshima Peace Institute in Japan. She is the author of *Securitization of Human Rights: North Korean Refugees in Northeast Asia* and the coeditor of *East Asia's Difficult Past: Essays in Collective Memory*.

Suk Hi Kim, a professor of international finance, is the discipline coordinator of finance at the University of Detroit Mercy. He is the founder-editor of *North Korean Review*, was the founder-editor of *Multinational Business Review* (1992–2002), and is the author of *North Korea at a Crossroads* and the coeditor of *Economic Sanctions Against a Nuclear North Korea*.

Sung-Hoon Lim is an associate professor of international trade at Konkuk University in Seoul. He has served as an advisor to the National Economy Advisory Council, Office of the President and has also been an advisor to the Presidential Committee on the Northeast Asia Cooperation Initiative. He has published in the *International Business Review* and the *Multinational Business Review*.

Mark E. Manyin is a specialist in Asian affairs and former head of the Asia Section at the Congressional Research Service of the Library of Congress. His area of expertise is U.S. foreign economic policy toward East Asia, particularly the two Koreas, Japan, and Vietnam.

Dick K. Nanto is a specialist in industry and trade and former head of both the International Trade and Finance Section and the Asia Section at the Congressional Research Service of the Library of Congress. He works primarily on U.S. international trade and finance and on U.S. economic relations with Asia.

Elliott Parker is a professor of economics at the University of Nevada, Reno, and also the department chairman. He specializes in comparative and international economics and his research interests include financial systems in East Asia, price deflation, and the comparative effects of fiscal policy.

Terence Roehrig is a professor in the National Security Affairs Department and coordinator of the Asia-Pacific Studies Group at the U.S. Naval War College. He is the author of *From Deterrence to Engagement: The U.S. Defense Commitment to South Korea* and *The Prosecution of Former Military Leaders in Newly Democratic Nations: The Cases of Argentina, Greece, and South Korea* and a coauthor of *South Korea Since 1980*.

Bernhard J. Seliger is the representative of the Hanns Seidel Foundation in Seoul, consulting NGOs and other institutions on questions of unification. He manages the capacity-building projects of the Foundation in North Korea, among them, from 2006 to 2009, the EU-DPRK trade capacity project. He frequently travels to North Korea, and is associate editor and book review editor of *North Korean Review* as well as founding editor of the website http://www.asianintegration.org.

Index

Academic exchanges 230–243
Acheson, Dean 14
Age of Freedom 100
Agreed Framework 20, 45, 87
Alamos National Laboratory 246
Angarsk 75
Armistice Agreement 15
Art of War 1, 36
ASEAN Plus Three 42, 67, 77–78, 80
Ashton Carter 248
Asian community debates 180–193
Asian continental powers 68
Asian Pacific Economic Cooperation (APEC) 42, 77–80
Axis of evil 16

Banco Delta Asia 89
Berlin Wall 24, 104
Big bang 103
Bretton Woods 108
Brezhnev doctrine 104
Bush, George W. 26, 49–50, 247

Capacity building measures 232–235
Carter, Jimmy 20
Chaebol 107
Cheonan incident 184–211
China–North Korea relations 116–134
China–U.S. relations 81–83
Choson dynasty 18, 30, 50
Choson Exchange 241–243
Chung Ju-young 88
Clinton, Bill 20, 26
Clinton, Hillary 250
Cold War 2, 28, 138, 220

Collapsists 138
COMECON 165
Commission based trade 91
Community 183
Confucianism 30
Cooperative SEZs 171–180
Country of Eastern decorum 30
Cuban missile crisis 220
Cultural Revolution 105, 107

Demilitarized Zone (DMZ) 24, 40, 68, 220
Deng Xiaoping 105
Denuclearization 117
Dictionary of Economics 163

East Asia 182–193
Eberstadt, Nicholas 46–48
Economic reform 99–101
Energy demand 142
EU–North Korea Trade Capacity Project 232–235
Eurasian Land Bridge 69
European Union 67
Eurotunnel 70–71
Exports 80–81, 219–222

Fifth SEZ 167–168
Fishing 203–204
Foreign exchange reserves 81–82
Four Pacific Powers 15–16
Four-Party Talks 21–22

Gorbachev, Mikhail 46, 103
Great China 193
Gross national product 17

Han Myung-sook 31
Hanns Seidel Foundation Korea 232–235
Hong Kong Management Association 237
Hunter, Helen-Louis 51–53
Hwang Chang-yop 55
Hyundai chaebol 88

Inter-Korean economic relations 86–97
Inter-Korean Red Cross talks 87
International Atomic Energy Agency (IAEA) 19, 20, 21, 23, 215–217
International nuclear club 36

Juche Principle 15–18, 32–34
June 15 2000 Joint Declaration 88

Kaesong Industrial Complex (KIC) 88, 94
Kaesong SEZ 161
Kelly, James 22
Kim Chaek University 239–240
Kim Dae Jung 47, 88
Kim Il Sung 13, 17, 32–33, 37–38
Kim Jong Il 13, 16, 18, 24, 33, 37, 89
Kim Jong Un 37–38
Kim Yong Sam 23
Korean Air 858 87
Korean Energy Development Organization (KEDO) 21, 22, 87
Korean unification 174–180
Korean War 4, 13
Kumgang, Mr. 161
K'ung Fu Tzu 30
Kyushu Island of Japan 70

Land bridge 70
Lee Myung-bak 90–91, 199, 246
Levkowitz, Alon 4
Light-water reactors 20, 21, 44
Lind, Jennifer 37
Liquefied natural gas (LNG) 76
London 70

Maritime boundary 200
Marx, Karl 31, 101
Military Armistice Commission 200
Military Demarcation Line (MDL) 68, 200
Military-first policy 18–19, 34–36

Mori, Yosihro 70
Mt. Kumgang tourism project 88
Mutual confidence building 249–250

Nakhodka 77
Nampo SEZ 167–168
National Press Club 14
Nautilus 138
Nautilus Institute for Security and Sustainability 235–236
Neo-Confucianism 29–32
Nobel Peace Prize 20
Non commercial trade 91
North American Free Trade Agreement 67, 80
North Korea: Asia Pacific Peace Committee (APPAC) 88; collapse 46–49, 137–158; economic sanctions 133–134; energy sector 137–158; famine 3; nuclear crisis 214–227; nuclear weapons program 19–24; policy 119–123; provocations 198–210; reform 108; survival strategy 174–180
Northeast Asian countries 66–68
Northern Limit Line (NLL) 180, 198–211
Nuclear Non-proliferation Treaty (NPT) 19, 20, 215–217

Obama, Barack 26, 247
Oceanic powers 68
Organization for Economic Cooperation and Development (OECD) 109

Park Chung-hee 109
Park Wang-ja 90
Perry Process 221
Prediction scenarios 38
Proliferation Security Initiative (PSI) 3
Pyongyang 14
Pyongyang International Business School 236–239
Pyongyang University of Science and Technology 240–241

Rajin-Sungbong 161
Regime implosion 148, 153
Reunification path 149
Rho Moo-hyun 31, 89
Rumsfeld, Donald 49

Sakhalin 76
Scott D. Sagan's Domestic Politics Model 222–224
Second Gulf War 49
Self reliance 3
Seoul-Pyongyang hotline 87
Siberian energy supply 76
Sino-DPRK's interaction 126–127
Sinuiju 161
Six Party Talks 3, 38, 124–125, 186
Socialist market economy 107
Socialist reform 101
Songun 18–19, 34–36
South-North Joint Communiqué 87
Sovereignty 204–205
Special Economic Zones (SEZs) 160–180
Standard Oil 73
Sun Tzu 1, 36
Swiss Development Cooperation 237
Syngman Rhee 13
Syracuse University 237–240

Taepodong-1 88
Targeted sanctions 251–253
Third wave of North Korean collapse 28–29
38th parallel 14–15
Threshold nuclear states 6, 65
Tokyo 70
Trading bloc 250
Trans Asian Railway (TAR) 5, 69–70
Trans China Railway (TCR) 68–69
Trans Korean Railway (TKR) 5, 68–69

Trans Siberian Railway (TSR) 68–69, 216–217
Truman, Harry S 14

Unger, Robert 61
United Nations 13, 27
United Nations Command 200
UN Council Resolutions 1718 and 1874 119
UN Economic and Social Commission (UNESCAP) 71
UN National Security Council 23
UN sanctions against North Korea 245–238
U.S. policy options on North Korea 245–254
U.S.–ROK Security Treaty of 1953 186
University of Applied Science in Switzerland 237

War path 146–148, 150
Weapons of Mass Destruction (WMD) 3
West Sea 204
World War II 13

Xenophobia 37

Yeonpyeongdo 246–248
Yongbyon 19, 215
Yugoslavia 103